MEMORIES
AFTER
MY DEATH

MEMORIES AFTER MY DEATH

The Story of My Father,
Joseph "Tommy" Lapid

YAIR LAPID

Translated from the Hebrew
by Evan Fallenberg

THOMAS DUNNE BOOKS ❀ ST. MARTIN'S PRESS

THOMAS DUNNE BOOKS.
An imprint of St. Martin's Press

MEMORIES AFTER MY DEATH. Copyright © 2011 by Yair Lapid. All rights reserved. For information, address St. Martin's Press, 175 Fifth Avenue, New York, N.Y. 10010.

www.thomasdunnebooks.com
www.stmartins.com

Designed by Steven Seighman

Library of Congress Cataloging-in-Publication Data

Names: Lapid, Yair, author.
Title: Memories after my death : the story of my father, Joseph "Tommy" Lapid /
    Yair Lapid ; translated from the Hebrew by Evan Fallenberg.
Other titles: Zikhronot aòhare moti. English
Description: New York : Thomas Dunne Books, an imprint of St. Martin's Press, [2017]
Identifiers: LCCN 2017028155| ISBN 9781250044013 (hardcover) |
    ISBN 9781466842472 (ebook)
Subjects: LCSH: Lapid, Joseph, 1931–2008. | Politicians—Israel—Biography. |
    Journalists—Israel—Biography.
Classification: LCC DS126.6.L35 L35513 2017 | DDC 328.5694092 [B]—dc23
LC record available at https://lccn.loc.gov/2017028155

Our books may be purchased in bulk for promotional, educational, or business use. Please contact the Macmillan Corporate and Premium Sales Department at 1-800-221-7945, extension 5442, or by email at MacmillanSpecialMarkets@macmillan.com.

Originally published in Hebrew in Israel by Keter

First published in English in the United Kingdom by Elliott & Thompson

First U.S. Edition: October 2017

10 9 8 7 6 5 4 3 2 1

MEMORIES AFTER MY DEATH

CHAPTER 1

I am writing this book after my death. Most people write nothing after they die, but I am not most people.

Or maybe I am. My biography is so full of contradictions that sometimes I used to think—and not only I—that I contain everyone I ever knew. At birth I was named Joseph after a grandfather I never met and Tommy after a Hungarian prince from a long-forgotten dynasty, and I held on to both names throughout my life. I was the most famous atheist in Israel, the public and bitter enemy of Orthodoxy, but I represented (faithfully, I hope) the entirety of Jewish fate. I was despised, but remarkably popular, a polite and educated European intellectual and a red-cheeked defender of the rights of the people whose outbursts were legendary. A conservative chauvinist who knew how to appreciate the figure of a beautiful woman and loved Rembrandt, Mozart and Brecht, and a folksy speaker who could fire up a crowd with pithy one-liners. A leftist who supported partitioning Israel and a rightist whom Prime Minister Menahem Begin chose to run the country's lone television station. I was an orphan who stepped off the boat with only the clothes on his body, and an affluent member of the upper middle class who stained his neckties at the best restaurants across Europe.

I entertained SS officers at the train station in the city of my birth, smuggled frozen horsemeat into a cellar in the ghetto, was sent at the age of seventeen to serve in the army of a country I was not familiar with under the command of officers who spoke a language I understood not a word of. In the service of said country, I was invited to the White House, 10 Downing Street, the Élysée Palace, Beijing's Forbidden City and Rashtrapati Bhavan in New Delhi. I lunched with Barack Obama, drank coffee with Yassir Arafat, raised a glass with Nicolas Sarkozy, marched in Winston Churchill's funeral procession, toured the Third World with David Ben Gurion, and yet my mother thought I had not amounted to much.

I lived my life with guilt-free passion the way only a person who has been spared certain death can. Long-legged girls shook their shapely bottoms for me from the Lido in Paris to the Mirage in Las Vegas. Louis Armstrong played for me, Ella Fitzgerald and Israeli singer Rita Yahan-Farouz sang for me, I presented an award at the German "Oscars" along with a dead-drunk Jack Nicholson, Danny Kaye was an usher at my wedding, I helped Jackie Mason with his gas mask during a rocket attack on Tel Aviv at the height of the Gulf War. I was an auto mechanic, a lawyer, a journalist, a businessman, a politician and once again a journalist. I wrote successful books of humor and travel guides, my collected essays were bestsellers just like my cookbook, and my comedies were big hits in the national theater, though everyone—including me—agreed that my wife was a better writer than me.

I disappointed Menahem Begin, I had a complex father-son relationship with Ariel Sharon, I shouted at Ehud Barak, Binyamin Netanyahu claims to this very day that without me he would not have been able to carry out the financial revolution that saved the country, and Ehud Olmert—one of my two best friends in the world—sat at my bedside and watched me die. Watched and bawled.

And I ate endlessly: Hungarian sausages, flaky French baguettes fresh from the *boulangerie* oven, pungent Dutch cheeses, steaming bowls of hummus with beans in Abu Ghosh, thick beef stews in North America, cream cakes in Vienna, wieners as thick as the arms of whichever Gretchen made them in Berlin, sushi in Japan, chicken tikka in Bombay; once I drank a frightful wine in Burma only to discover, too late, that it had been fermented in pitchers in which monkey fetuses had been placed in order to improve the taste. I ate everything, I ate more than everyone, and I always remained hungry.

But still I need to explain this strange act—by no means the strangest thing I have ever been involved in—that allows a man to write his autobiography after his death. Carlo Goldoni, the eighteenth-century Italian playwright whose most famous work is *Servant of Two Masters,* once wrote, "He only half dies who leaves an image of himself in his sons."

I am writing now through my son, Yair, but my voice has commandeered his own, just as it did more than once during my lifetime. Is this unfair to him, an injustice? I suppose so. But it is not the first injustice I have committed against him and yet he still loves me in that unswerving and occasionally undiscerning way of children who are willing to accept the image we have created for them.

Without his knowing it, I had been preparing Yair for this moment from the day he was born. I told him the story of my life again and again. As with every good storyteller (and what Hungarian Jew is not a good storyteller?) I studded my stories with anecdotes, ridiculous characters, good guys and bad guys, eternal winners and losers, vistas and flavors and scents, and clever and sometimes cruel observations about human nature and its weaknesses.

And Yair always listened. He was a sad and serious boy, nearly friendless, and I filled the emptiness in his life with exhilaration without ever asking myself whether I was the one who had created that emptiness in the first place. I can picture a scene, toward the end of the 1960s, when we had returned to Israel from London with a new record collection and I sat in my small study in Yad Eliyahu listening to Mozart's *Magic Flute* and enthusiastically conducting my battered stereo system with my chubby, white fingers (a part of my body I always hated). It took me a few minutes to notice that he was there, sitting on the floor and imitating me, conducting a piece he had never heard with the fingers of a child. At that moment I suspected—and continued to suspect for years—that that imitation would perpetuate itself and, like many children of successful people, he would become the Sancho Panza of my memories without bothering to develop an identity of his own. I was wrong, of course, but let it be said to my credit that I was happy to be wrong.

Death is a very centering moment. It places before you only the most important matters: parenting, family, love. When I look back on these things I have no regrets. Regret is not circumstantial, it is a character trait, and I admit that it does not exist in me. Time and again I said to my kids, "The proof of the cooking is in the pudding." If the pudding does not turn out well, no amount of talking about it is going to improve it. And if it does turn out well then the chef deserves an ovation. I had three successful children, and two of them have outlived me. Something was apparently working well in my kitchen.

I did not suffer from a surplus of modesty but I must admit that I would not have bothered to work on this book if my funeral had not been so impressive. It was without doubt a stunning success. The prime minister cried over my grave, many hundreds of people jammed the walkways, the press was there in all its glory, and of course I managed to cause one last scandal by becoming the first person to be buried in secular fashion in an Orthodox cemetery.

It was cause for celebration in the Orthodox press when word first got out that I was to be buried at Kiryat Shaul. Those are precisely the moments when religion pushes its way into our lives—at the beginning and at the end, when we have no possibility of refusing. Imagine how great their disappointment was when they discovered that instead of a recitation of the traditional Kaddish prayer, Frank Sinatra's "My Way" would be played. Truth be told, we very nearly failed: just before I was lowered into my grave, Chabad Rabbi Gloiberman appeared on the scene—one of God's wretched *makhers,* the kind of fixer I hated my entire life—and started mumbling some incomprehensible verses from the Bible, positioning himself quite naturally in front of the television cameras. Yair put his hand none too gently on Gloiberman's arm and told him to take a hike. Maybe I shouldn't have enjoyed it as much as I did in my present state, but I never missed a good fight or a good meal and there's certainly no point in starting now.

On her way out of the funeral, my wife, Shula, muttered to Alush (Aliza Olmert, Ehud's wife), "I'm so embarrassed." Aliza asked her why. "I always knew he was important," Shula said, "but I only just understood how important."

Don't be mad at yourself, Shulinka. I didn't understand either. People asked me time and again to write this autobiography but I always figured they wanted me to write their own biographies and took me for a suitable vessel. There are a few attempts at writing my life story still on my computer but I never got past the first few pages. After all, I was never good at distinguishing what is important from what is not. Everything I ever dealt with seemed, at that time, to be the most important thing. On the Internet site where I played Blitz Chess against opponents from around the world, I racked up 31,731 games, and every one of them, while I was playing, was like a matter of life or death to me. I guess it's no wonder that I wasn't able to take life or death themselves too seriously. In a letter I wrote to Barran, a friend from the ghetto, on his seventieth birthday, I noted that "in our case, it was a lot tougher to reach our fifteenth birthdays than our seventieth."

In fact, it was only after my death that I realized—or acknowledged— that I was the last one.

There is nothing remarkable about being the last of one's kind. In my case it is merely proof that apostasy and stuffed cabbage are a life-lengthening combination. Being the last is not an honor, it is a job. I was the last Holocaust survivor to be a member of the Knesset and serve in the government. After my death there will be no one else to sit on one of those buckskin armchairs who can recall the most horrific event in the history of the world's nations. I was also the last to remember pre-war Europe, an antique world of crystal chandeliers and women in satin ballgowns leaning gracefully against the shoulders of elegant men. I was the last of Israel's leaders to watch Churchill orate in Parliament, be present for the creation—and later the fall of—the Iron Curtain, make *aliyah* to Israel on a rickety boat, listen to the United Nations vote on the establishment of Israel over shortwave radio, serve in the army during the War of Independence in 1948, and to have been on hand, personally, to witness the death of God.

My good friend, the Nobel Laureate Eli Wiesel, once said that memory is his principal occupation. But with me, memory is only a hobby. I was always too busy, too lustful for life, to spend my present on my past. Only now do I understand—with surprise and no small measure of pride—that I was the last in precisely the same things in which I was once first.

CHAPTER 2

Most people do not know at what point they passed from being a child to an adult. I do. It happened one night when I was twelve, between 18 and 19 March 1944.

It was a clear night, the sky studded with stars. My father and I were walking alone down an empty street as I declaimed my Latin: "*Sum, es, est . . .*"

"It's a beautiful night," I said to escape from Latin.

"Yes."

"Has Mother arrived in Budapest yet?"

She had traveled to be with her sister, Aunt Edith, who had had an operation.

"Yes. She's at your grandparents, showing off your photograph." My father smiled.

"Can I sleep with you tonight?" I asked.

"Yes."

At six in the morning I was still a child. I slept in the huge bed next to my father, under the same blanket. My father was large and fat—even fatter than I grew to be—and his hot breathing was the metronome of sanity and consolation in a world that I already knew, the way a child does, was losing its mind.

This would not be my first brush with the war. It had seared me three years earlier, a few months past my ninth birthday, on April 5 1941, when the Hungarians invaded Yugoslavia. My mother was at that time, too, visiting her parents in Budapest (she would travel there three times a year) and my father and I had packed three suitcases and gone to Belgrade, the Yugoslavian capital, to hide out with relatives. That night Belgrade was bombed. It was the most serious bombing campaign the Germans had engaged in since Rotterdam, and the building in which we were staying was hit by an incendiary bomb. We escaped with our lives. I can recall the way the bombed building shuddered, but even more than that I recall the way each building on that street was aflame like so many giant books of matches. Frightened people ran about the streets, and my father said, "Let's go toward the Danube." Burning stones and beams fell from the buildings, and I began to run in a zigzag. My father shouted to me that it would not help because we could not see from where the debris was falling, but I continued running in a zigzag while he— wonderful, conservative Dr. Lampel, dignified and deliberate even in such circumstances—continued walking in a straight line, carrying his suitcase. As I ran I heard a noise behind me and looked back. A burning telephone pole had fallen next to me; I had run a zig and it had fallen in the zag.

I was in the habit of telling my Israel-born friends that they had no idea what war was, and this always offended them. What is that supposed to mean? they would protest: Wasn't the Yom Kippur War a war? And the Gulf War? And how about the Lebanon Wars—first and second? With a bit of arrogance, I would explain to them that real war looks nothing like any of those. In a real war the battles do not take place on the periphery, on the outlying edges. In a real war, 2,500 Israelis could be killed every day, with tens of thousands of wounded civilians and soldiers making their way (or not) to the hospitals. In a real war, ships would be sunk in Haifa Bay, the Defence Ministry in the center of Tel Aviv would disappear, the government offices in Jerusalem would burn to the ground and cities in the north, center and south would be razed.

Because that is what a real war is like: no electricity in most of the country; roads blocked with burnt-out cars; trains not running, ports mined, the country is cut off; air force bases wiped out, the Israel Defence Forces fighting admirably even though all contingency plans have been scrapped, the home front hanging on in spite of the fact that during the first week of war we sustained 15,000 fatalities and 100,000 wounded. There is no television, though the radio is still working, requesting blood donations.

My friends fall silent and stare at me. I fall silent and stare at them. I do not tell them one last truth, something I understood on the burning streets of Belgrade, where a man in a suit marched along, determined to maintain his dignity in the eyes of the child running circles around him: in a real war, people who have been saved do not feel any real relief, only guilt. I carried this guilt around with me my entire life. Why my father and not me? Why, from among twenty-four pupils in my class, was I one of only seven to survive? I hope this will not sound too strange, but I even felt doubly guilty because I was actually a good little boy who respected authority and always tried to please everyone. The problem was that everyone wanted me dead. The teachers, the neighbors, the government, the state—all the authorities I had been brought up to respect. Everyone made it clear that death was my job; still, I insisted on living. The war caused me to stop being a good little boy, and I never went back to that. I ran at a zig, not a zag.

In the years that passed I watched—first in anger, later with acceptance—as the Holocaust turned into a literary event (or worse, a cinematic event). "Why didn't you people get out of there?" I was asked again and again, even by those closest to me. The Holocaust seemed to them like some ongoing event in which people would fade out: first they would lose their jobs, then their property, then the flesh of their bodies, until finally they were loaded onto trains and transported to their imminent deaths. But for Jews like us, the Holocaust was a Mount Vesuvius erupting over a new Pompeii. We were trapped under the lava while preoccupied with the most trivial matters, dying at our desks or making love or walking with our children in the park or drinking our morning coffee and reading the paper without understanding the news was all about us.

Or while sleeping.

One morning, at exactly 6 a.m., I heard Grandmother talking softly. *"Ja, bitte, bitte,"* she was saying to someone in German, and then the bedroom door opened. "Bela," she said to my father, "a German soldier is at the door and he wishes to see you." The soldier did not wait. He followed her into the bedroom dressed in a gray-green uniform and carrying a bayoneted rifle, and was polite as could be. I pushed myself down under the blanket, peering out from beneath it through a slit. I burst out crying. My father rose from the bed and dressed.

"The rucksack," he said to my grandmother. She left the room and returned carrying his bag. There was no need to pack; since the outbreak of war we each had a rucksack prepared for the road.

My grandmother took a step or two toward the blond man with the bayonet and when she reached him, quite close, she grabbed hold of the headboard of the bed and slowly, in the manner of an old person, lowered herself to her knees and pressed up against his polished boots. She raised her head and looked into his blue eyes. "Sir," she said, "please do not forget that you, too, have a mother waiting at home for you." Then she added, "God bless you."

The German grimaced, then nodded to my father. Time was up.

Father bent down and took the blanket off me. He hugged me and uttered the words that turned me into an adult. "My child," he said, "either I will see you again in life or I will not."

I saw him one more time, five years later, but not in life.

It was during my first weekend furlough from the army. My cousin Saadia (his father, Dr. Waldman, was a fervent Zionist and called him Saadia without knowing it was a Yemenite name; he was undoubtedly the only blond-haired, blue-eyed Saadia in Israel) brought me to see Tel Aviv, the big city. I was profoundly disappointed. Even in the war-damaged city of Novi Sad that I had left behind, the central square was grander than Tel Aviv's Mughrabi, and the main street far more impressive than Allenby. When we reached the seashore, Saadia pointed to the Kaete-Dan guesthouse and informed me with pride that this was Tel Aviv's largest hotel. I began to understand just exactly where I had landed.

That evening, on the way to the home of Saadia's parents, we passed a balcony on which young people were dancing the tango. I watched the twirling couples and my heart cinched in a way that only that of a new immigrant can. Mere weeks earlier, I had been just such a young man, a high-school student who had survived the war and danced on balconies with girls I was wooing, surrounded by schoolmates and chattering away in our own language, singing popular songs that meant something to us, eating foods that suited our palates, laughing at the same jokes, looking at the vistas in which we had grown up. And suddenly here I was, amid the alien corn. Homeless. Deaf and mute and hopelessly, desperately, far from ever making anything of myself. When would anyone ever invite me to dance the tango?

That Saturday evening, Saadia took me to the Esther cinema. For the first time in my life I saw a translation from English that was not on the screen itself but next to it, and written by hand. In the intermission a young man carrying a sketch pad approached us. He had heard us speaking Serbian.

"My name is Lifkovitz," he said, introducing himself. "I am a painter."

"My name's Lampel," I told him.

A flash of recognition lit up his eyes. "Are you related to Dr. Bela Lampel?" he asked.

"I'm his son," I said.

"We were in Auschwitz together," he said just as the second half of the film began.

After the movie we sat on a bench in Dizengoff Square. Lifkovitz opened his sketch pad, pulled a thick pencil from his pocket, and said, "I'll draw your father for you." I sat beside him on my first Tel Aviv evening and watched with great excitement as the lines spread across the page. When he finished, he said, "Does it resemble him?"

"The contours of his face do," I said, "but he was fat."

Lifkovitz's face fell. He closed the sketch pad. "When I knew him," he said, "he was already thin."

I cannot imagine my father thin. I do not wish to. I prefer to retain my memories as they are.

CHAPTER 3

On the wall of my study, in a thick frame, hangs an eighty-year-old photograph of the Lampel family. After my death my wife, Shula, decided to leave it there as a memento of a vanished world, and a vanished husband.

Pictured in the photograph are my grandfather, Joseph Lampel, who died a year before I was born and for whom I was named; my grandmother, Hermina; my father; and his two younger brothers, Pali and Latzi.

I do not know how this photograph survived. It was snapped in 1928 at Foto Vaida in Novi Sad, the town in which I was born. The subjects are staged and formal, like some Dutch painting from the seventeenth century: my grandparents, starched and prim, sit beside a small table on which a large clock has been placed and set to the hour of six. My father and grandfather are wearing neckties; the two younger boys wear bow ties. No one is smiling.

I grew up in what is known as the Old World. It was a world of luxuriant tranquility, of honorable, heavy sloth, a world of marble palaces and stone bridges, of long afternoon naps and even longer evening meals, of brass phonographs and pure silver cuff links, of patient horses and puffing steam engines that run late because tardiness is no crime.

Only a few years later the palaces were blown up and the bridges crumbled. Grandmother Hermina was killed at Auschwitz along with ten other family members. My father died at the Mauthausen work camp only two weeks before the end of the war. Our smiling neighbors turned us in to the authorities, then set their coarse feet in our house and carried off the gramophone, the cuff links. The trains were derailed, the carriages left to lie on their sides like dice in a crazed giant's game. We ate the horses. During the daytime we could hear their screams after Russian bombardments and at night we stole from our cellar hideaways in the ghetto armed with makeshift knives and sliced away at their frozen flesh. I am not the kind of person who remembers his dreams, but the sound of those screaming horses stayed with me for long nights over many years.

Sometimes I look at Yair and Meirav and envy them. I envy them, and worry for them. They believe—wrongly—that the world in which they live is unassailable. Their careers, their beautiful children, the things that surround them—homes, cars, bank accounts—give them the illusion that what was is also what will be and that no one can come along and take their lives away in one fell swoop. But I know just how fragile reality is. The world in which I grew up seemed far more stable and permanent than the feverish modern world. It had moved along at a sleepily slow pace for centuries and then suddenly—in a day—the ice shattered and all the dancers plunged into the murky waters.

But it is best to begin at the beginning.

Novi Sad sits on the Danube River, some 80 kilometers north of Belgrade and 220 kilometers south of Budapest. For most of its history it was a border town that looked after the southeast corner of the Austro-Hungarian Empire. The first Jew in Novi Sad, a man named Kaldai, arrived in the seventeenth century. One hundred years later, in 1749, the town had 4,620 inhabitants, of which 100 were Jews. By 1843, some 1,125 Jews were registered in Novi Sad, among them several doctors and the "fat Jewess Pepi," the pushy madam of the Golden Girls brothel.

According to documentation, in 1836 she was fined when soldiers who visited her establishment contracted a venereal disease.

There were 80,000 residents of Novi Sad prior to the outbreak of World War Two, including 4,350 Jews. We were three of them: my father, Bela; my mother, Katalina; and me.

They seemed like a perfect couple. He was known as Bela the Bright and she as Kato the Beautiful. He was a dark-eyed, dark-skinned journalist and lawyer from the outskirts and she was a gorgeous blonde from Budapest, the metropolis, never letting anyone forget that we were, in her eyes, rustics. They met when she came to visit relatives of ours, the Korody family, a large suitcase filled with the latest fashions in tow.

In no time she grew bored—there was not much to do in a family whose favorite way of spending time was to paint on eggs—and persuaded the two younger daughters, Vera and Mira, to bring her to the community center for evenings of dancing. It was there that my parents met and fell in love. He was relatively old by then, and the fact that his two younger brothers had already married caused the family to spare no effort in matching him up with a girl from the local Jewish community. He refused them all, until my mother came on the scene: she was tempestuous, flirtatious, frivolous and without doubt exceptionally beautiful. Small cities are naturally suspicious, and eyebrows were raised. My mother came from a family of relatively meager circumstances and the rumor that circulated (thanks to the disappointed mothers of the city's unmarried Jewish girls) was that she was interested in him solely for his money.

On 5 July 1930, my father took a holiday at the Grand Imperial Hotel in the Dalmatia region of Croatia. Appropriately named, the Grand Imperial was an imposing building with ornate Corinthian pillars set on an enchanting strip of sand on the Adriatic coast. (In the 1980s, the building was razed and replaced by an ugly modern hotel that bears the same name.) It was there that my father sat and wrote—in neat, compact handwriting that concealed the tremendous storm of emotions he was experiencing—a letter to his father:

I am thirty-two years old and I long for the tranquillity of married life. My great loneliness is slowly grinding away at my nerves—I cannot find my place—I can no longer stand it. Sometimes it angers me that you and Mother did not appreciate my endless wandering, my constant malaise, my attacks of nerves which repeated themselves with growing frequency. And now you know the reason. It was my terrible loneliness that caused it . . . Throughout my life I have only been capable of glimpsing happiness from the side, which caused me to be increasingly bitter as I looked around. But now, as the decision to marry Kato has ripened in me (if in fact she will have me), I feel, for the first time in my life, what it is to be happy.

Father, this is what I wished to tell you, and I can only add what Luther said: "Here I stand, I can do no other."

I embrace you and Mother,

Bela

I read that letter again and again during my lifetime, trying to see the connection between the staid man I knew and the melodrama unfolding with his words. Perhaps it is decreed that we shall never know the truth about our parents, but it seems to me that this was a moment of loneliness of operatic proportions that occurred in a life that was otherwise remarkably calm and ordered. As far as I could tell, the power of the connection between them was that it suited them both. My father gave her the easy life she desired and he in return received the most beautiful flower in the city to put in his lapel. Is that love? Does anyone know what love is?

Our villa was three stories tall and capacious and faced Train Street. Rosebushes and pear trees bloomed in the large back garden. Father's law office occupied the ground floor, along with the servants' quarters. My parents' bedroom, my bedroom, my nanny's bedroom and a guest bedroom (which usually stood empty) occupied the top floor, while on the first floor there was a large living room, a separate dining room and another spacious room called "the master's room," which was elegantly decorated with heavy furniture that included an escritoire, a well-appointed library and a large armchair in which Father took his naps. Naturally, there was also a large kitchen presided over by our fat Hungarian cook who toiled over a gas oven, since the Novi Sad gas company had already by that time installed pipes through the entire city. (When I first came to Israel and discovered that gas was distributed in canisters, I understood I had arrived in a primitive country.) A dumb waiter operated from the kitchen to the roof terrace, in case we wished to dine up there.

Today it seems to me that only very rich people live in such a manner, but back then this was the norm for the bourgeoisie, who saw themselves—correctly—as the cornerstones of the entire society. It was a comfortable milieu of masters and servants, and no one gave too much thought to his or her status. The cook and the maid, who lived with us, were Hungarian. The gardener, who came once a week, was Serbian. Lizzy, my nanny, was a Swabian German. To my dying day I found it hard to polish my own shoes, and not just because of my extra poundage, but because in my childhood it was abundantly clear that this was a job for the servants.

But perhaps the most notable feature of status was not the size of one's house or the number of servants but the comfortable pace of life.

Father would rise at eight, read the newspaper, and eat a leisurely breakfast until Mother would remind him—from her bed, with the aid of a small bell—that he needed to be in court at ten o'clock. At nine he would descend to his office where his two legal interns awaited him with documents. He sat importantly at his desk while one of his two secretaries served him coffee in a Rosenthal china cup. From there he walked to court, after which he would spend time at the nearby café, where he would have a bite to eat, browse the weeklies hanging from bamboo poles and return home in a carriage.

After we ate lunch, he would retire to his armchair in the master's room and sleep for a quarter of an hour. From there he returned to his office, met with clients, perused documents, and dictated letters until six o'clock, at which time he would climb the stairs to our living quarters, listen to the radio, read a book or go out for dinner and then a game of bridge. Once a week he would travel one hundred kilometers to the city of Sobotica, where he would remain overnight in order to edit the weekend supplement of a Hungarian daily called *Unpel*, owned by a rich Jewish family. One evening a week he would devote to writing an article, usually by hand, which he would then type on his Remington. His opinions, which were the kind espoused by Jews of his type, were moderately liberal. On the day I was born—27 December 1931—he wrote a piece praising Mahatma Gandhi and his struggle against British imperialism.

The metronome of his life ticked at an astonishingly slow pace. He would speak on the telephone only two or three times a day; he listened to the news at ten in the evening; he had time to explain things to me and to listen to what I had to tell him. As an only child I had no competition. On Sundays he would take me to watch the Vojvodina football club play. To this very day I can feel my small hand in his large, warm hand as we walked into the stadium.

I wonder sometimes: to where did all that time that stood at my father's disposal disappear? How was it possible to maintain such a slow pace, no televisions or computers or cell phones or cars? Perhaps it is because all those appliances, designed to save time, did not eat away at his time?

And yet, my father's pace seems like a typhoon compared with that of my mother's. My nanny, Lizzy, would wake me up each morning, bathe me, prepare my breakfast, dress me and bring me to my parents' bedroom, where Mother was still in bed. We could not embrace because she was smeared with creams designed to prevent wrinkling, so she merely eyed me from afar, blew me an air kiss and sent me on my way to kindergarten or school.

Only after Father went to his office did my mother emerge from her bed. She would take a short walk around the house, checking to make sure the maid had done the cleaning and polishing. This was the extent of her daily labors. For what remained of the morning she would chat on the phone with friends, go shopping, or meet a girlfriend for coffee at the Dornstadter café in town.

Lunch was served by the white-aproned maid at the heavy mahogany table in the dining room. Throughout the meal I had to make sure my elbows were kept firmly at my sides and never on the table itself, heaven forfend. If I forgot for even a moment, my nanny would be asked to bring two books and I would be required to place them under my arms, one to a side, and eat without dropping them to the floor.

After lunch, Mother would simply be exhausted. She napped for two hours in order to awaken refreshed for the bridge game she looked forward to in the afternoon, either at our house or at the home of one of her friends. If she and Father were invited out in the evening, she would stay home and read in the garden or on the roof terrace. This was when she would play with me. She quickly discovered that I had no talent for musical instruments or singing or drawing, a fact she found singularly depressing since she wholeheartedly believed that the highest purpose in life was that of beauty. As compensation for my dearth of talents, she bought me a card game called Quartet, the object of which was to collect four paintings each by famous artists. That was how I learned, at age seven, that there was a Spanish artist named Bartolomé Esteban Murillo who had painted *The Little Fruit Seller*, *The Young Beggar*, *Two Children Playing Dice* and *Beggar Boys Eating Grapes and Melon*, in which the grape-eating boy held a bunch of grapes over his head and slipped them into his mouth much as Greta Garbo did in *Queen Christina*.

It is not by chance that my favorite painting was of children eating. Years later, when I had already earned a reputation as an insatiable glutton, I pretended to be making up for what I had lost in the ghetto. That may have shut people up, but there is not an element of truth to it. I was always a big eater, from as early as I can recall. Not only me, but everyone in my life. Today, the papers are full of cooking columns and restaurant reviews but all that is nothing compared to the monumental role that eating played in our lives.

The lion's share of my childhood memories is connected to food: talking about food, secret recipes, arguments about whose cook was the best, visions of a pantry in which Pick and Herz sausages swung lazily, and behind them stood colorful bottles of winter preserves: plum, strawberry and apricot jams; cherry, pear and peach compotes; cucumbers pickled in vinegar and cucumbers pickled in brine—rows upon rows of tempting jars waiting their day.

Each morning, Mother would speak with the cook about the day's menu. It was a deep and lengthy discussion in which the courses would be selected according to the season. Calories were not a consideration, even though on occasion Mother would force Father to diet. At such times, Father would sneak off after appearing in court to Café Sloboda for a little dish of chicken livers with paprika. If school let out early he would have me join him, and for me he would order a pair of sausages with horseradish, on the condition that I not tell Mother, of course. Each summer, during the court's recess, Father would spend two weeks at the Carlsbad spa in Czechoslovakia, where he would shed ten kilos that he would quickly regain at home.

My two uncles—partners in a mirror manufacturing factory—and my father, the elder brother, would often go hunting together, and on occasion I was invited to join them. We would rise at five in the morning on a Sunday and travel a few dozen kilometers to the area surrounding the village of Kac, where there were ample hunting fields. (The pride of the townspeople of Kac is native son Milos Maric, a Serbian officer born in 1846. Maric's daughter Mileva was one of the first women to study mathematics and physics in Europe and was Albert Einstein's fellow student and, later, his first wife.)

The youngest of the Lampel brothers, Latzi, was the most serious of the three hunters. Stag horns adorned the walls of the hunting room in his villa and the sofa was covered in the skin of a bear he had hunted in the Carpathian Mountains. Uncle Latzi had a hunting dog he prized, a pedigree pointer named Lord who went about with his head held high and his tail erect, as befitting an aristocrat. Once, on a morning we were supposed to hunt, Uncle Latzi was ill. After much argumentation he was persuaded to let my father and Uncle Pali take the dog with them. We went out to the field, where Lord uncovered a flock of pheasants that he dispersed. My father and Uncle Pali fired but no bird lost even a single feather. We trailed along behind Lord, who sniffed this way and that, until once again he pounced on a flock of birds hiding in the underbrush. Once again the birds took flight and once again the amateur hunters failed to down even one of them. Lord gave us a scornful look, turned on his heels and headed home.

I am not only recording here the biography of the life I lived, I am also recording the life I missed. My father wished for me to be like him and I wanted the same. In some ways, I have even succeeded: it is not by chance that, like him, I became a lawyer and a journalist. The difference is that I did so in a different country, as a different person. Sometimes I wonder what would have happened if a single year—March 1944 to June 1945, the sixteen-month period that constituted the Hungarian and Serbian Holocaust—were removed from history. Would I have lived in the villa next to my parents, maybe even in the very same one, after inheriting my father's thriving practice? Would I have married a beauty by the name of Ruzy and napped in the master's room each afternoon facing his portrait? Would I have spent evenings writing nostalgic articles about the late Mahatma Gandhi for *Magyar Hírlap*, the largest Hungarian newspaper?

CHAPTER 4

"If you don't believe in God," some angry ultra-Orthodox politico shouted at me during one of the *Popolitika* television programs, "then who defined you as a Jew?"

"Hitler," I shouted back at him.

For once there was silence in the studio.

God was not a major preoccupation for me during my childhood, and after the Holocaust I stopped believing in Him altogether (in my present situation I am in possession of information that I am sorry I did not have access to during my lifetime; it could have done wonders for my political career). But all this does not mean that I am not a Jew. In fact, I am a Jew in the deepest way possible. Judaism is my family, my civilization, my culture and my history. The people who insist on holding inquisitorial investigations in order to classify me as a first-class or second-class Jew amuse me. There is something ridiculous about the idea that faith in God turns Judaism into a rational matter. After all, the very act of believing in God is irrational, which is why it is called "faith." Thus, in the very same measure and with no less conviction, I believe in my Judaism with all my heart and soul. To paraphrase Shylock's famous speech in *The Merchant of Venice*, I am a Jew because I have eyes, I am a

Jew because I have hands, sense, affection and love; if tickled I laugh like a Jew, if stabbed I bleed like a Jew, if poisoned I die like a Jew.

Two popular rumors swirled around my heresy, and both were imprecise. The first was that, like most European Jewry, I was a believing Jew but lost my belief in God in the ghetto. The second was that I was raised in a completely secular household in which pigs were slaughtered every winter (that's true) and that I had never heard a prayer service in my life (that's not).

I suspect that the former chief rabbi of Israel, my friend Rabbi Israel Lau, is the source of the first rumor. We were the two most famous Holocaust survivors in Israel and we argued a lot. He never grew tired of trying to persuade me to "return" to Judaism, and I never grew tired of explaining to him that I had nowhere to return to. After my death he published an article in which he described our final meeting, when I lay on my hospital deathbed, in which he wrote, "With regard to his attitude towards religion and religious people, it seems that Tommy has undergone some sort of transformation." As my doctors and family members can attest, this foolish statement has no grounding in reality, and if I were still alive I would settle accounts with him.

The source of the second rumor is one of the more embarrassing moments of my life. It happened some two weeks after I arrived in Israel as a boy of seventeen sent straight from the boat to basic training. Those were confusing times for me, and I had trouble sleeping at night, or, in the words of the great Hungarian humorist Frigyes Karinthy, "I dreamt I was two cats fighting with each other." One morning I awakened at dawn and stepped outside the tent to relieve myself. On the outskirts of the camp I caught sight of a man wearing a square transmitter on his forehead and an antenna which was attached to his forearm; he was rapidly muttering his report to the enemy. I raced to my commanding officer and informed him I had caught an enemy spy. The officer burst out laughing. "You mean to tell me," he said, "that you've never seen a Jew don *tefilin* for the morning prayers?"

No, in fact I had not. But that still does not mean we knew nothing about Judaism. Judaism played a meaningful role in our lives, even if it was carried out in the same relaxed manner that we did everything else.

The Jewish community of Novi Sad belonged to the Neolog stream of Judaism, a mild reform movement within Judaism, practiced mainly in Hungarian-speaking regions of Europe, which began in the late nineteenth century and would today fall somewhere between the Reform and Conservative movements. We had a large and beautiful synagogue, one of the loveliest to be found in central Europe, with an enormous organ behind which sang the choir. Men and women sat separately and the men covered their heads and wore prayer shawls. We could read Hebrew letters and chanted the prayers in that language, but without understanding a word of it. The rabbi gave his sermons in Serbian (the official language) but in the aisles of the synagogue and in the women's section, juicy gossip was spread in Hungarian. In fact, we all knew three languages equally well: Serbian, Hungarian and German, which was the preferred international language in our part of the world. We attended synagogue three times a year: on Rosh Hashanah, Yom Kippur and Passover.

Had our activity ended there it could have been claimed that ours was a feeble form of Judaism, but in fact it did not. Our synagogue was situated on a large piece of property on one of the main thoroughfares of the city. At the far end of the property stood the three-story Jewish community building that boasted a banquet hall, a cafeteria for Jewish students who came from the surrounding villages to study in Novi Sad, and an archive of documentation pertaining to the city's Jewish history. (The archive remains intact; it enabled Yair to find the communal grave of our family where he went to pay his respects, up to his knees in snow.)

Behind the synagogue stood the building of the Maccabi sports organization, with a large, well-appointed gymnasium where I worked out twice a week. There were rooms for the different Maccabi sporting groups: football, handball and even *henza*, a kind of handball for women that has since disappeared from the world of sport. There was a chess and checkers room that was mostly used for card-playing. On the top floor the youth movements had offices, everything from the left-wing *Shomer HaTzair* to right-wing *Beitar* (I was in the Scouts). There was even a spacious theater used mostly for concerts. My Aunt Ila—Latzi's wife—was a pianist who appeared there often, and the entire family would attend her performances.

But I have not mentioned the most important thing of all: the Jewish school, where I studied for nearly four years (elementary school in Yugoslavia lasted four years). The teachers' salaries were paid for by the community, and both the level of instruction and the well-equipped classrooms were of a standard higher than that of the public schools. Thus, the Christian elite of Novi Sad also sent their children to the Jewish day school. In our Judaism classes we learned the Hebrew alphabet, and I can still mumble the Shma Yisrael prayer without error, but with a strange accent. We learned the Bible stories and Jewish history in Serbian.

All of this created a very Jewish atmosphere, if not a particularly religious one. At our house we celebrated Hanukkah; at my grandmother's house there was a *pushke* for collecting money for the Jewish National Fund, and on the wall a print of Abel Pan's *The Shepherd*. Grandmother was the president of the local WIZO chapter; Father was, in his youth, secretary of the Zionist Federation and, later, president of Bnai Brith; and Uncle Pali was head of the Novi Sad Jewish community after the war. None of this required lighting candles on the Sabbath, or donning a prayer shawl or a pair of *tefilin*. The most religious thing that took place in my life, apart from my circumcision, was when Grandmother's brother, Uncle Sándor, swung a chicken over his head as part of the preparations for the Yom Kippur holiday of atonement. And that was funny, and not very convincing.

The two customs we did keep were the lighting of the candles at Hanukkah and the Seder meal at Passover. For that holiday, my father had a leather-bound Haggadah. Starting in 1931, he listed the participants at our Seder meal each year on the blank pages found at the beginning of the Haggadah.

Unlike my father himself, my father's Haggadah survived the Holocaust. After the Jews of Novi Sad were expelled, our Hungarian neighbors looted our property and made off with furniture, household utensils, paintings, clothing. Everything. Whatever was left behind was stored by the authorities in the city's large synagogue. Upon our return from the concentration camps and ghettos, we were sent to the synagogue to look for our belongings. I can still recall the scene: dozens of Jews, pale and thin, scrounging among the shattered furnishings, the faded piles of clothing, and the broken utensils that remained behind after the non-Jews had picked them clean and taken anything that appeared to have value. There were also quite a large number of books; among them, Uncle Pali was amazingly lucky to find the family Haggadah. Three years later he added to it the three most important words in the history of our family: *Moved to Israel.*

CHAPTER 5

Throughout my life I was blessed—or cursed—with an exceptionally good memory. I can recall flavors, scents, books that I read, people I met and conversations in which I took part. Even after Google came on the scene, my eldest grandson, Yoav, an insatiable trivia addict just like me, continued to phone with questions like where the first May Day was commemorated (at a rally in Chicago) or which monks wear brown cloaks (Franciscans). I would answer and he would thank me and ring off before I could ask why the hell a staff sergeant in the Israeli army would need such trivial information. It is only with respect to myself that my memory is hesitant. I know that Uncle Latzi was assertive and Aunt Ila was fragile, but what kind of child was I? Philip Roth, one of my favorite authors, once wrote, "Memories of the past are not memories of facts, but memories of your imaginings of the facts."

My earliest true childhood memory was also my first trauma. One day, when I was about five years old, a farmer brought my father a lamb as payment for drawing up a contract for him. My father gave it to me as a gift for me to play with in the garden. I named him Mickey. I fed him milk and lettuce leaves, I played with him. This lasted for several weeks, during which time Mickey grew and the connection between us deepened. Then one day he disappeared. I looked all over for him; I cried, but Mickey was nowhere to be found. That evening at dinner, during the main course, I complained bitterly to my parents about Mickey's disappearance. My parents exchanged glances, and suddenly I understood that we were eating him. I jumped up from the table, ran to the bathroom and heaved the contents of my stomach into the toilet.

It could be that this was not an exceptional tale in a provincial town surrounded by villages, but at least it hints at the fact that I had protective parents who tried to spare me the difficulties of life. (Years later I ate a wonderful lamb roast with Ariel Sharon at his farm; the fearless warrior admitted that the meat was purchased from a butcher because he could not stomach eating an animal that had been raised on his farm.) My parents never raised a hand to me, I was permitted to speak during meals as much as I pleased though this was unacceptable in those conservative times, and I do not recall asking for something that I did not later receive. I was a spoiled only child, and to this day I believe that pampering a child does no damage as long as it is not a substitute for love. When I was forced to be resilient, which happened to be at a very young age, I proved to possess rather remarkable survival skills.

Father was the center of my world. I had many friends, but a patient father, one who was always willing to set aside time for me, was a true asset in those days. He could be very assertive when necessary, but he always had time to sit with me, to take me to a football match, to check my homework, to read the newspaper with me and to explain where Bosnia-Herzegovina was located, or who the Pharaohs were. At night we would raid the kitchen together, where he would make himself a Körözött (soft white cheese with anchovy spread, paprika and chopped onion), all the while describing for me with wildly gesticulating hands the heroic victory of Ilona Elek, the Jewish fencing champion of Hungary who took the gold medal at the Berlin Olympics right under Hitler's disappointed nose. (It is interesting to note that Elek's opponent in the finals was Germany's Helene Mayer, one of only two Jews permitted to compete for Germany in those Olympics.)

I was able to read from the age of four and I did so incessantly. I read Pinocchio, the Baron Munchausen, *Der Struwwelpeter, Max and Moritz,*

Peter Pan, Edmondo De Amicis' *Heart*, Cooper's *Last of the Mohicans*, and, to this very day I cannot forget how I cried when Little Nemecsek died at the end of Ferenc Molnár's *The Paul Street Boys*. However, my favorite book of all was *Old Shatterhand*. At the time I had no way of knowing that its author, Karl May, was a crook who had never set foot in the Wild West he described. Many years later, when I was a politician, each time I wished to end an argument I would bang on the table and say, "I have spoken!" which made a great impression of authority on everyone in the room. What no one knew was that I was simply quoting Winnetou, the book's Indian hero.

When I had finished reading all the children's books I could get my hands on, my father permitted me to browse his private library, where I encountered Edgar Wallace's spy novels, all bound in blue and first featuring that clever investigator J.G. Reeder and later stern Sergeant/ Inspector Elk. I was smitten. Wallace is a nearly forgotten writer today, but he was a talented and productive author who wrote one hundred and seventy-five novels, twenty-four plays and hundreds of articles in various newspapers. At one stage, one-fourth of all the books sold in the United Kingdom had been written by him.

This great investment in reading apparently paid off, since within days of starting school it was clear to me that schoolwork came easier to me than to the other children. Happily, that did not cause them to bear a grudge against me. It turned out that everyone expected the son of Bela the Bright not to be stupid. Although I was not particularly good at athletics, I became one of the class leaders. Physically, I was medium-sized for a Jew but was always looking up to my Serbian classmates. (The Serbo-Croatians are among the taller peoples of the world; it is no wonder that this small region has produced many noted basketball players.)

It seemed at the time that I enjoyed a normal childhood, a childhood like that of the other children I knew. It was only many years later that I came to understand just how deeply we were affected by the fact that we were caught between two warring cultures. In Novi Sad the Hungarians refused to learn Serbian, the Serbians refused to learn Hungarian, and only the Jews spoke both with the same ease. Our gym teacher was Hungarian, the teachers of our other subjects were Serbian, our headmaster was a Jew. At home we spoke Hungarian but the youth movement I belonged to was Sokol (Eagle), which was headed by Serbian Crown Prince Peter, and at every activity we sang the national anthem, "*Boze Pravde*," God of Justice.

I always detested the famed linguist Noam Chomsky, who is, in my opinion, the epitome of the Jew-hating Jew, but I am forced to agree with his theory of Universal Grammar, according to which language and cognition impact one another. As I grew up, my ambivalence increased. A second-grade teacher of mine handed back a homework assignment with a single written comment: DECIDE. When I looked at the pages I discovered I had written the right-hand pages in the Cyrillic alphabet used by the Serbian language and the left-hand pages in the Roman alphabet used by the Hungarian language.

By the time I was six or seven years old, current events had already found their way into my life. I read all the newspapers, listened to the radio, and participated in the worried conversations taking place around the table. War clouds were gathering over the skies of Europe. In December 1937, on my sixth birthday, my father published in his paper a poem he had written for me, called "My Young Son," the last lines of which were as follows:

> *Listen, my son—do not give your back to those who would whip you!*
> *For there is no value in tears or in laughter;*
> *If an enemy rises against you, ball your fists and clench your teeth*
> *Until you can return a blow for a blow—with valour, and heedless of law or convention*
> *Just do not give your back to those who would whip you!*

During all my years in politics I abstained almost entirely from the absurd pomp that most politicians pursue so excitedly. That is, except for one time. In 2003, when I was Israel's deputy prime minister, I visited Novi Sad. For the first time ever, I demanded—and received—a full military escort, an official limousine and two uniformed policemen on motorcycles with flashing lights and blaring sirens. I wanted everyone to see, to know, that I had not given my back to those who would whip me.

CHAPTER 6

On a sun-drenched Sunday morning during my time as the London correspondent for *Maariv* newspaper, I went to Speakers' Corner in Hyde Park, erected a sign that read *TACHOMETRIC ECONOMICS*, mounted a footstool and delivered an impassioned speech about an economic doctrine that does not exist. As is usual in Hyde Park, a crowd of curious onlookers gathered, several of whom began to debate with me. I continued to argue in favor of my revolutionary theory and found myself surrounded by dozens of Brits and tourists all discussing the merits and deficiencies of tachometric economics.

The fact that a person can speak passionately and persuasively about something that never existed and manage to win people over was nothing new for me. I learned that on the first day of the occupation of Novi Sad.

Throughout my life I quoted the German pastor Martin Niemöller: "They came first for the communists, and I didn't speak up because I wasn't a communist. Then they came for the trade unionists, and I didn't speak up because I wasn't a trade unionist. Then they came for the Jews, and I didn't speak up because I wasn't a Jew. Then they came for me and by that time no one was left to speak up."

In the Lampel family, however, there was in fact someone left to speak up. And he was the most unlikely person of all.

———

In April 1941, Hungary invaded Yugoslavia with the help of the Germans, and conquered it. By the time Father and I returned to Novi Sad from Belgrade, which was aflame, the fascists had already started hanging communists in the streets. The Jews cloistered themselves in their homes and asked if they were next in line.

A few days after our return, Father was arrested and sent to a labor camp. It was clear this was only a station on the way to the galleys or to eastbound trains. We did not know exactly where they were headed but we already knew that no one came back from there. Mother, however, had different plans. She seemed to understand—long before the rest of us—that in this new life that had been forced upon us there was only one principle: survive at all cost.

That fragile beauty queen, who had always needed a man's arms to support her, suddenly disappeared. She put on her best clothes, took her Hungarian passport, and, despite the snow, set out for the police station in high heels. Armed only with her habitual aura, that of the duchess from Budapest, she screamed at everyone, tossing about heavy hints of her (completely imaginary) connections with the highest authorities in the capital. The policemen regarded this furious woman with her gray-green eyes and decided that they did not want trouble; who knew what important personages she really did know. Father was released.

My mother and I had our share of misunderstandings over the years. Children tend to excessive morality, and it was impossible for me not to notice her explosive sexuality, her manipulations, her flirtations and her lovers. She had three husbands throughout her lifetime (all three of whom died while married to her; in Judaism that is what is called an *isha katlanit*—a femme fatale too dangerous to wed again), each wealthier than the last and each more servile in his turn. She was fond of them all, but only loved one person her entire life: me. When her cub was threatened she exposed her pampered Siamese-cat nails. More than once, and in different ways, she saved both our lives. This served to create a bond between us that was far deeper than words can express.

On that same day, my struggle for identity came to an abrupt end. My school closed. We were removed from our large villa and sent to live in an apartment in the center of town. Father lost his license to practice law. I was certainly no longer Hungarian, but neither was I Serbian anymore. People who had known us our whole lives peered at us from behind locked shutters as policemen took Father away—and did nothing. Of course I am familiar with the famous exhortation made by Anne Frank, who was two years older than me, that "despite everything, I believe that people are really good at heart," but I do not agree with her. Most people are not good at heart, they are indifferent. Whoever does not belong to their immediate group holds no interest for them. From that moment on, I was a full-time Jew.

After Father's release we were plagued, for the first time in our lives, by financial worries. No longer able to practice law, Father tried his hand as a real estate agent, but clients were not biting. Jews were interested in getting rid of their apartments and moving to America but the Hungarians understood that it was best to wait until they were expelled and they could simply take over their property. We began slowly to sell off everything we owned. Paintings and furniture would suddenly disappear, my mother's jewelry box emptied out at an alarming rate. After several weeks of this, Father suggested that we might be better off in Budapest, which was still under military control. Mother was pleased; her parents lived there and she missed them and worried about what would happen to them.

We arrived in Budapest in late May and went to live in two rooms in a small boardinghouse in District VII, quite near my grandparents. Mother registered me for the fourth grade at the elementary school in Senra Street. In the space of a single day I found myself learning the flip side of the history, geography and citizenship lessons I had previously learned, since the Hungarians and the Serbs had been at war with one another for hundreds of years. The teaching methods were different, the level was much higher and—most perplexing of all—everything was taught in a different language. I made an enormous effort to succeed; I was a ten-year-old who understood that his parents were in trouble and decided—in that secret way children sometimes use for taking responsibility upon themselves—to make them happy. All at once I was Little Nemecsek, the diminutive army private from *The Paul Street Boys* who decided to rescue his neighborhood.

At the end of the year I received my marks. In Hungary, the highest mark was a 5. I looked at the paper with a banging heart: I had one 4 and all the rest were 5s. I ran all the way home, ecstatic. My grand-father, who was a tall, cold man (and, in retrospect, an idiot), took the report card from me, gave it a passing glance, and said, "Our family does not bring home any 4s." I never ever forgave him for that.

I am well aware that this was not the most fascinating part of my life. The years during which our personalities are shaped is of interest mostly just to us. But in this case, those years carry added importance: they illustrate just how the trap clamped down on us—slowly, in tiny increments—while we waited for the world to return to sanity, surprised at each juncture that it refused to do so.

In 2007, after being appointed chairman of *Yad Vashem*, the Holocaust Martyrs' and Heroes' Remembrance Authority, I delivered the main speech at the Holocaust and Heroism Remembrance Day ceremony on Mount Herzl. These were my final words:

> *Six million of our dead speak to us from the earth. "We did not think," they say to us, "that such a thing could come to pass. We trusted others' benevo-lence. We believed there was a limit to the madness. By the time we awak-ened from these delusions it was too late. Do not follow in our footsteps." The enlightened world counsels us to compromise, to take chances in the name of peace. And we ask the enlightened world, on Holocaust and Heroism Remem-brance Day, we ask all those who preach and moralize to us: What will you do if we take chances and make sacrifices and put our trust in you—and then something goes wrong? What will you do then? Ask our forgiveness? Say, "We were wrong?" Send bandages? Open orphanages for the children who sur-vive? Pray that our souls rise to heaven?*

But perhaps I was troubled simply because the months that followed were, contrary to all logic, among the happiest of my life.

After finishing the year, I was meant to study in middle school, but no school would admit Jews any longer. This enforced inaction was the opening chord of the song my life would become over the next year and a half, during which I went from being a bright child to an educated person. My father, who could scarcely find work, decided to become my teacher, at home. Everything that I became, everything I was, sprouted from that period of my life. Ours was a two-person classroom filled with warmth and love. As was his wont, we worked methodically: each morning there were three or four hours of studies and the afternoon was spent on learning by heart and doing homework.

I learned everything, almost without discretion: there was literature, mathematics, physics, English, history and even Latin. From who knows where, he managed to obtain a high-school syllabus, but we only followed it very broadly. My father had an appetite for knowledge that led us to arenas that no child my age had the privilege of visiting: French Impressionism and Admiral Nelson's battles at sea; the poetry of Hungarian-Jewish poet Miklós Radnóti and the short stories of O. Henry; gossip about the quarrels between Michelangelo and Leonardo da Vinci in Renaissance Florence; and Romeo's suicide monologue, delivered in the midst of our tiny living room: "Eyes, look your last! Arms, take your last embrace! and, lips, O you, the doors of breath, seal with a righteous kiss."

Meanwhile, the news that reached us of our family in Novi Sad was far less righteous. In January 1942, the Hungarian army staged its first round-up of Jews, which lasted several days. They closed off the city and the surrounding villages, gathered a few thousand Jews, led them onto the frozen Danube, bore holes in the ice, then shot the Jews and dispatched them into the frozen river. For years after the war there were still Jews who refused to bathe in the Danube because of this memory. Quite a few of our acquaintances were killed, some of them while walking innocently down the street. When we returned, everyone spoke of the "red snow." It took me some time to understand what they meant.

In the summer of 1943 our permit to stay in Budapest expired and we were forced to return to Novi Sad. We lived in a small apartment and Father continued to try to make a living as a real estate agent while preparing me for the high-school entrance exams which—it was clear to us both—no one would allow me to take. We lived in constant fear. I have no way of articulating that feeling to someone born after the war. When you live in a constant state of fear—as we did from the summer of 1943 to January 1945—it becomes part of who you are, a piece of your DNA. Outside, bombs were falling and Jews were being picked up on the street and hunger gnawed at everyone, and all the while we stayed inside and pretended everything was fine. I lived in fear at eleven, at twelve, and at twelve and a half—I was still living in fear.

Am I explaining it well enough? I am not sure. Perhaps there is no way of explaining the fact that if you are fearful long enough it becomes a habit, a part of your life, even its most intimate details. Once, in Israel, I attended the premiere of a play that takes place in occupied Poland. One of the actors, playing a resistance fighter in a cellar, was charged with turning off the radio when the Germans approached. I sat in the theater recalling how Father and I would sit listening at night, risking imprisonment and death, merely to hear Churchill's voice, an oasis of warmth and sanity in a world gone mad, as he said, "We shall fight on the beaches, we shall fight on the landing grounds, we shall fight in the fields and in the streets, we shall fight in the hills; we shall never surrender."

After the performance, I approached the actor and told her that it was not enough for her to turn off the radio, that she had to move the dial because when the policemen entered they would check to see where the dial was pointed even if the radio was off. In every show thereafter, the actor did as I instructed, as I myself had done.

And then Mother went to Budapest and on 19 March 1944, Father and I went to sleep together in the big bed and at six in the morning all our fears came true.

CHAPTER 7

Father was forty-four years old when he was apprehended, younger than Yair is today. Mother was thirty-seven at the time, younger than Meirav. I was twelve and a half, younger than my second oldest grandson, Lior.

I missed Lior's bar mitzvah by only three months. When he awakened that day, he found a pressed white shirt that his mother had hung over the back of the chair next to his bed, because children of that age do not choose their own clothing. He was taken to the synagogue, because children of that age do not drive. The checks he received as gifts were deposited for him in the bank, to be used after his release from the army, because children of that age do not yet know how to take care of their own money. Was I any different at his age? I believe I was. When Father went away with the Gestapo officer I understood that I would have to leave Novi Sad. I decided to prepare for the trip. I took a small bag and put inside it the most essential belonging I could think of: my marble collection.

And with that, my plans came to an end. A gray morning dawned and Grandma Hermina stood crying in the kitchen as we waited without knowing what we were waiting for. One of our upstairs neighbors came down and said, "The Germans are here. We're in the hands of the Germans." Only then did I begin to understand what had happened. The Jews were rounded up at the train station and from there were sent to the east, to Auschwitz. Father was there for nearly a year before being moved to Mauthausen, where he died. Mother was stuck in Budapest, because at once the Jews were forbidden from traveling by train. It took two or three days before I managed to make contact with her by phone and to tell her what had happened. "Wait there," she said. "Someone will come to fetch you."

Once again there awakened in Mother the very thing no one ever suspected she possessed. She went to my grandparents' Christian neighbors, the Nakovsky family, who had a son, Peter, who was my age and with whom I would play during the summers we spent in Budapest. After a brief negotiation, she purchased from them his Lavanda certificate indicating his membership in the Hungarian Youth Organization and replaced Peter's photograph with my own. The invasion was barely three days old and my mother had already become a forger.

From there, she went in search of Uncle Alfred.

Until that day, I had only heard vague mentions of his name, mainly whispers that ceased whenever I drew near. Uncle Alfred was the black sheep of the family. Already in his twenties he had rebelled against his parents, become a Christian, and, of all the professions in the world, had chosen to be a detective in the Criminal Investigations Unit of the Budapest Police. He was baldheaded and fat, did not look at all Jewish, and spent his life among whores and thieves, crooks and pickpockets. The family had ostracized him and my mother had not seen him since she was a little girl.

On that day, however, she knocked at the door of his apartment. "I am Kato," she told him the moment he opened the door. "Your sister's daughter. My son is trapped in Novi Sad, alone, and you've got to go there and bring him to me here."

Uncle Alfred's Christian wife went hysterical. "Don't you dare!" she cried. "For thirty years they haven't spoken to you, and now that they need something she shows up. I want her out of here."

No one, however, was better at histrionics than my mother. She quickly crossed the apartment, went out to the balcony and climbed on top of the narrow railing. "If you don't go bring Tommy here," she shouted, "I'll jump."

Uncle Alfred took one look at the two women, went to the hat rack, fetched his black leather cap and put it on, then removed the forged papers from my mother's hands and left without a word.

Several days later, a man I had never laid eyes on, wearing a black leather cap, showed up at our apartment in Novi Sad. "I am your mother's uncle," he told me, "and now you must dress yourself, say goodbye to your grandmother, and come with me."

I looked at Grandma Hermina and she looked at me. "Go with him, Tommikeh,' she said. "I will manage."

Grandma Hermina was a fine-looking old woman, her white hair always in place. She was well aware that she was going to die. I replayed that moment in my mind thousands of times during my lifetime, and each time it was clear to me that my grandmother understood what I could not. Shortly after I left with Uncle Alfred, the Germans sent her to Auschwitz, too, and she died there without knowing that I had been spared.

It was a strange journey: Uncle Alfred in his gangster's clothing and shiny pistol in his gun belt, with me tagging along behind with my bag of marbles. He stopped at the tram station and waited. "Jews aren't allowed on the tram," I told him quietly. He removed my forged documents from his pocket and handed them to me. "Learn this by heart," he said without looking at me. "You are Peter Nakovsky from Budapest and we are not Jews."

We reached the train station, a long and impressive two-story building built of wood and metal and fronted with stone, like a church. The station teemed with baggage-laden travelers and soldiers with duffel bags and weapons. Hungarian policemen moved among the people checking identification papers and looking for Jews trying to escape. Uncle Alfred looked worried. He knew that my papers would not withstand scrutiny. We went up to the second floor, where there was a large workers' restaurant with a balcony overlooking the platforms. Soldiers milled about there as well. A group of SS officers in gray-green uniforms and the eagle emblem glittering from their caps were sitting in the middle of the restaurant. "Do you speak German?" Uncle Alfred asked quietly. I told him I did.

He took my hand and began acting like a drunk, weaving and mumbling his way through the restaurant until we came to the German officers' table, where he sat down with them and promptly put his head on his arms and pretended to fall asleep. This amused the Germans. "Your father had a bit to drink, eh?" one of them asked me. I do not know what I answered. I recall that I talked, I recall that we laughed, I recall that they were friendly to me, these people who wore the exact uniform worn by the man who had come to take my father. I recall that this lasted half an hour, the longest half hour of my life.

But Uncle Alfred's trick worked. As long as we sat with the SS officers the Hungarian policemen did not dare approach us. When the train blew its whistle downstairs, he suddenly "awakened," took my arm, mumbled something incomprehensible in parting and led me quickly to our carriage. The train whistle sounded one more time and we were off toward Budapest, though the nightmare was not yet over.

After traveling some fifteen minutes, I fell asleep, exhausted by all the stress. Uncle Alfred was just beginning to relax when two Hungarian policemen threw the door to our compartment open and entered. One put his fingers to his lips to keep Uncle Alfred from awakening me. They took my papers and examined them; something made them suspicious. They approached me cautiously and then, all of a sudden, shone a flashlight in my eyes, shook me and shouted in Hungarian, "What is your name? What is your name? Tell us what your name is!"

Later, Uncle Alfred told me that he had never, in all his years as a detective, been so frightened. His life would be determined by whatever a child he had never met before would say—a child who had learned his new name from dubious identification documents only two hours earlier. He was certain that I would instinctively give my real name the moment I awakened.

However, a far more primitive instinct was at work here. I opened my eyes and said, "Peter. Peter Nakovsky."

The policemen eyed us with suspicion for another moment, then left.

CHAPTER 8

In Graham Greene's short story "A Shocking Accident"—which I thoroughly enjoyed and even quoted on one of my radio programs—a boy studying at an English public school is summoned by the housemaster in the middle of a lesson. He understands, judging by the man's serious demeanor, that something terrible has happened and indeed, the housemaster begins in an ominous tone: "I'm afraid I have bad news for you . . ." In fact, he is having trouble keeping his laughter under control.

He manages to inform the boy that his father has died. The astonished boy asks, "Did they shoot him through the heart?" The housemaster turns his back so that the boy cannot see him. "Nobody shot him, Jerome," he tells the boy. "Your father was walking along a street in Naples when a pig fell on him."

I found this story, a kind of Neapolitan *Appointment in Samarra*, highly amusing, mainly because it felt familiar. During the course of 1944, Death and I met so many times that if he had materialized in the form of a pig falling from a balcony, the only thing that would have surprised me was the possibility that there were still any pigs left uneaten in the whole of Budapest.

Uncle Alfred left me at my grandparents' house and disappeared forever. Years later, long after the war, I discovered by chance that he was in financial straits; I sent him packages containing food and money until his dying day, but we never met again.

It will perhaps sound absurd but we felt lucky since we were among those permitted to remain in their own homes. We were joined there by my uncle Irwin and aunt Edith and two other families.

During that period, Adolf Eichmann, the *Obersturmbannführer* of the city, had managed to squeeze tens of thousands of Jews into the ghetto, but we had fallen, for the time being, through the holes of German bureaucracy. There were too many Jews to deal with even for a demon like Eichmann. Pre-war Budapest was one of the largest Jewish cities in Europe and in 1944 there were still a quarter of a million Jews residing there.

The four-room apartment we lived in at 5 Géza Street was on the third floor of a large, six-story building built in a horseshoe shape. There was a piano in the living room. Mother and I occupied a small bedroom off the kitchen where, in days past, the maid had slept. The others were spread around the flat, with one mattress abutting the next. The adults were irritable and frightened, and they argued all the time. I spent most of my time on the narrow patio on the ground floor of the building. I wanted to ask Mother if Father would return, but I did not dare.

Running through the building a few days later, I bumped into the building's Hungarian custodian. He pushed me and said, "Dirty Jew-boy, watch out." The fact that I answered him is, in my mind, proof that my notorious big mouth was not born on Israeli television. I looked at him and said, "A man in a uniform? You should be ashamed of yourself talking like that." In response, he gave me a stinging slap across the face. When I fell back I saw Uncle Irwin looking down at us from the staircase, frightened and speechless. From that day on, I shifted the center of my activity to the small park facing the building, where I spent most of my time playing marbles with children from the neighborhood. They were apparently better players than me, because within a few weeks I had lost my entire collection. My last possession from Novi Sad was gone.

The slap administered by the custodian was not, of course, the only violence I encountered. To this day it astonishes me how the Hungarians, who were nearly as hungry and dirty and frightened as we were, found the time and energy to continue persecuting Jews right to the end of the war; each passing month brought more bullying. Come fall, our rations were cut for the umpteenth time and we were forbidden from leaving home before eleven o'clock in the morning so that we would have no time to reach the shops. Once, I went out to buy food and decided to sneak to the head of the line, where Jews were not allowed to stand. Unfortunately, I had forgotten I was wearing my yellow star; when those in line noticed it, they attacked me and beat me brutally. I ran away from there crying and bloody but I did not return home. Instead, I went to another shop to try my luck sneaking to the head of that line.

Back then it was not only the non-Jews you had to fear, but the Jews as well. We are accustomed to thinking of the victims as pure and innocent, but human nature does not work that way. People who are starving and angry are capable of anything. And where I was concerned, the danger was double: in addition to everything else, I was an illegal resident in Budapest on dubious false papers. One day I fought with Andreas, the son of the people who lived on the top floor of our building, and he stepped onto the balcony and began shouting, "Tommy Lampel is an illegal resident! Tommy Lampel is an illegal resident!" Luckily, his parents dragged him inside before anyone had a chance to hear him. I still wonder whether he ever comprehended the fact that he tried to have me sentenced to death merely for beating him in a race on the stairs.

Before the war, Andreas's parents were quite wealthy people and had many aristocratic friends. One of them, Baron Lipansky—apparently a very decent man—continued to visit them and bring them food. On one of those visits he noticed Mother. In spite of the hunger and poverty, she was still exceptionally beautiful and took as much care as always with her appearance. It did not take long before a romance developed between them. They were discreet, out of their fear of two very powerful institutions: the Nazis and me. But in the crowded circumstances in which we lived it was nearly impossible to keep anything a secret, so it did not take long for me to figure out what was going on. I was confused and angry; we still had no idea what had become of Father, even though we could guess—but I did not say a word. Mother was simply not the faithful Penelope I had read about in the children's illustrated version of *The Odyssey*, waiting silently for her husband and turning away all suitors.

Baron Lipansky gave Mother the identity card of his first wife, the Baroness Yaslasky, who had died several years earlier. She placed it in her purse alongside her real documents, as a kind of insurance policy. Several weeks later we had arranged to meet my aunt at the tram station facing the police station for the purpose of looking for food. When we arrived we were just in time to watch as members of the Arrow Cross, the Hungarian Nazi party, detained my aunt and brought her into the station. We stood there not knowing what to do. Trams came and went while we stood waiting.

Finally, one of the guards on duty noticed this strange pair waiting outside. He came up to us and informed us we were being arrested, then escorted us into the police station. Scores of Jews were lying around there—beaten, bloodied, injured, broken-limbed, shot, many of them in the throes of death. I was paralyzed with horror, but my mother did not bat an eye. She removed the Baroness Yaslasky's passport from her handbag, presented it to the guard and, with a haughty look, ordered him to summon his superior.

The officer approached us and looked us over with suspicion. Mother drew herself to her full height and began to shout at him as I had never heard her shout at anyone before. "I am the Baroness Yaslasky," she roared so loudly that they could hear her down at the Danube. "How dare you people detain me! The moment I leave here I will be contacting the German ambassador, Doctor von Jagow, a close personal friend of mine, and I will lodge a complaint against each and every one of you. Is this how you treat a Hungarian baroness?! By putting me in a courtyard filled with these Jews? How dare you?!"

The officer took a deep breath and made a quick decision. He turned to the guard who had arrested us and began shouting at him: "Idiot! (Pardon me, Baroness.) Cretin! (Excuse me, Baroness.) Don't you have eyes in your head? Can't you see that this is a baroness? Wait until I take care of you later, just wait!" With that, he bowed deeply, kissed Mother's hand and escorted us out, all the while muttering apologies.

From the distance of many years, the Holocaust seems to many people like one long story during which Jews march through the snow to their deaths, shrinking as they go and finally disappearing in concentration camps. In fact, to most of us who were actually there, it looked quite a bit different. It went on for years, during which time people fell in and out of love, moved homes, raised children, were famished, stole food, lied, forged documents and were saved (if they were saved) not once but over and over again, each time by some new miracle.

We tend to forget this, but something else was taking place during those years—a little skirmish called World War Two. So if you managed to survive the Germans and the Hungarians and the informers, you could still be killed by the Allied forces. By this time the Americans and the British were staging nightly air raids, with hundreds of bombers strafing the city. Our building shook like a leaf and the cellar to which we descended for protection filled with coal dust from the earthquakes shaking us from above and below. Once again I was living a zigzag life.

One morning, when we left the cellar of our apartment at 5 Géza Street after a bombing raid, there was no longer a 3 Géza Street or a 7 Géza Street—and hundreds of people were buried in the ruins. We stood there shaking with cold and shock. No fire trucks arrived, no ambulances wailed, it seemed that no one cared at all, until suddenly the postman appeared at the corner of the street. He walked along at his usual pace, his large sack slung over his shoulder. When he reached 3 Géza Street, he removed the envelopes addressed to that building, glanced at the ruins, thought for a moment, then returned them to his sack. He moved on to our building and slotted the mail into the postboxes, then continued on down the street, all of us watching him as he delivered the mail or returned it to his sack when there was no one to whom to give it.

This was the period during which my career in journalism began. On one of my treks around our apartment I came upon Uncle Irwin's portable typewriter. I stood looking for quite a while at the black keys; a typewriter for me held only one meaning: Father.

An original idea struck me then: I would write a house newspaper. I gathered all the children from the building and turned them into my correspondents. Children from every floor would bring me the latest gossip and I would print it up on my uncle's typewriter, and in the evening

I would distribute it among the residents. This was sensationalist journalism at its finest, a local paper that found no news item unworthy of printing. *Uncle Schwarz Threatens to Hit Aunt Green on Fifth Floor* screamed one of my headlines. *Gross Family Stops Speaking to Feuersteins* was another. On occasion, the headlines penned by the twelve-year-old editor were more serious: *Yet Another Suicide, Third Tenant to Jump from Roof in Past Month.* Years later, in 1986, I traveled to Budapest with Yair.

This was the first time I had been back in the city since the war and I was naturally quite emotional about it. The communists were still in power, and within a day or two of our arrival, we noticed an amusing phenomenon: whenever I opened my mouth to speak, everyone was taken aback. The Hungarians looked at me and saw a fat, authoritative man in a Brooks Brothers camel-hair coat and Bally shoes in the company of a sturdy young man who looked like a bodyguard. They assumed I was a tourist until I spoke and proved myself to be one of them, Hungarian-born. As expected, they all came to the same incorrect conclusion: that I must be a high-ranking communist official.

I must admit I enjoyed every minute of it. I have a long historical and personal account to settle with the Hungarians, and the moment I understood what was happening, I began to order people around with all kinds of strange demands. It was my chance to pay them back just a little of what they had done to us, as well as a way of showing Yair what it was like to live in a totalitarian state, where one grows accustomed to asking no questions.

One morning, I took him to see our apartment at 5 Géza Street. We went up to the third floor and I knocked on the door. A man of about forty opened it, while a woman and two children stood behind him. "Everyone out," I said, without bothering to explain why. The four of them left the flat without a word and waited nervously in the hall while we made a tour of the rooms. Everything was familiar and unfamiliar at the same time. The furniture was of course different, as well as all the things that make a house a home: the wallpaper, the carpets, the pictures on the walls. "The only thing that has remained the same," I told Yair, "is the smell. It smells exactly the same." It was only when we got back to the hotel that I realized what it was that I had smelled: fear.

CHAPTER 9

During my tenure as minister of justice, I was once invited to speak at the Academy of Justice in Budapest. At such events it is customary for the guest of honor to mumble some timeworn polite phrases then clear the stage. Instead, I positioned myself in front of the microphone and said, "Good evening. I am very pleased to be here this evening, since the last time I stood facing this building there was a sign hanging from it that said: *NO ENTRANCE FOR JEWS AND DOGS.*"

A heavy silence fell on the audience, and I could see the looks on my hosts' faces, sorry that they had invited me. I did not care. Someone had to state this truth aloud.

For a brief moment in September 1944, it began to seem as though the end of our nightmare was at hand. The Russians were closing in on Budapest and the Hungarian government had decided to try to come to an agreement with them and had asked Eichmann to leave the city. However, our hopes were dashed when, as I reported in the 15 October issue of my house newspaper, the pro-Nazi Arrow Cross Party took control. Two days later, Eichmann returned, as enthusiastically active as ever. On 20 October, 50,000 men were drafted into digging ditches meant to slow the advances of the Russian army. A second detail of women and children set out on 23 October. Those who managed, somehow, to survive working in the cold and snow and dodge the incessant onslaught of Russian artillery, were handed over to the Germans and sent for extermination.

A man named Alfred Place, who succeeded in slipping away from one of those gruesome enforced labor marches, came to hide out in our apartment. No one knew him, and I was the only one to speak with him. "I don't know what they want from me," he said again and again in desperation. Like many other Hungarian Jews, Place had had no use for anything Jewish in his life. He was a Hungarian nationalist who even then refused to remove his prize possession from his breast: a gold military decoration from World War One. I did not respond. I did not understand what they wanted from me any better than he did.

Within weeks, Eichmann had organized the transfer of all the city's Jews into two large ghettos. The first was behind the Dohány Street Synagogue—then as now the second largest synagogue in the world (after New York's Temple Emanu-El)—in the cramped Jewish quarter of Budapest with narrow alleys and kosher restaurants and Judaica shops. The Nazis walled off the quarter, removed the few non-Jews who lived there, and pushed 70,000 Jews inside.

Incidentally, Theodor Herzl, the founder of political Zionism, grew up in a house next to the Dohány Street Synagogue. In the 1950s, before communist Hungary broke off relations with Israel, the Israeli ambassador to Hungary took great pains in persuading the authorities to allow him to affix a brass plaque attesting to the fact that the visionary of the State of Israel had been born there. The ambassador was my father-in-law, David Giladi, who died a year after I did, at the age of 101.

We were moved into the second ghetto, the International Ghetto. It was not exactly a ghetto, but a collection of fifty-three large buildings above which flew the flags of one of the neutral nations: Sweden, Spain, Portugal or Switzerland. We were in the Swedish building, at 14 Pozhony Street. They put us in the cellar along with three hundred other people. Above us, people slept on mattresses, in the hallways, in every corner. The men had disappeared, leaving behind only the aged, women and children. On occasion, the Nazis would enter and pull Jews out for a "death march" in which they were forced to drill holes in the frozen Danube then were shot and rolled into the holes. Whoever left did not return. We were starved, frightened, lice-ridden; the wounded horses outside did not stop bellowing and the number of suicides grew every day.

I do not know why but my most vivid memory of this time is not the bodies we piled on the roof, one atop the other so that they would freeze, or the flavorless melted snow we would drink, but the fact that I constantly had to pee. There were not enough toilets available and we were afraid to risk stepping outside only to be caught in a barrage of Russian Katyusha rockets, so we were always waiting in line, dozens of people jumping from foot to foot, their faces contorted. I do not believe in the concept of heaven, but I have seen hell and there are no toilets there.

One morning, they took Mother.

They came and took the youngest women, those who were still able to march. We were given only a few moments to say our goodbyes, which were almost identical to those I had with Father. She did not use the same words, but Mother hugged me and Mother kissed me and Mother went, and I remained completely alone. No grandmother, no father, no mother. Alone in a building under bombardment, with hundreds of starving people with far bigger problems to worry about than taking care of me. Then suddenly, toward nightfall, Mother returned. "He rescued us," she said.

She did not say who this "he" was and there was no need to. There was only one "he" in Budapest at that time: Raoul Wallenberg.

At the corner of Wallenberg and Barzel Streets in Tel Aviv there is a bronze sculpture of Raoul Wallenberg. Two meters tall and weighing a ton, the work was created by the Hungarian sculptor Imre Varga. Wallenberg is depicted as tall and thin, with his arm raised as if attempting to stop something from happening. I am very familiar with this sculpture since I arranged for it to be brought to Israel, financed it, and convinced the authorities to place it. This was the little I could do, and it was too little.

At the time, Raoul Wallenberg was only thirty-six years old. He was the scion of a bored, aristocratic Swedish family of businessmen (and who isn't bored in Sweden?), a man who had studied architecture, pursued beautiful women and was a partner in a successful commercial concern. Nothing in his background could have foretold that he was poised to become a Righteous among the Nations, perhaps the most important of them all. In my opinion, he was and always will be the proof that human conscience—like human evil—is likely to pop up in the most unlikely of places.

When the Hungarian Jewish Holocaust began, Wallenberg decided to turn himself into a one-man rescue operation. In his capacity as first secretary of the Swedish legation in Budapest, he issued "protective passports" which identified the bearers as Swedish subjects awaiting repatriation and preventing their deportation, thus saving tens of thousands of Jews. My mother and I were two of them. Our passports were in fact of no practical value, but Wallenberg had them filled with all sorts of impressive stamps and signatures and symbols, all in an elegant binding. It worked wonders with the Nazis, who always paid great respect to paperwork.

But Wallenberg did more than that. He confronted the entire Nazi bureaucracy, wheedling and making promises and lobbying them, all the while saving more and more Jews. He threatened to ensure personally that General Gerhard Schmidthuber, commander of the German army in Hungary, would be tried as a war criminal if he did not foil Eichmann's plans to eliminate what was left of the ghetto. In many cases, it worked. In others, as with Mother, he did not make do with merely speaking with the commanding officers. He actually went out into the streets in order to save a few more of "his Jews."

After Mother recovered, she told me what had happened.

The Germans had gathered a convoy of hundreds of young women and were marching them through the empty streets. One of them dared ask, "Where are we being taken?" and was told, strangely enough, "To Vienna."

Just then, however, Wallenberg discovered that this march was taking place. He showed up suddenly in his long black car with the diplomatic license plates. He emerged from the car and said to the Nazi colonel leading the march, "I am the Swedish ambassador. There are women here with my protective passports. I demand that you free them."

Today perhaps it is hard to comprehend just how surreal this scene was. Winter, snow, the end of the war, killing in the streets, bombs, total anarchy. Then, suddenly, in the midst of it all, there appears a well-dressed Swedish diplomat in a black car making demands of the convoy commander. Had the commander pulled out his pistol and shot Wallenberg dead on the spot, nobody would have known, nobody would have noticed, nobody would have intervened.

But that is not what happened. The Nazi officer acquiesced, muttered something, then ordered the release of all the Swedish protective passport holders. Wallenberg—their guardian angel—escorted them back to the ghetto and went on his way.

Wallenberg himself did not fare so well. When the Russians entered Budapest, Wallenberg was summoned to their headquarters for interrogation. He was later brought to Moscow, where he fell into the cobwebs of the Soviet gulag system, never to return. Many prisoners claim to have seen him throughout the 1950s and even later, but the Russian government gives his official date of death as 1947. It has never retracted or amended this version of events.

The Nazis were not the only ones who posed a threat to us. On occasion, gangs of Hungarian thugs would appear and try to steal the little we had left. Two or three club-wielding Jews always stood at the entrance to our building in the hopes of keeping them out. We children were appointed to be "runners" whose job it was to run inside and inform the adults that they should close all doors because the thugs were coming, or to rush out in order to have time to buy provisions. I was the commander of a group of runners. On 25 December, several children from my group asked if they could go out to find a fir tree. "A fir tree?" I said. "What do you need a fir tree for?"

"Today is Christmas," they told me.

It took me a moment to understand. These were the children of the non-Jews among us, people who had been baptized in order to progress in their careers or marry a non-Jewish woman. But none of it had helped them much. The Nazi racial laws did not recognize them and they were sent to the ghetto along with us.

"In this building," I told them, "there will be no fir trees and we will not be celebrating Christmas!"

Many years later I was speaking at a kibbutz in the north of Israel. At the end of the speech a woman from the kibbutz approached and asked, "You're Tommy Lampel, aren't you?"

"Yes, I am," I said.

She began to cry.

"Why are you crying?" I asked her.

"Because you wouldn't let me have a Christmas tree," she said.

I became a bar mitzvah two days after that Christmas, on 27 December 1944. We were sitting in the cellar, hundreds of people pressed one against the next. Mother opened her bag and pulled out a small bottle of Chanel perfume, a leftover from better days. "My son," she said, "today is your birthday. I cannot bake you a cake. You cannot invite your friends over. And Father cannot be with us. But at least it shouldn't stink at your bar mitzvah." With that, she broke the bottle on the floor and for a moment—only a moment—a beautiful scent enveloped us. I may be a secular Jew but I believe I had the most Jewish bar mitzvah imaginable.

CHAPTER 10

They came to take us at dawn.

Members of the Hungarian Arrow Cross Party, in the company of several SS officers, surrounded the building on Pozhony Street, brought us all outside and began to march us through the snowy streets of the empty city. From windows overlooking the street, people peered down at us and said nothing.

They marched us down the length of Pozhony Street, toward the Margaret Bridge, and it was then that we understood they were bringing us to the edge of the Danube, where they would shoot us and leave us to die under the ice.

When we arrived at the foot of the bridge, a Soviet reconnaissance aircraft appeared out of nowhere over our heads. The death march stopped, and there was a moment of chaos while the Nazi guards sought refuge in the entrances to buildings and shot their Schmeisser submachine guns skyward. Mother and I were standing next to a small public toilet made of metal and painted green. Mother pushed me inside. "Pretend you're peeing," she said.

I stood there, frozen with cold and fear, but I could not pee; when you are thirteen years old and frightened you cannot pee. The Soviet plane had meanwhile disappeared and the march was resumed. Not a soul noticed that Mother and I had remained in the toilet. Half an hour later, not a single person from the march was left alive.

This was the key moment of my life, the moment that defines me more accurately than any other—more than anything I ever did, more than any place I ever lived or visited, more than any person that I ever met. Not because I was spared—every survivor has his story of a private miracle—but because I had nowhere to go.

In Australia, between Sydney and Perth, there was kilometer after kilometer of dry earth where no foot had walked. The American Midwest was blessed with thousands of miles of open land, where rivers flowed and animals grew wild. Paris had been liberated, along with Rome and even Novi Sad. But I had nowhere to go. In this big wide world there was not a single place for a Jewish boy of thirteen whom everyone wants to kill.

So we went back to the ghetto.

Years later, on the trip I took to Budapest with Yair, we took a walk and found ourselves, without planning to, at the Margaret Bridge. We strolled along, chatting merrily, when suddenly I stopped and, shaking, pointed at something ahead of us. At first Yair could not understand what it was that I was pointing at, but there it was: the public toilet, made of metal and painted green. We stood there, two grown men, hugging and crying and stroking the green walls of the public toilet that saved my life, while the Hungarians who passed us on the street did so with caution, convinced that they were looking at two lunatics.

"My boy," I said once I was calm enough to speak, "it was at this place, without my even knowing it, that I became a Zionist. It is the whole Zionist idea, in fact. The State of Israel is a problematic place, and we'll all always have our arguments with it, but this is the very reason it was established: so that every Jewish child will always have a place to go."

I hope that Yair understood. I am certain he did not forget.

Before returning to the ghetto, we made one final, unsuccessful attempt to restore our faith in the world. Mother removed our yellow stars and said, "Listen, when we still lived on Géza Street there were two doormen who were friends of ours. One of them will certainly agree to hide us until the Russians come." We went to the first of them, a Slovakian named Elidyod; the moment he spied us he panicked and began shouting at us to leave because he was not willing to endanger his family. The second, Mr. Vincer, reacted similarly, though he gave us a little food before slamming the door in our faces. Sometimes it is difficult to remember that while the Holocaust was carried out by evil people, it was the cowards who enabled them to do so.

It took us some forty-five minutes to return to the building on Pozhony Street, which was now empty. All the Jews had been taken. There was something surreal about it. The accused were late for their death sentences and the executioners had gone home. We wandered about, but the only sound we heard was our own footsteps and the thunder of Russian heavy artillery and Katyusha rockets that were moving toward us from afar. In the end I told Mother, "A friend of mine from school, Latzi Anchel, lives at 4 Tatra Street, not far from the post office. He's Jewish, but they're still in their apartment. Let's try his place."

Mother was too tired to argue and followed behind me. Anchel opened the door suspiciously, but his face lit up when he saw it was me and he let us into his apartment. At first we were alarmed; the flat was full of Hungarian policemen. Soon, however, it became clear that this was an entire department of twenty-five policemen from a nearby station who had made a deal with the building's tenants: the policemen would keep them safe from the Nazis and when the Russians arrived the Jews would save them in return. They were dressed in street clothes and mixed among us, lowering their gazes when they met us in the hallways. It was very nearly funny: since leaving Novi Sad I had been saved again and again by posing as a Hungarian, and now the Hungarians suddenly wished to pose as Jews.

We laid down empty sacks on the kitchen floor to sleep. There was no food, and the only water was a leaky tap in the cellar where we stood for hours on end collecting water in mugs and pots. Incessant fighting took place around us, growing closer and closer. "We must turn Budapest into a Soviet graveyard, the reverse of Stalingrad," Hitler ordered in a telegram he sent that December. "I command you to defend the city building by building."

We knew that the Russians tended to appear suddenly from underground, since beneath Budapest there was an entire city, hidden to the eye. The city's buildings were connected by a system of tunnels and caves spread out below the crowded city streets like spiderwebs. The Hungarians, fearing invasion, had decided to prepare the city for prolonged trench warfare. They destroyed the barriers between the cellars of adjacent buildings and built thin walls in their place which could be knocked down with a few good kicks, so that if one building was bombed and caved in it was possible to escape via the neighboring building. But in fact it was the Russians, who were experts at belowground warfare, who exploited the winding system of tunnels better and would often pop up like rats in their brown uniforms, shoot in all directions, and then disappear back underground.

One morning I woke up early because I could hear voices. I awakened Mother. "Someone is speaking Serbian," I told her. She lay still and listened. "That's not Serbian," she said. "It's Russian." (Russian and Serbian are related Slavic languages and sound very similar.) For a moment we did not move. Finally, she asked if I knew how to speak with them. I told her I could manage a few words. She rose to her feet, found a piece of red, white and blue cloth—the colors of the Yugoslavian flag— wrapped it around my arm and told me to go and ask them for food.

I went down to the cellar, where I found several dusty, sooty soldiers. They looked at me, surprised and suspicious. I pointed to myself, then at the rag wrapped around my arm, and said, "Yugoslavian. *Shtoy Yugoslavi*, Marshal Tito, Yugoslavi." They relaxed, the metal on their teeth shone with their smiles. Marshal Tito, commander of the Serbian anti-Nazi resistance movement, was the most famous resistance fighter in Europe. One of the soldiers poked around in his bag and handed me a loaf of bread and a few onions. This was my first meal in weeks and I never tasted a more delicious onion.

We were liberated. My war had ended.

CHAPTER 11

There were 825,000 Jews in Hungary before the Holocaust, of which 596,000 were murdered in less than a single year. In the space of eight weeks alone, nearly half a million Jewish Hungarians were sent to Auschwitz. We tend to blame only the Germans for this, but they could not have managed such a feat on their own. There were peoples that actively opposed the annihilation, like the Danes and the Bulgarians, and nations that did not lift a finger, like Belgium. The Hungarians assisted in the extermination of the Jews, often enthusiastically. Until the very last moment, the pro-Nazi government of Ferenc Szálasi continued to dispatch Jews to the concentration camps by the thousands. I love Hungarian culture, its poetry and its sausages, but I will never, ever forgive the Hungarians.

Incidentally, Szálasi escaped to Germany after the war, where he was apprehended by an American-Jewish colonel. He was returned to Budapest and hanged. Unbelievable as it may seem, the name of the American-Jewish colonel was Himmler.

After we parted from Latzi Anchel and his family, we returned to the only address we knew: 5 Géza Street. We found my mother's parents there, along with Aunt Edith. But not Uncle Irwin.

Irwin—tall and handsome and very quiet—had worked his entire life for a Swiss concern that assembled transformers at radio stations. He had been taken on one of the marches and had reached Dachau, where he managed to survive, miraculously, until the end of April, when the American 45th and 47th Divisions liberated the camp. The American soldiers, shocked by the skeletal humans they found there, stuffed them with all the food they had in their possession. No one had warned them that the bodies of people starved for so long a period could not withstand such quantities of food and could suffer from intestinal spasms that would endanger their lives. Poor Uncle Irwin ate and ate until he died.

Perhaps it will sound strange, but what happened to Uncle Irwin's body also happened to my soul. In the first weeks following liberation, I found it difficult to adjust to the fact that I had survived. For many long months my days and nights had been filled with constant, ongoing fear of all sorts of bizarre and terrible deaths. And then, all at once, there were no more Nazis, there was no more war, nobody wanted to kill me any more. I remember the strange, unnatural feeling of waking up in the morning and knowing that no one wished to harm me.

It did not help that a mere few hundred meters from where we were, the fighting continued. Across the river, in Buda—the ancient part of the city—the forces of Lieutenant Colonel Otto Skorzeny, a commando fighter and one of Hitler's favorites, was waging a battle literally to the last man. The Russians were on our side of the river, the Germans on the opposite bank, and all the bridges had been destroyed. You could walk down the street that ran along the Danube, stop to buy something, chat with someone, but the moment you reached the corner you had to run for your life, because the Germans shot at anything that moved.

When one fear leaves you, another comes along in its place. I hope this does not sound ungrateful of me, but we feared the Russians. They were the best fighters on earth, but they were rabble, scum. The first words every Hungarian learned in Russian were "Give me your watch." There were Russians walking around with three watches on each arm.

They raped women as well. We all knew about it, even before they reached Budapest. Rumor had it that when the Russian army occupied a city, the commanders gave their soldiers one day to drink and do whatever they wanted. In most cases, the preferred activity was rape. My mother was terrified. She made herself up to look like a wrinkled old woman, gathered rags from all around the house and shoved them under her clothing so that her body appeared lumpy and shapeless. My beautiful mother, who, during even the grimmest days in the ghetto, had carried on behaving and looking like Greta Garbo, suddenly turned ugly.

One day, a Russian soldier knocked at our door. We were terribly frightened and Mother said, "Don't answer, don't answer!" but the soldier continued to knock and shout and in the end, Grandmother broke down and opened the door. It took us a while to recognize him beneath the uniform and the dirt, but it was Uncle Latzi, my beloved uncle, Latzi the lively and energetic, Father's youngest brother. He had recalled that Kato was from Budapest and had come to look for her.

After we had all calmed down, he told us his story. When the Germans occupied Novi Sad he was sent, like all the young men, to a work camp. He escaped several weeks later, crossed the front line and joined the Soviet army as a translator. He advanced with them, through ceaseless fighting, to Budapest, determined to find the remains of his family. "And now that I've found you," he told us, "my war has finally ended."

In some childish way I must admit I was disappointed. My uncle the hunter, with the Kalashnikov rifle hanging from his shoulder, seemed like the most suitable person to rush to Berlin at the head of the Red Army and rout Hitler. Instead, he went to shower and emerged dressed in one of Grandfather's old suits and Uncle Irwin's hat. "Marshal Tito took control of Yugoslavia several weeks ago," he said. "It's time to go home."

Mother looked at her parents. They were old and sick and we all knew they had little time left. "Take Tommy with you," she said. "I'll stay on here a little longer."

Early the next morning we set out, Uncle Latzi and I, for the Budapest railway station. There were no ticket sellers and no guards, but freight trains were running from this ghost town. We climbed into one of the carriages and sat on the floor like the drifters you see in American movies, and this was how we started our journey home. There were several other people in the carriage and they looked just like us: hungry and restless. We chatted with them; nearly all were Jews who had been spared the valley of death and were traveling to find what was left of their families—if there was anything left at all.

When we reached Sobotica, Uncle Latzi decided we should disembark. He knew some people there, friends of Father's from his time as a journalist, and we set out to find them to ask for some money. Then, we walked around the center of town. People were coming and going, men and women were sitting in cafés, most of the buildings were intact and even the Russian soldiers behaved graciously toward the Serbians, who had been princely in their anti-Nazi resistance. I could not imagine a more different sight than that of starved and razed Budapest. While I was still thinking these thoughts, Uncle Latzi stopped at a restaurant and invited me to breakfast. Menus were placed in front of us. Menus! I had not seen a menu for more than two years.

I ate and ate without stopping. I ate until my entire body ached. One basket of rolls emptied and was replaced by another. I inhaled eggs and sausages and cakes and cookies, I gulped down cream and spread thick layers of butter on everything, then I ordered a meat pie with pickled cucumbers and stuffed cabbage; I do not believe there was a single item on that menu that I skipped. My hunger may have begun in Budapest but my famous appetite was born in Sobotica.

An hour later, we were back on a train—this time a regular passenger train—headed for Novi Sad. Next to us sat an elderly couple, Mr. and Mrs. Buxenbaum. Before the war, Mr. Buxenbaum had owned a Bakelite factory that made an early form of plastic, and they had lived in a large villa they were certain would be returned to them as soon as they returned home. They invited us to come with them and spend our first nights in Novi Sad in their guest room, at least until we found somewhere to sleep. We alighted from the train and went with them to their villa. When Mr. Buxenbaum proudly opened the tall wooden door, the first thing we saw was two Russian soldiers—one male, one female— having sex on the rug. The adults were stunned; I was riveted. The male soldier pulled his pants up and faced us. "This house has been confiscated," he told us calmly. "Get out."

The fate of our own home was similar. The communists had taken it over and declared it a municipal building. We could not argue. We were refugees with no papers, no identity, my uncle was a deserter, and they were the new authority in town. I returned only once more in my life to that house, during a visit to Novi Sad in the late 1970s with a group of Israeli journalists. We stopped the car next to the house and I showed them where I had grown up. An elderly woman in a black dress emerged from the house and came up to us. "Where are you from?" she asked.

"From Israel," I told her.

"Israel? Perhaps you know an Israeli journalist by the name of Tommy Lampel?" she asked.

"That's me," I said.

She patted my arm. "Wait a moment," she said, and she disappeared into the house, returning a moment later with a small envelope full of photographs. "I have held on to them for thirty years, in case you came back," she said. These are the only family photographs I have from my childhood.

In the end, only Uncle Latzi's house remained empty, and we returned there. Several houses away there lived a man named Rudy Gutman, who would become, a few months later, my stepfather.

Mother came back to Novi Sad two months later, more quiet and pensive and beautiful than ever. One evening we sat in the warm kitchen and the adults chatted among themselves. Someone mentioned Father. I grew tense. "Well," Uncle Latzi said, "you know he died there." I ran from the room. To this day I do not know if he had forgotten I was sitting there or whether this was his way of breaking news to me that everyone else already knew.

I did very little with what remained of that spring. I walked the streets looking for classmates, watched the flow of refugees that continued to trickle into the city. Everyone looked the same: gaunt, quiet, somnambulant. One evening, Uncle Latzi came home and announced that Hirschenhauser the tailor had gone mad. Mother asked what he meant. "He was in some place called Auschwitz," Uncle Latzi said. "He says they incinerated all the Jews there." Mother said nothing, she merely shrugged in disbelief.

People today have trouble understanding how it was that we did not know. The answer, apparently, is that the human brain is accustomed to seeking out the logic in everything, and in this case there was no logic at all. The extermination of the Jews had begun when Germany was at the height of its powers, but by 1944 it was clear to all that the Third Reich was about to lose the war. In Berlin, fifteen-year-olds were rounded up and sent to dig trenches, German industry collapsed, cities like Hamburg, Mainz and Dresden were being so thoroughly bombarded that they became nothing but heaps of ruins, the Allies were marching from the east and the west toward Hitler's bunker—and still, throughout it all, tens of thousands of German soldiers, along with hundreds of thousands of collaborators, were busy trying to kill more and more and more Jews, up to the very last moment. They hated us so much that they preferred to continue exterminating us even though they knew it was bringing about their own destruction.

I am an educated man, and in the way of educated people I tried to understand my enemies. I read *Mein Kampf* and *The Protocols of the Elders of Zion*, I browsed Voltaire's anti-Semitic letters, and even the speeches of Karl Lueger, Vienna's anti-Semitic mayor and the founder of modern anti-Semitism. And still, I cannot figure out what it was about me that was so disturbing to them. Why such an enormous apparatus for killing me needed to be built. What they actually gained from it, and what they could have gained had they not been stopped.

CHAPTER 12

I once read a letter to the editor published in the *New Statesman*, in which the writer claimed to be a poet writing his autobiography and was interested in hearing from anyone who might have some idea of what he had been doing for the past three years.

I lived in Novi Sad after the war for three and a half years and I, too, would be interested in hearing from anyone who might have some idea of what I was doing there.

It was my town, but at the same time it wasn't any longer. The fact that everything looked the same only deepened the empty spaces. The bronze statue of Svetozar Miletic, the nineteenth-century Serbian freedom fighter, still stood in the town square, his arm lifted to the masses as if he were about to give a speech, but there were no longer any masses. Some 80,000 Jews lived in Yugoslavia before the war, but only 10,000 remained. Silence prevailed everywhere.

Once again, I was required to adopt the identity of a boy I did not know, but this time it was me, my own identity. Other than crazy Hirschenhauser, nobody talked about what had taken place "there." I did not know what had happened to Father. I did not know to where my grandmother had disappeared. Nobody volunteered any information about the seventeen members of my class who had been murdered. I did not pass through any of the five stages of grief according to the Kübler-Ross model: not disbelief, not yearning, not anger, not depression, not acceptance. Instead, I hid everything that had happened to me like one of those sealed jars in the pantry of the house that was also no longer. My new job was to pretend that I was a normal young man in a normal world. To move like a normal young man, sound like a normal young man, think the thoughts of a normal young man, all in the hopes that one day that normal young man—whom I imitated so loyally—and I would merge into one.

Mother was not much help. The war ended and she went back to her old ways with the ease of a woman slipping into a mink: relaxed, self-centered, turning the heads of every man in the vicinity. We spoke very little, as if we feared that the Nazis would suddenly jump out and remind us of the past.

I hope that I do not sound angry with her. In my opinion there is something pathetic about adults who continue to be angry at their parents about real or imagined injustices done to them as children. From a certain age, every person is responsible for his or her own destiny and, sometimes, to blame for it. "In my days of *Sturm und Drang*," as Goethe called it, she saved me more than once and I was grateful for that to my dying day. In fact, this probably took a greater toll on her than I had imagined and she was in need of a pair of consoling arms.

Three months after she returned to Novi Sad, Rudy came into our lives. Rudy Gutman was a chubby, cheerful man, as dark-skinned as a Creole and known for his pleasant demeanor. He was not particularly handsome—Mother was of the opinion that handsome men were likely to be self-absorbed—but he enjoyed being around other people and was always surrounded by them. One of my first memories of him was the sight of him sitting in the kitchen late at night with his aged mother, Margaret, their heads bent close together telling racy jokes for hours and laughing hysterically.

His hasty marriage to Mother was not unusual in those days, when an entire generation was trying to stitch together its tattered lives. Like Father, Rudy had been married to a Jew from Budapest, and he and the Lampels moved in the same social circles. When the fascists took over in Yugoslavia, Rudy was sent to a work camp, escaped, and joined Tito's resistance fighters. His wife escaped to her parents' along with Margaret and their young son, Peter. She died of a brain tumor in 1943.

Peter spent the terrible winter of 1944 hidden at his grandparents' home and was returned to Novi Sad immediately following the war, when he was seven years old. At fourteen, I suddenly found myself with a younger brother. I cannot claim I was thrilled.

Peter was a quiet boy, and very spoiled by the three women who had raised him. He followed me around almost from the start. I would go to the river with my friends and when I turned around, there he would be, right behind me. When I played football he would be standing at the sidelines. After school I would spy him by the fence, waiting for me.

To my embarrassment, I must admit that he made me angry. Nobody had asked me whether I wanted a brother, and certainly not one who had turned himself into my shadow. I had enough of those already in my life. Mother took me aside for a chat, perhaps the most serious talk of our lives. "This is your family now," she told me in no uncertain terms, "and you will behave nicely toward Peter whether you like it or not."

It is probably safe to say that I was unpleasant toward both of them, father and son. I liked Rudy and I could not ignore the effort he made at having a relationship with me, but I still retained my loyalty to Father. Less than two years had passed since he was taken away from me, and miracles were happening around us on a daily basis. People declared dead suddenly appeared; others sent letters that arrived in very roundabout ways from the frozen wasteland Stalin had established in Siberia; the Iron Curtain had dropped with a sudden bang and cut us off from Western Europe, but the entire continent was awash with people wandering its length and breadth on foot and trying to make their way home (no one described it better than Primo Levi in his book *The Truce*). Who knew? Perhaps Father was sitting in a café in Zurich or Rome wearing a white suit and waiting for the right opportunity to let me know he was still alive. Something inside me knew this was a false hope, but I waited for him for years. Nice as he was, Rudy went to sleep each night with my mother, on Father's side of the bed. I had trouble forgiving them both for this.

Unlike most of the people around us, we were not undernourished. Before the war, Rudy had been a talented businessman who owned a small shipyard where industrial rafts were built for transporting merchandise on the river. Upon returning to Novi Sad, he understood that the new government would soon nationalize most of the private businesses, so he brought one of his fellow resistance fighters, a high-ranking official in the local communist party, into the business as a partner. Under the patronage of his new partner, he managed in the early days to smuggle part of his wealth to England and, even more importantly, to preserve his place of employment. Peter and I were very fond of "the carpentry shop"—our name for the shipyard—and we spent no small amount of time wandering among the stacks of long planks of wood and the yellow cranes that would transport the rafts to the water.

Rudy also managed to retain his house, a large white villa on a corner lot on Vodina-Brigada Street. It had a circular balcony at the front of the house that resembled the archer's perch in a Crusader fortress, and a nice garden in the back. Peter's two grandmothers also lived with us, and they spent most of their time chasing the boy around with sweets in their hands. At first, they tried to bring me into their game, but the distance I had sworn myself to quickly had an effect on everyone. We lived together, wordless, as courteous to one another as passengers on a night train.

Spring came, then passed. Summer came, followed by winter. Then one morning Mother awakened me to say that the time had come for me to go back to school. My second childhood was about to begin.

CHAPTER 13

I spent most of my life in a noisy, tumultuous democracy in which every single person has something to say. On occasion, when our chaotic Israeli mess tends toward anarchy, I notice how people long for a strongman, someone who will spare them the indecision and confusion of free choice. I for one have no such longing; in fact, I feel a deep disdain for it since, at the age of fourteen, I found myself suddenly, like a hamster on a treadmill, in the midst of the largest social experiment ever conducted: communism.

The years during which I lived under a communist regime left me with a very strong, almost violent, inner opposition to people who speak in the name of justice. Human history is littered with more crimes committed in the name of justice than for any other excuse. A sense of divine justice was the oil that stoked the flames of the Inquisition. A sense of racial justice was the oil that stoked the flames of fascism. A sense of social justice was the oil that stoked the flames of communism. Justice is the biggest criminal in the history of nations, because in the name of justice it is permissible to do what is impermissible in the name of mercy and kindness and charity.

I got my first lesson in socialist justice some two months after I began my studies in secondary school. We had a Jewish teacher named Kishna who was an ardent communist. She taught us about the structure of the family as dealt with in a book by Friedrich Engels, friend and co-author of Karl Marx. When we got to the chapter dealing with polygamy, I recalled something I had read in one of the colorful books by the Turkish writer Assad Bey (who turned out to be a Jewish writer from Baku, Lev Nissenbaum, in disguise).

I raised my hand and said that in the east there was an inverse phenomenon to polygamy called polyandry, in which one woman was married to more than one man. The teacher glared at me. "Engels wrote nothing of the sort," she informed me.

That day, before I went home, the janitor summoned me to Headmaster Adamovic's office. I was taken aback. What did he want from me? In his office, the headmaster seated me facing him and said, "Listen, Kishna paid me a visit. She wants you expelled from this school."

"Why? What have I done?" I asked.

"She says you're inciting people against the teachings of Marx and Engels."

Luckily, Headmaster Adamovic was a decent man. "I won't expel you," he said, "because I know what happened to you in the hands of the Germans. But starting today I will ask you to take precaution."

And starting that day, I did. On Marshal Tito's birthday I stood with the other children in the schoolyard singing with artificial gusto the march written for him, "The White Violet," all the while restraining myself from making eye contact with any of my classmates. We all understood how ridiculous it was to compare our esteemed leader—who weighed more than 250 pounds and had three chins and the eyes of a drowsy sea lion—to a delicate flower like the white violet. But if we had dared break into laughter, we would have been swiftly taken for interrogation by the OZNA, the terror-inspiring Yugoslavian secret police. An acquaintance of mine, the historian Jennie Lebel, was sent to a labor camp for two years simply because she told someone a joke about old, angry Tito. If the communists had decided that he was a flower, then Tito was indeed a flower.

I was not, of course, the only child to feel this way. Our class was divided between communists and anti-communists, and a bitter fight broke out between us. Pupils from the upper grades would steal out at night to write LONG LIVE THE KING on the walls and the police would show up at school in the morning to interrogate us and clean the walls.

The younger among us had our own form of rebellion: in the summer we would go about in shorts with the hems stitched upward with a thick thread. I no longer recall why this was considered an act of rebellion, but those up-stitched hems made us feel very daring and underground. One day, after school, the communists were waiting for us on the other side of the fence. They attacked us and knocked us to the ground and used knives to cut our hems. The revolution had failed.

Mother hated the communists even more than I did. She could not swallow an ideology that forbade her to put on makeup in the evening and go out to dance waltzes with her new husband to the tune of Strauss's "Blue Danube." Every aspect of her life, from her bridge games to the porcelain mugs she used for drinking coffee, became anti-revolutionary events and signs of "materialistic corruption." Poor Mother. That is exactly what she wanted to be her whole life—a corrupt materialist.

However, it was not the ideological confrontation with communism that occupied most of my time in those days. I was in love.

I suppose that people who remember me as the fat guy on television will have trouble believing this, but once upon a time I was not only thin, I was one hell of a dancer. Our school had set up a Serbian folkdance troupe with a girls' school in town and, thanks to my impressive grasp of the intricacies of the Paso Doble, I was accepted to its ranks.

Meza Kovchevic was the principal dancer. She was a slight, captivating blonde who devoted most of her time to training and, despite her youth, was already performing as a dancer at the Novi Sad opera house. I became an opera enthusiast, attending eight performances of *Rigoletto* and twelve of *The Magic Flute*.

But nothing helped. Just like in *Rigoletto*, I was haunted by my own raffish Duke of Mantua in the form of Zhazhy, the guitar player in our troupe. He was a tall, dark Serb with the long eyelashes of a gypsy and he wore tight-fitting embroidered shirts that flattered his muscular body. Meza, like most of the girls in the troupe, fell prey to his charms. I suffered greatly from what Shakespeare called the "green-eyed monster" but I swore I would not give up. I wooed her enthusiastically for two whole years, which resulted in a single stolen kiss. That was all I came away with, but I held that kiss in my heart for many long days.

Years later, Meza dumped the guitar player and married a Serbian football player with whom she moved to Australia. They divorced and she became a stylist in a small Sydney hairdressers. In the 1960s, an elderly Jewish woman originally from Novi Sad happened into her salon. While the woman's hair was drying, Meza said, "Would you happen to know what ever became of little Tommy Lampel?" In fact, she did. "Little Tommy is actually a big journalist in London these days," she told her. "I'll find his address for you." Several weeks later, I received a letter from Meza. My wife, Shula, is a clever woman and suggested that I respond. We corresponded for years and then, in 1982, when I visited Australia as director general of the Israel Broadcasting Authority, I invited her to lunch. She still looked good, but the years had taken their toll on us both. Some things are better left as memories.

In my second year at school my life finally settled down. I was the best student in our class, but what was far more important was that I had become the goalie and captain of our football team. In later years, Yugoslavia became a basketball powerhouse, mostly thanks to the late Dražen Petrovic, a star in the NBA. But in those days football was the only sport that interested us.

One day our teacher entered the classroom with a gaunt student. "This is Vujadin Boškov," he said. "Vujadin moved here this week because his father works for the railroad. Please make him feel welcome."

The communists treated railroad workers with particular respect, and we all made an effort to be nice to the new boy in class. A few days later, he took me aside and asked me to include him in our football training, which I did with pleasure. Vujadin came to the field and began to play. I watched him from the goalposts and saw at once that he had no talent whatsoever. I said nothing. The next day he showed up for practice again and was even worse. I spoke with him in private. "Vujadin," I said, "we both know that you're no good at football. We have a tennis court, why don't you try your hand at that? I have a feeling you'll be great."

Vujadin lowered his gaze. "You're kicking me off the team?" he asked. I was forced to admit that that was indeed the case.

"It's a waste of your time," I said, trying to sound encouraging. "It's clear that you'll amount to nothing."

Vujadin Boškov was for many years the captain and undisputed star of the local Vojvodina football club. He had fifty-seven appearances as a player on the national team, which took the silver medal at the Helsinki Olympics. He also played for a while for Sampdoria in Italy and, after retiring, became a successful coach. From 1979 to 1982 he coached the legendary Real Madrid and even led the Yugoslavian team to the quarterfinals of the Euro 2000 championships.

I've made better assessments in life.

Was I happy at the time? I am not sure. The German poet Richard Dehmel once wrote that grief occurs alone while happiness happens with others. Life has its own dynamic. The basic forces of human nature—sex, love, ambition, lust for knowledge—flowed powerfully in me, perhaps even more powerfully than feelings of loss and ruin. I was still trying to find out what had happened to Father, but I put no less energy into trying to find information about members of the Aston Villa Football Club, of which I was a fan. I played tennis twice a week, I danced, I pursued Meza gallantly and my blonde neighbors quite a bit less gallantly, I read ceaselessly, and while learning Russian at school as a gesture to the somber-eyed bear who kept watch over us from the other side of the border, I also made a great effort to learn English thanks to back issues of *Time* magazine that I found in Rudy's shipyard.

However, the most earthshaking event of all during that time was decidedly unintellectual.

On Sundays I would visit Uncle Latzi and eat dinner with him. His Serbian maid was a woman of about twenty-five who was in the habit of opening the door only halfway on my arrival so that I had no choice but to brush up against her when I entered the house. It took me several weeks to understand what she was doing, but the moment the penny dropped, those arrivals at the house turned into the most prolonged part of my visits. Several weeks later, I waited until my uncle had gone to sleep, and when I got to the door I tried to kiss her. She burst out laughing, took me by the hand and led me to her small bedroom, where I quite dramatically lost my virginity.

The affair lasted several weeks, until the day my uncle caught me sneaking out of her room. He brought me to his study, sat me down facing him and, with a most serious expression (only years later would he admit how difficult it had been for him to keep a straight face), he said, "There is a rule in such matters. One does not do it with the maid. I will not do it with yours, and you will not do it with mine." Red-faced, I apologized. Only later, at home, did I remember that we did not even have a maid.

CHAPTER 14

The noted British playwright Sir Arnold Wesker once wrote the following postcard to me:

> *Dear Tommy,*
> *People in London are saying are that the Israelis are torturing Palestinian prisoners. Is that true?*
>
> *Yours,*
> *Arnold*

I responded:

> *Dear Arnold,*
> *I do not know if it's true, but I hope it is.*
>
> *Yours,*
> *Tommy*

Wesker, a wise Jew, naturally understood that while of course I do not support the torture of prisoners, I was irked that a man like him could sit in the comfort of tranquil London and permit himself to criticize life in a country riven by terror, a country with whose day-to-day reality he is not familiar.

After that, he stopped pestering me with questions.

Just as I could not explain life in Israel to Sir Arnold, I am not sure I can explain to someone who has spent his entire life in a free country the feeling of slow, ongoing strangulation to which life in a police state gives rise. In Belgrade at that time, staged show trials were being held for supporters of the exiled king, while at the same time the secret police imprisoned and often assassinated the supporters of Stalin, who aspired to turn Yugoslavia into a satellite state of the USSR. A heavy cloud of suspicion hung over us all. The free press disappeared, uniformed soldiers patrolled at night, there were informers everywhere.

And we were poor.

This may sound strange, but I was not aware of this fact. Poverty—like wealth—is a relative matter, and everyone around us was no less poor than we were. (Against our will we had fulfilled the communist dream: we all had exactly the same—nothing.)

I only comprehended just how poor I was some sixty years later, when my cousin Sadi (Professor Saadia Touval) was invited to serve as a research fellow in Washington. While unpacking his belongings in his new home, he found a stack of letters that I had sent from Novi Sad to Israel. In one, from the spring of 1946, I wrote, "If you by chance have a pair of shoes or socks that you are planning to throw away, please send them to me. I only have one pair of socks that I wash every evening and that's not always convenient. My shoes have holes and it would be nice to have another pair, even used. My underpants situation is also pretty weak."

Shortly after my sixteenth birthday, Rudy received a secondhand Czech-made motorcycle, and when he felt like it he let me ride it. Of course, I did not have a license, and it scares me to think how many times I was nearly killed, or nearly killed others. Most of the time my good friend Sasha Yvoni, the only other Jew in my class, was seated behind me. We would go down to the Danube, sit on the bank of the river and talk about the lives we would build somewhere else, in America or England.

I have to admit that at that time, we did not think of Israel as an option. In spite of Sadi's frequent letters, I failed to be impressed by this mosquito-infested nation filled with enemy Arabs which the BBC referred to—even back then—with patronizing derision. My plans were different. I wished to return to the bosom of the cultured world in which I had been raised, to escape from gray and gloomy Yugoslavia and build a new life for myself in a place where I could become a lawyer, or a journalist, where I could sit at a mahogany desk by day and return to an elegant home in the evening, where a beautiful wife and rosy-cheeked children would be waiting.

Like every Jew in the world, I was glued to the radio on 29 November 1947 in order to listen to the UN resolution declaring statehood for Israel, but unlike most people I had trouble believing that the nation would indeed rise. The pale merchants and clerks I had grown up around did not seem to me like people capable of taking up arms and fighting for their lives. What's more, it was clear that nobody was going to let us leave Yugoslavia. The country was sealed shut.

Naturally, I followed with great interest, and fear, the reports in the Yugoslavian media about the battles taking place in Israel between Arabs and Jews. In the wake of one such skirmish I published a pathos-filled poem in my school newspaper in support of "our brothers in Palestine." It was accepted politely with a raised eyebrow, but there were no repercussions. Yugoslavia—which had abstained from that famous vote—was complacent about what was happening in the Middle East, and my poem was thought of as just another whim by a rather eccentric young man with too many opinions.

In spite of the complacency, or perhaps because of it, the authorities at one stage permitted the formation of a local branch of the Shomer HaTza'ir Young Guards' Youth Movement in the old Jewish community center. Another Jewish friend, Barran, dragged me to a few activities, but when the student leaders began speechifying about the glories of socialism, I got up and left. I had enough of that at school. Barran, on the other hand, stayed, and apparently listened as well, because after moving to Israel he joined a kibbutz and remained there his entire life.

In the spring of 1948, I reached the pinnacle of my inner dissatisfaction with the regime. At the time, Yugoslavia was building a railway line between two tiny godforsaken villages. The communist party had decided to make the laying of this line a show of loyalty by Yugoslavian youth. *YOUNG PEOPLE ARE OUR FUTURE* the posters proclaimed loudly on every wall. *THEY ARE BUILDING OUR NEW HOMELAND.* Slightly more quietly, we were told that whoever did not sign on as a "volunteer" during the summer holidays would not be eligible to sit for matriculation exams.

One morning, Sasha called me to come with him to sign up.

"I'm not signing," I said.

"They won't let you go to university," Sasha said, shocked.

"I don't care," I told him. "This isn't my country and I'm not a communist. I'm not signing."

He tried to persuade me, but I would not budge. In one fell swoop I had cut myself off permanently from the chance that I might still build a life for myself in my old homeland.

With regard to where I was supposed to find myself a new homeland, I had no clue.

Reality, as often happens, would decide matters for me just a few months later, in the form of a moustachioed and heavy-jowled man I had never met.

Moša Pijade was "Tito's Jew." An ardent communist, Pijade translated *Das Kapital* into Serbian, was imprisoned by the monarchists, and while in jail became Tito's closest friend. During the war they fought side by side in the ranks of the freedom fighters, and after the Nazis were vanquished he received the Order of the People's Hero of Yugoslavia and was appointed president of the Federal Assembly. He was a large, stern-faced man who resembled an Andalusian farmer, but he was the unofficial intellectual of the party and Tito, who was a very primitive man, relied on his opinion in every matter.

Three months after the declaration of Israel's independence, Pijade asked to meet with his old friend alone.

"Comrade Tito," Pijade said, "I have never, in all the years we fought together and have been friends, asked you for anything. Today I am asking."

"What is it you want?" asked Tito.

"Let the Jews go," Pijade said.

Several weeks later we got the news. We were being allowed to leave, even take the little we owned with us. But we would have to make the decision at once: there were two ships leaving and whoever was on them could leave and whoever stayed behind would not be given a second chance. There were members of the Jewish community who preferred to stay. The young State of Israel seemed too fragile to them, and full of dangers. There is no point, they claimed, in surviving one Holocaust only to die in another.

For us, however, there was no question. We were positively feverish about it. My two uncles, Latzi and Pali (who had also, in the meantime, made his way back to Novi Sad), converted all their belongings into gold on the black market. They then took over Rudy's shipyard and built a small wooden container with a secret compartment in the middle where they could stash their gold. (In retrospect, it was an act of madness. Had they been caught, they would have wound up in prison, not Israel.)

Mother ran about like a madwoman, packing suitcases and taking them apart again, shouting at Peter and me for no good reason, showering good-natured Rudy with Hungarian curses and me with instructions in German, sobbing one moment and devising grandiose plans the next. I shut myself up in my room with a Hungarian-Hebrew dictionary I got from the community center but grew discouraged at once, convinced I would never manage to master such an impossible language.

Four days before our scheduled departure, I experienced terrible stomach cramps and wound up in the local hospital, where a young and seemingly efficient doctor examined me. "His appendix is about to burst," he told us. "We must operate at once." From my bed, I could see the different expressions of relief and disappointment on the faces of the people surrounding me. If I had the operation, we would not be on the boat to Israel. I got up, went to the little cupboard where my belongings had been placed, and got dressed. "I'm feeling much better," I announced. "We're leaving." My appendix never bothered me again, right up to my dying day.

On the morning of our departure, I packed a single suitcase for myself, with underclothes and shirts. I did not even have marbles to bring with me this time.

In December 1948, we traveled by train to the city of Bakar, on the Adriatic coast. Thousands of German dockworkers, whom Tito refused to repatriate, swarmed about, and we marched out to the end of the pier in a long line where we met the most ungainly ship I had ever seen tossing about in the waves. The *Cephalus* was an aging freighter whose captain, a known criminal, had in the past smuggled arms from South America. The navy had asked if he could transport 1,500 Jews to Israel, and for a large sum of money he agreed to turn his ship into a passenger vessel. That morning, he stood on the deck and was astonished to see that the true number of passengers was closer to 3,000. More and more and more people climbed aboard, packed in like sardines, sitting on one another's laps, and retching even before the anchor had been reeled in. I had not experienced such crowding since the ghetto.

It was only years later, during my university studies, that I read *The Republic* and learned that Plato's friend Cephalus believed the meaning of justice to be that each person was due what was his and that one must tell the truth even when it is unpleasant. I believe that during my public life I realized rather successfully the teachings of the man who gave his name to the ship that brought me to Israel.

Before we set sail, representatives of the nascent Israeli navy moved about among us and gathered the young people. They explained that the sea was still full of mines left over from the war, and that it was our job to sit on the prow of the ship and warn the sailors if we spied something. I sat at the prow, with my friend Sasha Yvoni at my side, our legs dangling over the railing. Thus began my career as an Israeli: a human watchdog of mines.

CHAPTER 15

"I'll warrant him for drowning," Shakespeare wrote in *The Tempest*, "though the ship were no stronger than a nutshell and as leaky as an unstanched wench." From then on, these images from Shakespeare always brought a smile to my lips.

On the morning we set sail, the forecasters were predicting stormy weather on the Adriatic Sea, but there was no way of postponing our departure. Tito's directive had been clear: whoever does not leave by midnight stays in Yugoslavia. Late that afternoon, the ship departed. The sea seemed determined to prevent us from arriving in Israel. For a period of three straight days, enormous waves broke on our rickety boat, whose weary engines were trying in vain to cope with the wind. Everyone was ill, gripping the wooden railings with all their strength as we shivered with wet and cold that seeped into the marrow of our bones. Next to me sat a dark-haired beauty named Tamar Friedman, younger than me by two years. We huddled close to one another to keep warm, and little by little our shivering turned into a different kind of quaking. By the end of the second day I was the only person aboard who hoped the storm would not end.

The sea finally calmed down on the fourth day and I began to speak to the people around me. The first thing that amazed me was how little I knew about them. For the first time in my life I was meeting Jews from Croatia, Jews from Bosnia, Jews from Montenegro, Jews from the south

of Yugoslavia, from cities and villages, the ultra-Orthodox, the traditional, dark-skinned Sephardic Jews from western Serbia and *shtetl* Jews
who looked as though they had never been exposed to the sun in their
lives. One group was speaking broken German mixed with words from
Hebrew in a very strange accent. I asked them what language they were
speaking.

"Yiddish," someone told me.

"What's that?" I asked.

They eyed me with suspicion and moved away. How could I expect
them to understand not only that I did not know how to speak Yiddish
but that I had never even heard of its existence?

With regard to another aspect of my ignorance, however, I am actually quite proud.

One of the young people at the prow of the ship asked if I were Ashkenazi or Sephardic. I answered that I did not know, which surprised
him. "How can you not know?" he asked. I went to find Mother and
asked her. "I'm not sure," she said, "but I believe we're Ashkenazi."

Years later, as part of the demonization campaign against me run by
the Shas Sephardic Jewry Party, I was accused more than once of being
a racist with regard to Sephardic Jews. Of all the slander slung at me—
most of which amused me—this was the only one that truly offended
me. Racism, like any prejudice, is something fixed in one's childhood. I
was seventeen years old when I first heard about the different Jewish ethnic groups. Even then it sounded stupid and disappointing to me, and
particularly irrelevant. Hitler taught me that every Jew has the same destiny. In these matters I am, and always was, absolutely color-blind.

After eleven nightmarish days at sea, the *Cephalus* skittered into an
unknown port at dawn on 26 December 1948. The sun rose behind a
range of hills we did not yet know was called Mount Carmel, its rays lit
up a city we would later learn was Haifa, and someone raised an Israeli
flag on the mast. We all stood there looking at it, thousands of drained,
hungry, slightly terrified people, and we sang hesitantly—since we did
not know all the words—the national anthem, "*HaTikvah*," "The Hope."
It was as simple and beautiful as a kitschy Israel National Fund propaganda film. The ship groaned once or twice then docked at the pier.

I arrived in Israel one day before my seventeenth birthday.

———

Before we even descended the gangplank, we were made to stand in rows and were disinfected with DDT. I know, of course, that there are thousands of people, especially those coming to Israel from North Africa, who were traumatized by this humiliating experience. Here were the patronizing "whites" spraying the lice-infested, sickness-bearing foreigners, no longer proud Jews and scions of illustrious communities who had set out to reach the Promised Land. I am not passing judgment on them, but I felt differently. Being disinfected filled me with pride. All my fears of coming to an enfeebled, backward nation evaporated at once. Here I was, not even having set foot on shore, and the health services of my new country were already taking care of me, concerned with my hygiene and that of the public, just as should happen in a developed nation.

An elderly, German-speaking Jewish Agency clerk placed a table on the pier and began registering us one by one.

"Name?" he asked me.

"Tomislav Lampel."

He gave me a bewildered look. "Do you have a Hebrew name as well?" he asked.

I recalled that Father had once told me that at my birth I had been given the name Joseph, in memory of my grandfather.

"Joseph," I told him.

After registering, we were led to a meeting point, where one of the clerks stood before us. "Everyone between the ages of eighteen and twenty-five," he said, "has to enlist in the army. Everyone above the age of twenty-five and below seventeen will be going to an immigrants' camp at Beer Yaacov."

"What about seventeen-year-olds?" someone asked.

"Seventeen-year-olds can decide if they want to enlist or not," was the answer.

As with most of the major decisions of my life, this one too was made in a moment. An inner voice told me that this was the right thing to do, that this was how I should begin my new life, that without this I would never be a true Israeli. I turned to Mother and Rudy and said, "I'm going to the army."

My mother became hysterical. "This is what I saved you from the Nazis for?" she screamed. "This is what I saved you from the communists for? So you could die here in a strange land?"

I gave her a strong hug. "I'm going," I said. "I'll come and visit you all the first moment I can."

Several hours later they were already on their way to the immigrants' camp and I had said my goodbyes to Tamar, who went with her parents to Nahariya. We remained a couple for several months, until she met another boy and fell in love. Forty years later, Yair presented to me the woman who would become his first wife, a stunning blonde who stuck out her hand and said, "My name is Tamar Friedman." To both of their surprise, I burst out laughing. "What's so funny?" Yair asked. "Nothing," I said. "I just remembered something." It turns out that when history repeats itself it does so blondely.

By the time that army trucks brought us to an absorption base, night had fallen and we were sent to eat dinner. I entered the mess hall and stopped, thunderstruck. On the wall there hung a portrait of Lenin. Was that what I had come to Israel for? Was this why I had escaped from communist Yugoslavia? To find a portrait of Lenin on the wall of an Israeli army base?

"Don't worry," someone said, "it's not Lenin. That's the president of Israel, Chaim Weizmann."

We each received a mess kit with our first Israeli meal: a hard-boiled egg, soft white cheese, slices of tomato and little green things I could not identify. I put one in my mouth and nearly lost a tooth. That was my first encounter with an olive.

In the morning we were put in a lineup, under the flag, a rabble of new immigrants still wearing their travel clothes and grouped according to their country of origin. An officer recited from a prepared text that we understood not a word of, then placed his hand on a Bible and shouted, "I pledge allegiance!" After a moment's hesitation we realized that we were expected to shout as well, and we did.

The next morning we were outfitted with a uniform, boots, belt, kit bag, and a funny hat with a little curtain in the back to protect our necks, like those of the French Foreign Legion. Inside the hat was a tag announcing that our hats were a gift to the Israel Defence Forces from the Yiddishe Hitelmachers—the Jewish Milliners' Union of New York.

The seventeen-year-olds were then separated from the other new recruits. Only years later did I learn that Prime Minister Ben Gurion had made a promise to a delegation of distraught parents that seventeen-year-olds would not be sent to the front. There were twelve of us from Yugoslavia. We were loaded onto an army truck once again and sent to Basic Training Camp 80 in Pardess Hanna, where we were housed in a huge tent with all the new recruits. The Romanians' tent was to our right, the Moroccans' to our left, and nearby the Germans,' the Bulgarians,' the Tunisians,' a crazy mix of languages and customs and colors and sounds that we were completely unable to decipher.

It took only two days for the fighting to begin, everyone stealing from everyone; the line at the mess hall became a battleground. Our squad commander, Corporal Fisher, was himself a new immigrant from Budapest and did not seem like someone who knew what to do with us. It was utter chaos. The company commander gave the platoon commander instructions in Hebrew, the platoon commander translated them into German and passed them along to Fisher, who translated them for me into Hungarian so that I could translate them into Serbian for the rest of the soldiers and in the end, as could be expected, nothing got done at all.

I was proud to be wearing a uniform, but it was not really me. Only three weeks earlier I had been in the eleventh grade of high school, doing math homework, and now, some doppelgänger had taken my place and was playing the role of a soldier in some bizarre film. The world around me was still one, but I was two. It was the first time that I was on my own, a private in an army at war, the citizen of a country where olives were eaten for dinner and a language that I would never understand was spoken. At night, in the darkness, I cried myself to sleep.

CHAPTER 16

Djordje lost his mind in the middle of the night. He was the only one among us who had been at Auschwitz, sent with his parents at age thirteen. He returned alone, an old man of fifteen.

He slept in the bed next to mine in the new recruits' tent. After a week there, Djordje jumped from his bed in the middle of the night and began screaming in Serbian, "They want to kill me! They brought me here to murder me!"

He went wild, overturned his bed, threw his belongings around, shouted at us and tried to beat us, or himself—it was hard to know which. Fisher, our squad commander, entered the tent in a panic and asked me in Hungarian, "What's going on here?"

"He had a nightmare," I told him. "He was in the camps."

"Calm him down," Fisher said as he turned to leave.

Djordje jumped him from behind and gave a blow to his neck. "Nazi!" he shouted. "You're a Nazi! We have a Nazi here!"

Fisher got away and returned with the camp doctor, who instructed us to hold Djordje down while he sedated him. Once Djordje had calmed down, the doctor said he would sleep at the camp clinic and then be taken to the hospital the next morning. Djordje asked that I keep watch over him with my gun, to which the doctor agreed. I sat beside his bed holding my heavy Czech rifle, protecting him from imaginary enemies. Before he fell asleep, Djordje explained to me that he was one of the only children to survive Auschwitz, and that the Nazis knew he was a witness to their atrocities so they were now looking for him in order to silence him. "This camp is full of SS officers posing as Israelis," he whispered to me. "You have to watch out for yourself, too. If they find out you're Jewish they'll kill you as well."

The next morning an ambulance came to take him to the hospital but they forgot his belongings.

"Where did they take him?" I asked Fisher.

"To Beer Yaacov," he told me.

I remembered that as I was departing from my sobbing mother on the pier in Haifa, she had said again and again, "Remember that they're taking me to Beer Yaacov. The immigrants' camp at Beer Yaacov."

I told Fisher that Djordje's belongings were still in our tent and that I had to take them to him.

Fisher raised an eyebrow. "You've only been in Israel one week," he said. "How will you find Beer Yaacov?"

I explained that I wanted to find my mother. Fisher scrutinized me; for a moment it seemed he noticed that beneath my uniform there was nothing but a boy.

"All right," he said. "Bring him his kit bag. But you'll have to get around by hitchhiking."

Even in Hungarian I did not know what a "kit bag" was or "hitchhiking" but I agreed. I got a ride to a nearby town from the base with a supply truck. When he dropped me off, the driver pointed me in the general direction of Tel Aviv and explained how to stop cars, then left me on my own. My destination was written on a slip of paper in Hebrew and Hungarian along with a map of the army psychiatric hospital at Beer Yaacov that Fisher had drawn.

I believe that if I had been left in the middle of the Sahara Desert I could not have felt more alone. The fact that I made it within a few hours to the Beer Yaacov hospital is only because in those days virtually every driver stopped for a soldier, and when I showed them the slip of paper they understood that I spoke no Hebrew and they went out of their way (and not only verbally) to help me.

The female soldier sitting at the hospital reception desk pointed to the cottage where I would find Private Djordje, and as I made my way there through the hospital grounds a white-coated doctor stopped me. "How are you?" he asked me with concern.

"I'm fine," I answered in German. "Thank you."

The doctor persisted. "How are you feeling?"

"Fine."

"Are you sure?"

Suddenly, I understood. "Herr Doktor, *ich bin nicht verrückt!* I am not crazy!"

"Of course you're not," he said with a smile as he patted my back. "Perhaps you'd like to talk to me a little?"

At this point I began to feel hysteria rising in me. After all, no crazy person ever believes that he himself is crazy. Maybe I had gone insane? Maybe Fisher had sent me here on doctor's orders? So many things had happened to me in the past few weeks that perhaps going mad was the only possible reaction. And even if I had not gone crazy, how was I going to convince this doctor that I was sane? How exactly do sane people behave? The person who saved me was the soldier from reception, who guessed what was happening and came to explain the situation to the doctor. He sent me on my way with a few more pats on the back, but when I moved away from him—as quickly as I could—I felt his suspicious eyes still watching me from behind.

I found Djordje in his room in the cottage with three other patients. He signaled to me to step out in the hall with him and then he whispered, "Those three are nuts! I'm the only sane person in the room." Then he disappeared to fetch us tea. I went back into the room, where one of his roommates said, "Poor guy. He's crazy. Don't worry, we're looking out for him."

I never saw Djordje again after that day, never heard about him, and I have no idea what became of him.

I found Mother, Rudy and Peter on metal cots provided by the Jewish Agency in a wretched building in an abandoned British army base housing five hundred other new immigrants. There were fifty other people in their area, and the only way to have any privacy was to hang blankets on clotheslines around their beds.

At first, Mother could only stare at me: here was her little Tommy in uniform. She hugged me and cried and then looked at my ridiculous

French Foreign Legionnaire's hat and burst out laughing. Everything seemed like one big mistake to her. What were we doing in a horrible building in a deserted army camp in some end of the world place in this odd country? How could we get out of there, return home to the apartment we had left behind, to our classrooms, to the shipyard on the Danube, to our friends, our bridge games, the language we spoke and wrote, to normal lives led by people in their natural surroundings? What did we expect to find here? There was no understanding this guttural language, the food was unpalatable, one had to stand in a line to shower, there was sobbing and noisy fights at night, people milled about all day with nothing to do, the future was a big unknown. What did we need this for?

From the distance of many years and the depths of my well-tended grave under a flowering purple bougainvillea tree in the Kiryat Shaul cemetery, I look back at the child I once was and am amazed by his sense of purpose. For sixty years I lived in the State of Israel and my identification with this country was absolute. Apart from my family, this was always the greatest source of my strength—the knowledge that I was in the only place in the world where a Jew could live and the only place in the world where I could live. My patriotism was stormy, often noisy, and with the conviction of a convert, because I knew it could have been different. The ghetto had taught me that I needed a place where I could be, but no one can imagine the feeling you are filled with when you actually find that place at last.

The country owed me nothing, but I owed it. Unlike Mother, Israel did not seem foreign to me; I was foreign to it. So I had a job: to become Israeli. Several years later, when I was discharged from the army, I came upon a registration brochure for the Hebrew University in Jerusalem. I did not even have a high school matriculation certificate, and I could not understand ninety percent of what was written there, but I wrote the following sentence on the first page: *I SWEER I WILL GIT THERE.*

I hugged Mother and went back to the army.

After two weeks in basic training, we boys from Yugoslavia were sent to Kibbutz Yagur for a week in order to see what life on a kibbutz was like.

I knew of their existence even though I did not really understand what they were. I went there happy and excited to take part in this authentic Israeli experience. But the kibbutz members did everything in their power to justify my preconceived notions about life in a socialist society. To put it bluntly, they did not do a thing. They provided us with two rooms and someone to look after us and put us to work in the kitchen, in the fields, and as cleaners.

When we came to the dining hall no one made any contact with us. At an evening sing-along event we sat to the side and no one thought to include us. There were quite a few young people our age who ignored our existence entirely. The boys did not invite us to join them when they played football on the grass and the girls treated us as if we were invisible. At some stage we understood that even though the army had brought us there to meet the kibbutz, the kibbutz members were not interested in meeting us. They were only interested in free labor.

With Djordje in hospital and another of our group booted out after being caught stealing at the training camp, we remained ten little Yugoslavian boys. The army, in its infinite wisdom, decided that we—a pack of spoiled members of the bourgeoisie—were particularly suited to work as auto mechanics: "You'll have a profession by the time you leave the army," one officer told us. We found ourselves in an army training workshop in a small forest overlooking the town of Afula.

The next morning we were split into different departments: I was sent to electronics; Rozhy to radiators; and all the rest—Albert, Braza, Mirko, Big Metu and Little Metu, Zalatko, Barran and Oskar—were placed in mechanics.

The commander of the auto mechanics workshop was a bespectacled German Jew, Captain David Schechner, who seemed very old to us. Today I know that he was only twenty-seven years old. When Schechner discovered that I understood German, the unit switched languages: instead of receiving our instructions in Hungarian, we—a group of Holocaust survivors—were told what to do in German.

Several weeks after our arrival at the workshop, I asked Schechner, on behalf of the Yugoslavians, if we could learn Hebrew. He went to Afula and found us a teacher, Rachel, and twice a week, at six in the evening, she would visit the camp in order to teach us Hebrew. She was young and attractive and very devoted. So devoted, in fact, that after several weeks of intensive study we discovered that after our lessons she was staying over in the room of the commander. Several months later they wed and lived together happily, even after David Schechner left the army.

Several years ago, Rachel Schechner phoned to let me know that David had passed away. "You brought us together forty-five years ago," she said, "so you deserve to know that he is no longer with us."

The mechanics workshop was a madhouse, with some one hundred people working round the clock. The Israel Defence Force vehicles were in particularly bad shape as a result of the War of Independence and all that interested Schechner was fixing the maximum number of vehicles in the minimum amount of time, and to hell with discipline. We had one prisoner of war with us in the camp, Ahmed from Acre, who was occupied with peeling potatoes and cleaning the kitchen. At some point Schechner decided it was a waste of time to have mechanics on guard duty so he made Ahmed the full-time guard at the front gate of the base. I believe this was the only base in the history of the IDF in which an Arab prisoner of war was given a gun for the purpose of guarding one hundred Israeli soldiers. This convenient set-up came to an end only when the security officer of the Northern Command came from Nazareth to have his jeep serviced. Schechner's impassioned explanation that he was trying to save on manpower did not pass muster, and Ahmed was returned to the kitchen.

No one taught us our job. Everything was carried out by trial and error as if we were some guild from the Middle Ages. However, in time I learned how to fix a starter, adjust a regulator and replace contact breakers, not to mention simple jobs like wiring and replacing headlights. My fingers were constantly black from oil and friction tape, but after a year I passed the test at the IDF central garage and earned my certificate as a licensed electronics mechanic.

Of all the diplomas I received during my lifetime, I was particularly proud of this one. To my dying day I was convinced that there was not an electrical appliance I could not fix. My family members tended to hide broken appliances from me (from bitter experience) until the technician showed up, in case I had one of my uncontrollable dismantling-reassembling urges.

I look back with a secret smile as I watch myself make my way among the collection of anecdotes that comprise my life, trying to understand which of them shaped me into the person I later became. I always loved reading biographies. I would lie on my bed at one o'clock in the morning, leaning Stalin or Roosevelt on my billowing belly and following with astonishment one's progression from studying for the priesthood to becoming the biggest mass murderer in history, or the other's progression from spoiled only child of one of the richest families of New York to savior of America during the Great Depression. I do not, of course, mean to compare myself to these people, but there is one story that just kept repeating itself: the will of the outsider to belong.

It is no coincidence that Napoleon was Corsican, that Hitler was Austrian, that Stalin was Georgian, that Roosevelt was a victim of polio and confined to a wheelchair and that Churchill was a political leper ostracized by his peers. They all had something to prove, and prove it they did, each in his own way. My own dreams were quite a bit less grandiose, but every contact breaker that I replaced brought me another centimeter closer to the goal I had set for myself: to become a true Israeli.

For the meantime, however, my reference group remained intact. Rudy managed to pull his money from the bank in the UK so that he and Mother were able to leave the immigrants' camp and move into a small flat they purchased with key money on King Solomon Street in Tel Aviv. They sent Peter to board at Kibbutz Kfar Szold, where they visited him only twice a year. These days this would be considered a terrible thing to do to an eleven-year-old, but in those years of austerity and economic hardship, it was not at all unusual. I felt sorry for Peter but there was little I could do.

One Saturday morning I discovered that a command car had been left over the weekend at our workshop. I "borrowed" it and went to visit Peter. He cried when he saw me, and many years later still remembered how his status among the other kids improved dramatically thanks to a command car appearing at the gates of the kibbutz and his stepbrother stepping out of it wearing the uniform of an IDF soldier.

CHAPTER 17

I am in a car traveling between Zurich and St. Gallen. The air is clear, the Alpine peaks are still covered in snow and the tinkling of bells means that a herd of cows is close at hand. This is what the world looks like through a hole in a chunk of Swiss cheese.

In front of me a tractor pulls a large piece of farm equipment. Everything is serene but something feels wrong; something is bothering me, making me feel anxious. I glance at the instruments on the dashboard, but everything is in order. Still, I am muddled and ill at ease.

Then my wife says, "Look at what's written on that combine in front of us."

I read the writing and at once understand what has been troubling my subconscious. On the combine, in huge letters, is the word *MENGELE*.

I recall that in reports about the monster from Auschwitz it was mentioned that his family produced farm equipment. They could have called their company by a thousand other names but were apparently proud of the family name and chose to announce it loudly.

I drive along behind Mengele and I want to go home.

Immigrants are always looking for home; it is part of the mythology of immigration. In every city in the world there is a wood-covered Irish pub with a Paddy and a Caitlin sitting at the bar doused with whisky and full of nostalgia for the green hills of their old homeland. Americans meet up at McDonald's, Chinese congregate in Chinatowns, Italians gather at Luigi's restaurant (because in every city there is an Italian restaurant, and in every Italian restaurant there is a chef, and every Italian chef is called Luigi), where they eat spaghetti bolognese atop red-and-white checked tablecloths and sing "Santa Lucia" at the end of the meal.

I, on the other hand, was longing for a home that did not yet exist.

I do not know whether it is possible psychologically to miss something yet to come, but that is precisely what I felt. I longed for the master's armchair I did not yet own, the career I had not yet embarked upon, the family I had not yet started. Mostly, I longed for that clear knowledge I possessed as a child, that I was in a place where I belonged and a place that belonged to me in return.

And I was not the first man to be rescued from loneliness by an Eve.

I met Hava (Eve) Horowitz at a party organized for us by Captain Schechner. One Sabbath he had stayed on the base and discovered that when all the other soldiers went home, his ten little Yugoslavians stayed behind because they had nowhere to go. Most of us had no parents to visit, and in my case it was clear that Mother and Rudy had no place to put me up. I preferred to remain with my friends.

Schechner made a few phone calls and persuaded the nurses at a nearby hospital to spend a Friday evening with us. They came straight from the hospital, several still dressed in their white uniforms like a scene from Hemingway's *A Farewell to Arms*. Hava's mother was the head of the hospital's laundry and made her daughter come along as well to spend some time "with those poor soldiers."

The poor soldier that stood with his back against the wall could not take his eyes off her. She was a student in the eleventh grade, a delicate, beautiful blonde who looked slightly overwhelmed; she caught my eye from the moment she walked into the dining hall. I went up to her and began trying to speak in my broken Hebrew, but in no time I discovered she spoke German with a soft Viennese accent. Her mother, who had come from Austria before the war, chatted with me for a few minutes, decided that I was "a boy from a good family," and allowed me to take my first walk with Hava.

It was an innocent romance between two children that lasted for more than two years. Evenings, she would wait for me by the gate of the base and we would walk together, hand in hand, to the road and back, or we would climb the water tower and sit on the tall cement rim and look down at the city spread out before us. From above, Afula looked almost pretty.

Our greatest adventure together took place after a letter arrived from my uncle Pali. He wrote that he had used the gold he had smuggled into the country to lease a small hotel in Tiberias, and he invited me to visit on the first evening I was free. That Sabbath, Hava managed to get her hands on two bicycles and we rode off to Tiberias, where we spent a weekend pretending we were John Barrymore and Greta Garbo in *Grand Hotel*.

For me the most attractive feature about Hava (who would later be known as the sociologist Professor Hava Etzioni-Halevi) was her Israeliness. Like all girls, Hava was eager to introduce her soldier boyfriend to her jealous girlfriends, and I found myself surrounded by girls who gazed abashedly at me, talked and giggled and giggled and talked, while I tried—sometimes desperately—to keep up with their rapid Hebrew. Through Hava I learned about the Holy Trinity: falafel, salad and *gazoz*—flavored soda water; from her I first heard about politics and higher education; she translated Hebrew literature for me; she read newspaper headlines to me and introduced me to a popular young singer by the name of Shoshana Damari and her hit song, "Anemones." I did not know what anemones were but I liked the song—and the singer.

She spoke and I listened (I now admit this was probably the last relationship of my life in which that was the case), and I could never get enough. My Yugoslavian friends were still trapped inside their glass cage—the Serbian language—while I had begun to break away to the world of real Israelis.

Captain Schechner, who kept track of our relationship with a fatherly interest, recognized the opportunity that he himself had created, and as the date of my discharge approached (obligatory service in those days lasted two and a half years) he persuaded me to sign on for another six months in order to save up a little money. From the moment I agreed I leaped tempestuously into the rank structure and was promoted to corporal.

My Yugoslavian friends and I went our different ways. Barran moved to a kibbutz and married a beautiful Yemenite Jew who bore him five children and thirteen grandchildren. Big Meto became a pimp in Frankfurt, Little Meto moved to Argentina and prospered there, Oskar worked in a sugar factory, and all the others got along as well. We kept in irregular touch over the years, but every Sukkoth holiday we met in the Ben Shemen forest along with all the other immigrants who arrived on the *Cephalus*—and, later, their children and grandchildren, too. Someone would produce an accordion, a circle of dancers would form, fat sausages would be grilled on the barbecue and bottles of golden Slivovitz would be passed hand to hand. All year I was a Hungarian—except for Ephraim Kishon, I was probably the most famous Hungarian in Israel—but once a year, for a single afternoon, I was a proud Yugoslavian.

My extra six months in the army came and went and, in spite of all Schechner's efforts at persuading me, I refused to continue my military service. Several days before my twentieth birthday I parted tearfully from Hava, both of us uttering pledges of undying love that would never be realized, and I left for Tel Aviv.

For the following year Hava and I continued to meet once a week, every Thursday, but with the passing months we grew apart. I plunged deeply into my new life while Hava enlisted in the Intelligence Corps and remained the same delicate, introverted girl she had always been. Eventually we broke up, in T.S. Eliot's words, "not with a bang but a whimper." We both believed, but did not dare say aloud, that if we had met several years later our story might have ended differently.

Fifty-three years later, during a lecture tour she was giving abroad, Hava had trouble falling asleep one night. She rose from her bed, turned on her computer, and connected to the Internet. The main item on the news was my death. She stood up from her chair, lit all the lights in her hotel room and remained awake the whole night long, sitting on a chair gazing out the window until the first gray light of dawn filled the sky.

It was not the future that preoccupied me at that time, but whether I even had one. For several months I wandered aimlessly about, lost and confused, trying to decide what to do with my life. At night I would meet friends from the army and we would play poker until the early morning. One of my friends from Novi Sad, Tommy Yagoda, had a one-room apartment in Ramat Gan, and we spent a lot of time there. Yagoda had a boundless charm about him, and a parade of curious young Tel Aviv women passed through there every night to make sure the poor new immigrants were not having too many absorption difficulties.

At that time, Rudy opened a mushroom factory with two partners. This was during the days of austerity, when people were rationed seventy-five grams of meat per month, so he and his partners figured there would be a demand for mushrooms. The factory was housed in a large building on the outskirts of Tel Aviv, and the three partners did not have enough money between them to paint the walls. Rudy cleared out a small storeroom with constantly leaking walls; I put a mattress and a desk in there and turned it into my first home. With the arrival of winter a few months later, it turned out that the factory was sitting on a channel of the Ayalon River and was subject to constant flooding. Quite a number of times I awakened to find myself drenched, my few belongings floating around me like paper boats in a fountain.

The factory had a cooling system that regulated the varying temperatures in different rooms, which enabled the owners to control the rate of growth of the mushrooms. (Mushrooms are seasonal and react to heat and cold.) The factory was filled to the brim with wooden crates, each one meter square and full of mushroom spores on a bed of reddish sand. Each time the company received an order from a food distributor they would raise the temperature in one of the rooms and by the next day the mushrooms would sprout.

Several weeks after I arrived in the city, the air-conditioning system suddenly broke down and all the mushrooms sprouted in a single evening, thousands of them growing at a dizzying rate while we looked on in stunned panic. It was a forest of white mushrooms, carpets of mushrooms, white sheets of moist, meaty mushrooms that stuck to your hands.

The three partners were in a state of hysteria. We stood there all night scraping the mushrooms into large containers; for every two that went into the containers, three more sprouted in their place; with each crate we finished, we discovered another producing more mushrooms. In the morning we ran from factory to factory, from camp to camp, with the mushrooms, trying to sell hundreds of kilograms of mushrooms that no one wished to buy. "It's all over for us," Rudy said. "We're destroyed." No one answered.

From that day on, I could never stand mushrooms.

I did not have a job. Everyone expected me to become a car electrician at one of the little garages springing up in South Tel Aviv, but I was adamantly opposed to the idea. I had amassed enough grease under my fingernails for an entire lifetime. Mother, who was worried about my descent into unemployment, convinced Dr. Waldman, my father's cousin, to employ me as a messenger in his legal office at 4 Rothschild Boulevard. After several weeks on the job he gave me an envelope containing several documents that I was to bring to the home of a Mr. Metzkin, the owner of a large clothing store on Allenby Street, for him to sign. I got on my bicycle and rode off. The door was answered by a maid, her hair covered in the style of religious women.

"I'll take that," she told me.

"I'm sorry," I said, "but I was asked to deliver this personally."

She raised an eyebrow but let me in. Mr. Metzkin was entertaining guests, some fifteen people seated around small tables laden with the best produce money could buy; foods I had not seen since before the war: smoked salmon, platters with black caviar, cream cheese, baskets of baked goods, Dutch butter, different colored jams, Swiss chocolates, bottles of French brandy.

Mr. Metzkin was embarrassed by my presence. Outside there was rationing and hardship; people lived on sixty grams of flour and five biscuits a day, the entire country was in an ascetic mood—and here, people were living it up. I did not utter a word. I had Mr. Metzkin sign the documents and I left, my nostrils still full of delectable scents. I knew I was meant to feel a deep moral outrage, but in fact I felt the opposite: if there were people who lived in that manner, I told myself, I wanted to be one of them.

That evening, I told Tommy Yagoda I wanted to be a lawyer. Yagoda laughed. "You don't even have your matric," he said. Two days later I registered for an external diploma program, where I would study to complete my high-school matriculation exams.

Of all the intellectual challenges I faced in my life, this was the greatest. I was capable of speaking the broken Hebrew of an immigrant soldier, but I was not yet capable of reading or writing properly in the language. Those little dots and dashes that appeared above and below the letters looked like ancient Egyptian hieroglyphs to me and I had trouble differentiating between certain letters. Suddenly I was going to have to study history and geography and literature and the Bible and would be surrounded by thick books whose meanings I could only guess at. The Bible in particular seemed impossible to me. How could a young person whose native tongue was not Hebrew understand a verse like "Dan shall be a serpent by the way, an adder in the path, that biteth the horse heels, so that his rider shall fall backward?" What the hell did it mean?

I worked days and studied by night, bent over my books, a small petrol heater lit behind me while my feet dangled in the water that covered the floor. That winter of 1952 was to become notorious. Terrible floods struck the entire country, and most especially my wretched storeroom in Tel Aviv. One night I fell asleep while studying and woke up to find my clothes aflame. I had apparently fallen backward toward the heater and my coat caught fire. I threw myself into the water and rolled about until the fire went out. Rather shaken, I rode my bicycle to Mother's home. She took one look at me and said, "You're staying here." Rudy Gutman, as always, simply smiled. Looking back, I am filled with gratitude toward the man. In their tiny studio apartment there was a single room, a minuscule kitchen and a laundry room. He had sent his only son to a kibbutz but I was given the laundry room.

Several months later, the time came for me to sit for my first matriculation exam, in composition. I opened the exam book and nearly fainted: "Write an essay about Israel as a democracy." I knew that my Hebrew was insufficient for such a task (or any other, to tell the truth), but I realized that my only chance was to signal to the anonymous person who would be marking the exam that I was not an ignoramus but an educated and intelligent new immigrant. Perhaps he would take pity on me.

I wrote an awful essay full of mistakes, but I sprinkled it with every foreign-language reference I could come up with. I recalled Abraham Lincoln's "Government of the people, by the people, for the people" and Goethe's last words *"Mehr licht!"* ("More light!") and Dumas' *"Cherchez la femme"* and the Italian *"Dolce far niente"* ('The sweetness of doing nothing') and I ended with Julius Caesar, in Latin no less: *"Alea iacta est"* ("The die has been cast").

And I passed. Not the Rubicon, but at least the exam. That anonymous marker of mine apparently understood my plea made to him from the pages of my essay and, in spite of my many mistakes, decided to pass me, just barely, with the sensational mark of sixty.

CHAPTER 18

Our parents are our own dress rehearsals, and we are the dress rehearsals for our children. I had that thought for the first time on the night that I rode to the hospital in an ambulance with my mother, who was in a critical condition.

The second time I had that thought was when I opened my own eyes in the hospital after having collapsed at home, unaware that the cancer had spread through my body, and found Meirav sitting beside my bed, tense and frightened. Through a fog of medications I asked myself whether she understood that her father was the dress rehearsal for her own life, for the stage play that lay ahead—the comedy and the tragedy, the drama and the melodrama.

Once, I danced with my wife in an elegant place where wine was poured into crystal goblets and the pearls around the women's necks were real. The orchestra played an English waltz. Against the backdrop of familiar, faraway sounds on a silvered screen of childhood memories, I could picture my parents, gracious and brimming with confidence, enmeshed and smiling, dancing on the balcony of a hotel on the Adriatic Sea while I, a small child, sat on a wicker chair drinking fruit juice and watching Mother, a glittery princess, and Father, a brave knight, as they glided across the shining parquet floor. My parents were staging a dress rehearsal for the dance I would dance many years later with my wife to the very same English waltz.

———

Father traveled by train each week to Sobotica to work for a newspaper. I traveled to my career as a journalist on the No. 4 bus that runs the length of Ben Yehuda Street in Tel Aviv.

Just as on the day that I refused to work on the Yugoslavian railway line, or the day I decided to enlist in the army instead of going to the immigrants' camp, I also made this decision—to become a journalist—in a fraction of a second and without a clue of what lay ahead. Was it really a decision? Or maybe it was some deterministic response, a given, to a path in life laid out for me by previous generations?

Thanks to this decision I met my wife, established my path in life, became a politician, entered every home in Israel via television and divided the nation between those who loved me and those who hated me. But when I stepped onto the bus at the Frishman Street bus stop I still thought I was on my way to somewhere else entirely.

This was during my second year of studying for my matriculation exams, most of which I had already passed, and I only had a few months of studies left ahead. I was still working as a bicycle messenger boy when one day Mother asked to speak with me and informed me ceremoniously that she had obtained the ultimate dream job for me: a taxi dispatcher.

I nearly fell off my chair. How? Where?

Their next-door neighbor, it turned out, was Mr. Frankel, who was one of the owners of the Tel Aviv Taxi company. Mother had met his wife at the greengrocers and told her what a difficult time her son was having making ends meet as a messenger boy. That evening, Mrs. Frankel told Mr. Frankel that it was a Zionist imperative of the first order to come to the assistance of a twenty-one-year-old new immigrant who had served three years in the army and needed a proper job. Mr. Frankel consented. "Have him pay me a visit tomorrow morning," he said. "I'll try him out as a dispatcher."

It was almost impossible for me to sleep that night. In the early 1950s, working at a taxi stand was like finding a job today with a hi-tech start-up firm. The next morning I woke early, showered, and caught the bus. It was moving slowly and I sat watching the passersby out the window. For some reason they seemed grayer than ever, as if they had been defeated by life.

The bus reached Rothschild Boulevard and the doors opened with a sigh, but I did not disembark.

The No. 4 bus line ended at the Central Bus Station. I knew that on one of the small streets nearby were the offices of the Hungarian newspaper *Új Kelet*. I got directions from someone, ascended to the second floor, and walked into one of the offices. A man in a suit glanced up at me with a questioning look.

"My name is Tommy Lampel," I said.

"And?"

"I know how to write."

"So?"

I tried to figure out if I could make a hasty escape, catch the bus in the opposite direction, and still get to my appointment with Mr. Frankel.

"I'm looking for work," I said. "Any work."

The man, Dezsö Shen, the assistant editor of the paper, took a good long look at me.

"You can hang out here," he said. "We won't pay you for the time being, but we'll see how you work out."

I was not sure what that meant, but I did as he said and walked about, peering into offices. In those days, *Új Kelet* was a relatively important paper that sold 35,000 copies a day. In one of the offices sat a thin man named Ephraim Kishon, a humorist, who kept writing and erasing, writing and erasing. The man who would become my closest friend for more than fifty years barely acknowledged me when I introduced myself. In another office sat two caricaturists, Dosh and Zeev, one lanky and mirthless, the other short and cheerful. They shook my hand warmly and wished me luck. In a third, I saw Avraham Ronai, an actor with Habima theater, who sat with his feet on the desk drinking cognac (at nine in the morning!) while giving an interview in his booming voice about his most recent play. Only a few years later these people and I would be called the Hungarian Mafia, but at that moment they were demigods to me.

Of all the people I met I was most impressed by the night editor, a dark-skinned and elegant man who did something I would never see again in all my years in journalism: on Wednesdays he would stand in the middle of the floor and dictate simultaneously from his head two different articles, the Thursday piece to one typist and the Friday piece to another. This was Israel (Rudolf) Kastner, who was later to become the hero—and victim—of the infamous Kastner trial.

I hung out at the newspaper offices for four days with nothing to do, until Kastner summoned me. "I understand you want to be a journalist," he said.

"Yes," I answered, nearly choking.

"Wonderful," he said. "So go buy me a pack of cigarettes."

He took a few bills from his pocket and I ran downstairs, returning with two packs and some change. He took them from me and said, "You're hired."

Kastner stood by his word, because the next morning Shen called for me. "There's a press conference taking place in a town called Ashkelon," he said. "It's being organized by the head of the local council who says he's going to make it into a city based on tourism and archaeology. Get down there and bring back an article."

For the first article of my professional life I traveled on two buses. When the driver announced "Ashkelon," I looked out the window and saw nothing but sand and a few buildings in the distance. I alighted and began to walk in the direction of the sea, until I reached the local council building. The council head was standing on a podium and speaking excitedly, his hands flapping. I understood almost not a word of what he was saying, but I wrote down several sentences in the notepad the secretary had given me. When all the other journalists raced to catch the bus back to Tel Aviv, I decided to stay. I walked between the buildings, interviewed several residents, paid a visit to the archaeological site and watched tanned archaeologists poking around in the ruins. That night I caught a ride back to Tel Aviv and wrote the first article of my life. Shen read it, looked at me, smiled, and repeated the two words Kastner had said to me: "You're hired."

I had become a journalist.

CHAPTER 19

At an official luncheon in Shanghai, over shark-fin soup (a questionable delicacy that the Chinese serve to important guests they wish to torment), I asked the city's vice mayor, Ho Zhan Chang, who was sitting across from me in a red armchair adorned with tiny gold dragons, how he dealt with the growing rate of crime in his city.

From the look of distress on the translator's face I understood that this was not a proper question to ask in communist paradise, but he translated it nonetheless. Chang looked out the window at the skyscrapers of the noisiest city on earth, and after a long moment of thought, said, "You have come during the rainy season but to your good fortune, today the weather is clear."

During the four years I worked at *Új Kelet* I felt that way more than once. Outside, the real world moved along, a world in which Israel was coping with war and poverty, with crime and the difficulties of absorbing immigrants, with periods of austerity and the first terrorist attacks on civilians. But inside our offices it was Little Budapest, where men wore suits and ties to work, flirted a bit with the secretaries, then drank a cup of tea with cookies before translating another erudite article from German.

The staff of the paper divided into two states of minds. Many among us were only too happy to remain on our peaceful Hungarian island, removed from the tense and sweaty reality that was this new country, Israel. Others—including me—viewed *Új Kelet* as a way station on the trip to the main destination. This may sound paradoxical, but I felt we had not come all the way to the Jewish State in order to live like the Jews had in Europe: in a small group, closed to outsiders, maintaining our own language, trying to reduce contact with the outside world to a minimum.

Ephraim Kishon was our undisputed star. He was seven years older than I and quickly became the older brother I never had. Many people lived in fear of his cool misanthropy, but I understood its sources: he was a Holocaust survivor who had escaped from the train taking him to the extermination camp Sobibor and had decided that the world was such a bleak place that there was no choice but to become a humorist. He was also a young writer who had been silenced by a communist regime (his first book had been banned by the Hungarian authorities) and had decided to put everything behind him and come to the new land of Israel. His first job in Israel was as a toilet cleaner, and he learned Hebrew in a very original—and particularly fitting—way: he got himself a second-hand copy of a dictionary and learned it by heart while scrubbing toilets.

From that tattered dictionary were born some of the greatest pearls of comedy ever written. In 1952, alongside his work at *Új Kelet*, Ephraim was summoned by Azriel Carlebach, the legendary editor-in-chief of *Maariv* newspaper, to write a daily satirical column, which he called *Had Gadya*. *Had Gadya* was enormously popular, and Ephraim kept writing it for thirty years. He wound up selling some 42 million copies of his books in twenty languages, won the Golden Globe award three times and was nominated twice for an Oscar. The characters he created—most notably Salah Shabati and Constable Azoulay—became an integral part of Israeli and world culture.

I was asked many times about the secret of Ephraim's talent, and in response I always told the same story: during the Second World War the British used color-blind soldiers for deciphering aerial photographs because they could not be fooled by camouflage. Kishon was emotionally color-blind. He saw the cruel truths hiding behind layers of camouflage of social hypocrisy and exposed them without a second thought. It was funny, because we always like to see liars stripped bare, but it left him a sad man because he had no delusions about his fellow humans.

Several months after I received my first salary, I finished my matriculation exams and registered at once for the College of Law and Economics, which later became the Law Faculty at Tel Aviv University. At the
same time, I left Mother and Rudy's cramped apartment and went to
live as a subtenant at the home of my father's cousin Dr. Waldman.

This time, my studies were pleasant. After having succeeded with the
Bible the year before, the laws of torts suddenly seemed simple, and I
enjoyed arguing during lectures on the philosophy of law.

"Without the courts," the lecturer, Professor Shaki, once shouted, "democracy is a regime in which sixty-one members of the Knesset can
hang the other fifty-nine."

"It's clear you've never lived in a dictatorship," I called out from the
audience.

"In fact I did," he said. "I left Mussolini's Italy at the last moment."

I was silent, but this was excellent preparation for the days to come.

My double existence grew more pronounced. Among Israelis I was just
a young student with a foreign accent who sat in the front of the classroom and asked too many questions. But among Hungarians my fame
was growing, thanks to the colorful reports I was publishing and the social commentary I was writing, inspired—and carefully monitored—by
Ephraim.

Even my mother, who had not forgiven me for missing out on an illustrious career as a dispatcher, had trouble hiding her satisfaction when
her friends quoted from my articles.

One day I handed an interview I had conducted with a young man
I found smoking hashish in Independence Park to Mr. Shen. In those
days—the early 1950s—this was as rare as if I had interviewed aliens
whose spaceship had landed in the center of Tel Aviv. Shen read the piece
and burst out laughing. "Young Lampel," he said, "this article is good
enough to be published in *Maariv*."

Instead of amusing me, this comment made my face flush with envy
and anger. If the piece could appear in *Maariv* (Israel's largest newspaper

at the time), then why wasn't it? That evening, I recounted my woes to Ephraim. "Patience, Tommy," he said. "You're not ready yet."

After I had spent two years on the job, Avraham Ronai invited Dosh and me to Café Roval with a suggestion: why shouldn't the three of us, along with Ephraim, create a show for Hungarians in Israel? He would perform a Shakespearean monologue or two, Kishon and I would read sketches we had written and Dosh would place a large block of paper on an easel and draw caricatures of the crowd. We would divide the profits among the four of us. We loved the idea and went straight to the home that Ephraim shared with his first wife and her elderly parents to tell him all about it.

The only thing we forgot to take into account was Ephraim's legendary miserliness (when one of his children called to ask how he was, he was in the habit of answering, "How much?").

"No problem," he told us. "But I want eighty percent of the proceeds and you can divide up the rest."

"But Froikeh," I protested, "we'll all be putting in the same amount of work."

"That's true," Ephraim said, "but the difference is that I can put on such an evening without the three of you, whereas you can't do a thing without me."

This simple lesson in practical capitalism silenced us all. He was right, of course. After all, Ephraim was the star while we had only begun to make our names. We discussed it briefly and concluded that Ephraim would receive sixty percent while we would divvy up the rest. At the conclusion of our chat, Dosh and I felt the need to take revenge, so we filled his mailbox with spaghetti and tomato sauce.

We put on the show and I was mildly surprised to discover that I enjoyed being in the limelight. The others suffered from occasional stage fright, and even Ronai, the most experienced among us, had trouble going onstage without the help of a bottle of cognac. But I was in my element. I answered questions, told stories, even let myself show my temper here and there at those pests who always show up for such evenings. Our show ran a few dozen times, and I learned from it a lesson that held me in good stead my entire life: anyone who stands on a stage is an actor, even if he is playing himself.

One year later, I finished my law degree. I stood among three hundred students wearing a black gown and received a diploma rolled shut and tied with a ribbon. Mother and Rudy stood in the crowd, excited and emotional. My gaze caught my mother's for a moment and the two of us thought the same thing: what a pity that Father could not be there to see how his son had become a lawyer like he had been, and a journalist like he had been. At the same time, incidentally, I was beginning to thicken around the middle and I began to wonder whether I was going to be fat like him as well. I fought the tendency all my life but I must admit with sorrow that that was one battle I lost.

Several weeks later, Mother asked me to join her for a talk in a coffee shop. She was pale and sad. "Rudy is sick," she said quietly. "Throat cancer."

I looked at her, unable to take it in. She was forty-seven years old and men still stopped to look at her on the street, a radiant blonde who seemed as though she did not have a care in the world. Yet here she was about to lose a second husband. We went to their apartment and I embraced Rudy. Even then, his eternal optimism had not abandoned him.

"We'll get through this, Tommy," he said by way of encouraging me. "Don't worry, we'll get through this."

But he did not. The disease brought him to his knees within only two months, as we sat by his hospital bed and watched him deteriorate. The only thing left of him near the end was his ever-present smile. As I walked behind his coffin, my hand on Peter's shoulder, I could not help thinking about how yet another thread connecting me to my past had been severed. Novi Sad was becoming a blurry memory, growing further and further away.

On a rainy winter day in 1955, Kishon left a message in my mailbox at *Új Kelet*. "Tommy," it said, "I've made an appointment for you at noon tomorrow with Azriel Carlebach at *Maariv*'s offices. He is looking for a personal assistant. Be humble."

CHAPTER 20

Will it surprise you to learn that I was always in search of a father?

I suppose my external appearance hid that fact well: the ruddy face, the hair already graying, the burgeoning belly, the flailing, expressive hands. Still, I always had a weakness for father figures, older men more authoritative than I. Most of the time I was unaware of the fact until much later, and perhaps it was best that way, since most were unsuited to the task: Kishon was melancholy and complex, Robert Maxwell eccentric and irresponsible, Rudolf Kastner arrogant and despised. The only person who recognized my need and even exploited it was Ariel Sharon, and it was only when we dismantled our political partnership that this tendency of mine disappeared once and for all, and I adopted instead two younger brothers who never disappointed me—Ehud Olmert and Amnon Dankner, a fellow journalist.

But for a single year of my life, and only one, I did have the perfect father.

He did not, of course, know this. How could he? All he did was to bring a young and overly ambitious immigrant into the small anteroom of his office to serve as his personal assistant. Did he see in me a reflection of himself? I do not believe so. Was he capable of understanding how our association affected me? Never.

Behind his back he was known as "The Indian Prince" due to his threatening, animal-like elegance, his exotic looks and the distant, romantic aura he maintained. A renaissance man with a *yeshiva* background, the sharp-witted Azriel Carlebach left his native Germany, where he wrote against the Nazis in German newspapers, and went to study communism in Moscow (where he became convinced of its eventual failure) before settling in Israel in 1937. After nine years as editor-in-chief of the *Yediot Ahronot* newspaper he founded *Maariv*, which quickly became the largest newspaper in the country. Government ministers and presidents (and not a few women) wooed him incessantly, while he crowned or dethroned them with open glee. Hundreds of thousands of people bought the Friday edition of the paper just to read his weekly column. "If you want to know what the public will be thinking tomorrow," said IDF chief of staff, Yigael Yadin, "read what Carlebach writes today."

When I entered his office for the first time, I realized that Kishon's instructions were unnecessary: I felt absolutely humbled. Carlebach looked me over briefly, then placed three photographs on his desk. "Give them captions," he said. I managed to improvise something even though I could not identify all the people involved. A shadow of a smile crossed his face. "You'll start work tomorrow morning," he said.

The work was not particularly complicated. The paper—which came out in the afternoon and comprised only eight pages—would be written at night and the proofs were brought to him for inspection. He went over every word, made changes, and then in the morning I would fetch them from him and take them to the printers. In addition, he would give me notes to present to the journalists with his comments and reactions, most of them sharp as a blade. I found these notes highly amusing, but they brought me enemies. Everyone knew I was the only person who read them and they suspected (unjustly) that I would share the insults with others. For the first time in my life I was working for a true leader, a man whose strength of character alone caused everyone around him to work round the clock. When he rebuked them they trembled; when he gave one of his rare compliments, the recipient would glow for days.

Carlebach taught me the delicate art of controlling people, their need to be listened to, the difference between what was important and what was trivial, and especially the hidden power of a person who always tells the truth. Often, it is unpleasant in the short term but in the long term—and management is only concerned with the long term—it is always the best policy.

Once, Carlebach saw me shouting at a typist. His face darkened and he asked me to step into his office.

"What happened?" he asked.

"I was angry," I admitted.

"If you're so angry then take it out on me. Truly angry people shout at their bosses, not their secretaries."

I never forgot that lesson, and tried to behave myself accordingly my entire life.

Beyond that, he taught me to write. Whereas he may have been amused by the intrigues he caused in the corridors, when it came to the written word—perhaps because of his rabbinical background—he was absolutely reverent. With uncharacteristic patience he revealed to me the secrets of the profession, like the "inverted pyramid" or the way an adjective grows in strength when it follows a full stop. Enormously. Once I asked him what a makes a person a good journalist. "The skill of an artisan," he said. "The eye of a sharpshooter. The senses of a hunter. And the soul of a curious child."

Two months after I began work, we were sitting in his office and he was dictating something when suddenly he raised his eyes.

"What's the meaning of the name 'Lampel?'" he asked.

"A lantern, in Hungarian," I told him.

"You need to change your name," he said. "You're a Hebrew journalist, you need a Hebrew name."

"I'm the last Lampel," I said. "My uncles have no sons."

He looked as though he did not hear me.

"Lapid," he said. "You need to change your name to Lapid, a torch. It's close enough in terms of the meaning and they won't be angry with you."

His influence on me was so great that two days later I went to the Ministry of the Interior, waited in line for two hours, and changed my name. Carlebach was right about the name because it was easy to remember, but he was wrong about my uncles: they were so mad at me that they did not speak to me for several long weeks.

Would I do the same thing today? I suppose so, even though I still feel a little guilty with regard to my ancestors for cutting off the Lampel line. There was something cruel in this decision that I gave no thought to in my youth. Ever since the eighteenth century, when Jews under the Habsburg Monarchy were ordered to adopt family names, Lampels had been born and Lampels had been buried, and I had decided offhandedly and arbitrarily to be the last Lampel.

It was not long at all before Carlebach's trust in me was so absolute that he handed me a sheaf of blank pages with his signature at the bottom. "I don't have the patience to answer letters to the editor," he said. "Write to them in my name." The assignment amused me until I thought about the endless teasing I got from the proofreaders about my misspellings. Never mind me, the new immigrant, but there was no way that Carlebach could respond to his admirers in erroneous Hebrew. In order to hide my distress from him, I sat at home night after night with a dictionary writing the letters with tremendous effort, only to put them casually on his desk in the morning as if they had taken me only minutes to write.

One day, he sent me to fetch an article he needed. In the cool gloom of the archives I encountered a beautiful black-eyed twenty-one-year-old woman sitting at one of the desks. She raised her face and smiled at me, but before I even had a chance to smile back she looked back down at her papers. When I left, I asked someone who she was. "That's David Giladi's daugter," he told me. "She's on a break from the university and came here to work."

David Giladi was one of the Fabulous Seven who left *Yediot Ahronot* with Carlebach to found *Maariv.* I wanted to go back in and speak with her but I did not dare. I had grown up in a class-conscious society in which servants did not mingle with the aristocracy, and I knew I had no chance with her.

In February 1956, I entered the building one afternoon and found the secretaries sobbing and red-eyed editors running back and forth like decapitated chickens. Carlebach was dead. He had been enjoying himself in bed with one of his many lovers—this one the wife of a well-known Tel Aviv physician—when he suffered a heart attack. I still find it hard to believe, as I write these words, that he was only forty-eight at the time of his death.

Ultimately, it was decided—against the policy of the newly departed Carlebach—that there was no choice but to lie to the public. One of the senior staff members wrote a moving piece describing how Carlebach's heart had given out as he sat in his armchair listening to Beethoven's *Ninth Symphony*. After that, the junior members of staff were asked to leave the room and Aryeh Disenchick—known to all as Chick—was chosen to be the new editor-in-chief.

Two days later, Chick summoned me to his office. Without looking me in the eye he informed me that he was sending me to be the paper's correspondent in Beersheba. We both knew that this was a form of exile; at the time there were only 20,000 people living in Beersheba, the vast majority of them new immigrants. The city still had no hospital, no university, no theater—only sand, a jumble of languages and exhausting heat. This was revenge by the veterans for Carlebach's affection for me, and for the fact that I knew too much about them all.

"What about my studies?" I asked. "At some stage I want to begin my internship."

"When you want to study," he told me, "you can come back."

On the way out of Chick's office I felt a mix of anger and relief. I did not want to go to Beersheba, but I was pleased they had not fired me and that my days as a personal assistant were over. From that moment forward I was to be a full-time journalist.

CHAPTER 21

I left Tel Aviv in the winter and arrived, two hours later, in summer. The Beersheba sun seemed as though it had no plans whatsoever to set; steam rose from the cracking asphalt on roads, flat-roofed one-story buildings were strewn about the sand like a child's building blocks, and life was as slow as the sluggish camels that the Bedouin rode to market on Thursdays.

The feeling I had when I stepped off the bus was akin to what Greek writer Nikos Kazantzakis once wrote (and which would later be inscribed on his tombstone): "I don't hope for anything, I don't fear anything, I'm free!"

The small town correspondent for a large newspaper is a kind of local sheriff. *Maariv* had rented a room for me in the only hotel in town, and within two days of my arrival I already found myself seated in the office of Mayor David Toviyahu, both of us lazily drinking sweetened Turkish coffee that had been prepared in a copper *finjan*. "Not a lot happens here," I noted.

He thought about this at length before answering. "Things happen," he said finally. "But at a different pace."

In order to shake off the lethargy that had settled on us both, I stood up and stretched my limbs.

"Where are you going?" the mayor asked me, surprised.

"To Cassit," I told him.

As a rural gesture to the big city, a café called Cassit had recently opened up on the main drag of Beersheba, and it boasted one of the only public telephones in the city. It was from there that I was in the habit of dictating my submissions to the paper.

Toviyahu had a small, thick Chaplinesque mustache that very nearly managed to hide the smile that appeared on his lips. "When you get there," he said, "ask about Betty."

I moved slowly down the street, my shirt clinging to my back, until I landed with a sigh under the ceiling fan at Cassit. "Is there someone here named Betty?" I asked the waiter. He smiled that same enigmatic smile I had seen on the mayor's face. Two minutes later, a woman slipped into the seat across from me. She was thin, with closely cropped hair, and appeared to be older than me, but her movements were youthful and sharp and a bridled energy encircled her like an aura. "Are you a journalist?" she asked in a fetching French accent. I told her I was. "I can't speak now," she said. "Come to my place at four o'clock." She wrote down the address on a napkin and sped away as quickly as a bird.

I arrived that afternoon at the spacious and well-tended villa that was very uncharacteristic for the area and clearly the home of well-to-do people. The gate was open, as was the front door. I knocked several times, then entered.

"Anyone home?" I shouted.

"I'm in the back garden," came the response. "Step out here."

I crossed through the house and came to a large, plate-glass window, where I stopped, astonished. On the other side, Betty was bent down on all fours in a large fish pond, poised and watchful as a bloodhound and naked as the day she was born.

When she saw I was hesitant, she motioned with her small hand for me to draw near. "Shhhh . . . she whispered. "I'm hunting frogs."

I continued to stand there, mesmerized and aroused. At twenty-four I thought I had fairly impressive sexual experience, but at that moment I realized that this was the first time I had seen a naked woman in broad daylight. Her skin was smooth and clear, her breasts small, and my gaze was drawn against my will to the thatch of dark hair between her legs.

Betty remained as still as a statue for another long minute, then sprang, disappearing under the water then reappearing, dripping with water and smiling, a surprised green frog in her hands. *"Mon chéri,"* she said cheerfully, though it was not clear whether to me or to the frog, "I've caught you!"

She stepped out of the water and into a colorful silk kimono. "So where are you from?" she asked.

"Tel Aviv," I stuttered. "But before that from Budapest. It's a long story."

"Très bien," she said. "I love long stories."

I never met another woman like Betty Knut. Not before and not after.

She was born in Paris in 1928, the daughter of White Russian nobility. Her mother was the niece of Soviet Foreign Minister Molotov and the granddaughter of the noted composer Alexander Scriabin (whose *Piano Sonata No. 9*, known as the Black Mass Sonata, I was familiar with and could not stand). With the occupation of France, Betty became active in the anti-Nazi underground at the age of fourteen, and later a military correspondent for the monthly magazine *Combat*; she was even wounded in battle. After the war she published her first book, *Circle of Flies*, which became a bestseller. The eighteen-year-old author was a hit among French intellectuals, but her tempestuous nature was restless and she became an ardent Zionist and joined *Lechi*, the Fighters for the Freedom of Israel underground movement.

On 16 April 1947, Betty went to the British Colonial Office in London wearing a fur coat and an enticing smile and left three kilos of explosives in a lavatory there. The bomb did not go off due to a mechanical mishap, but Betty managed to slip out of Britain at the last moment. Several months later, she was apprehended in Belgium, where she was trying to blow up British warships that were preventing immigration to Israel. Police found her carrying nine kilograms of explosives, forged documents and a double-bottomed suitcase, and she spent a year in a women's prison in Brussels.

"How was it there?" I asked out of curiosity.

"Like Dante's vision of hell," she said. "Only darker."

After her release she returned briefly to Paris and came to Israel immediately following the War of Independence. She was taken into custody for a short period after the assassination of Count Bernadotte but was released on lack of evidence, and she came to Beersheba in 1951 with her husband, a Jewish American who owned bulldozers that were involved with infrastructure around the Negev.

"Your husband?" I asked. "You have a husband?"

"Of course I have a husband, *chéri*. Every woman needs one."

We were lying in her bed sharing a cigarette after making love. A glowing orange sun was setting outside the window, and Betty said lazily, "In fact, he should be coming home soon so we'd better get dressed."

I rose quickly and gathered my clothing. Not fifteen minutes later we were drinking coffee in the living room when her husband, a genial, rosy-cheeked American, walked in and kissed her on both cheeks. If he guessed what we had just been doing he did not let on. "Any friend of Betty's is a friend of mine," he said while pumping my hand.

If Hava had exposed me to Israeliness, it was Betty who introduced me to Left Bank bohemian culture. It was on the record player at her house that I first heard the hoarsely sensual voice of Juliette Gréco; it was Betty who translated for me the pornographic books of Guillaume Apollinaire; Betty who danced for me (again in the nude) her version of a Diaghilev ballet; Betty who screened eight-millimeter films of Jean Cocteau and made me read his book, *Les Enfants Terribles*, which he wrote while trying to wean himself from opium. "Look how he drew him," she exclaimed, putting a portrait of Cocteau done by Modigliani in front of me. "He doesn't look anything like that!" I laughed. I had no idea what Cocteau really looked like but her excitement was contagious.

In addition to our affair, I was enjoying an unexpected high point in my career.

One year earlier, in 1955, a unit of paratroops commanded by Ariel Sharon had stormed Gaza as part of the Black Arrow operation and had killed several dozen Egyptian soldiers. When Gamal Adbel Nasser came to power in Egypt he decided to retaliate and began sending terror cells into the southern part of the country, where they murdered and plundered and planted mines. Suddenly, my enforced stationing in Beersheba became an unexpected prize. Instead of some standard pieces that would get buried in the middle pages of the paper ("Bedouin Sheikh Offers Twenty Camels for Daughter of Shoe Store Owner"), I was supplying nonstop page one headlines. Almost daily I was riding around the Negev in IDF jeeps, taking part in ambushes and interviewing officers fresh back from nighttime chases.

One evening I was sent to the home of a family whose son had been killed by terrorists at an oil-drilling site in the Negev. As the result of an error, the family had not yet been notified. "I wish to express my condolences at your son's death," I told the elderly woman who answered the door. She fainted.

Other than that incident, I loved every moment. This was journalism, steely and true, the kind I had only read about in books by Ben Hecht, where the unkempt journalist falls asleep fully dressed on his bed, wakes up to a knock at the door, takes his notepad and goes out into the field to get his story. Two hours later he is sitting in front of his typewriter, his hat still on his head and a bottle of whisky at his side. A cigarette dangles from his lips as he pounds out his latest scoop and leaves his frustrated competition far behind.

Like every journalist in that period I admired Ben Hecht, who had begun his career as a field reporter with a legendary nose for finding scoops and later became famous for screenplays like *The Scoundrel* and *The Front Page* and even won two Oscars. Hecht was such a fervent Zionist that during the British Mandate his films were banned in the UK for "promoting Jewish terrorists." I could never have imagined that only a few months later I would be sitting shoulder to shoulder with him as we both covered the Kastner trial.

On 29 October 1956, the Sinai Campaign broke out. For six days, swarms of soldiers crowded the south, some 175,000 Israelis and another 100,000 British and French soldiers who came to take part in the battles. At times I felt like I had interviewed every single one of them. I ran along the battle lines with a ridiculous British World War One helmet on my head, slept two hours a night and wrote furiously, endlessly. *Maariv* sent its more seasoned reporters to the area, and I was made to understand by the Tel Aviv office that I was to provide them with assistance.

I ignored this demand; it was my territory and I had no intention of becoming anyone's apprentice. Perhaps I should have recalled what US Speaker of the House of Representatives Joseph Cannon said upon completing forty-eight years in Congress: "The pendulum will swing back."

CHAPTER 22

Several weeks after the war ended, my mother asked me to come to Tel Aviv to meet her new husband.

Matitiyahu Nakhumi was the first-born son of the town of Hadera. As a child he had contracted polio and used crutches throughout his life. After completing his high-school education he went to study medicine in Germany and became a surgeon. When the Nazis came to power he left for the United States where he married an American woman. After several years of marriage, his wife began to suffer from hallucinations and was diagnosed as a schizophrenic. Nakhumi decided not to abandon her, leaving surgery behind instead and completing a second specialization in psychiatry. He looked after his wife until her dying day.

Concurrently, he began to work as a psychiatrist at Bellevue Hospital Center in New York and grew quite wealthy. At the time, psychiatry was far from being as fashionable as it is today, and I once asked him how it was that he, of all doctors, had made such a good living. "It's due to the Japanese," he told me. It turned out that in the hospital they spelled his name Nakumi, a common Japanese name. When Japanese patients arrived at the hospital they were happy to see that a Japanese doctor was working there and therefore asked to be treated by him. Later, when they discovered their mistake, they felt it would be impolite to ask to make a change, so Dr. Nakumi/Nakhumi from Hadera became the most popular Japanese psychiatrist in New York.

After the death of his wife, Nakhumi decided to return to Israel. He purchased a beautiful penthouse apartment on luxurious Dubnov Street in Tel Aviv. Mutual acquaintances introduced him to my mother, and after a brief courtship they decided to marry. I was slightly surprised by the decision, but I did not say a word. Peter was at the kibbutz, I was in Beersheba, and I figured they would relieve one another's loneliness.

Before we parted, Mother gave me the biggest gift I had ever received: a set of keys. "I've transferred ownership of the apartment on King Solomon Street to you," she said. "I don't need the place any more and maybe this will get you back to Tel Aviv to start your internship, so you can become a lawyer."

I could not believe my ears. No one I knew had his own apartment, and in central Tel Aviv no less. Loyal to my mother's advice, I went to the offices of *Maariv* and asked for an urgent meeting with Chick, the editor-in-chief.

"I want to return to Tel Aviv," I told him. "You promised I could come back for my studies."

"You're not returning anywhere," he said.

"I'll quit," I said by way of a threat.

"Don't bother," he said coldly. "You're fired."

For three days I walked around moonstruck, confused and utterly lost. After that I returned to Beersheba to gather my few belongings. I went to say goodbye to Betty and we drank coffee in her garden while I poured out my woes. "Don't worry, *mon chéri*," she said. "You're a talented boy, they'll call you back one day."

I kissed her one last time and we parted. A year later, she and her husband opened a nightclub called The Last Chance, which was a magnet for every crazy person in the Negev. Betty, who was always ahead of her time, was also the first to bring the 1960s revolution to Israel. In the end she became addicted to drugs and died at the age of thirty-seven.

———

After returning to Tel Aviv, I sat day and night in my new apartment, staring at the empty walls, until I realized that I was not depressed, merely bored. I had always believed that depression was not circumstantial but a natural part of our genetic makeup. In the ghetto I saw people who had lost their entire world and continued to be optimistic and full of vitality, while on the other hand I have met others who have everything—money, career, a successful family—but could not free themselves from the cloud of depression that hovered over them constantly. Fortunately for me, I was the first type. One morning I woke up early, took the good old No. 4 bus and rode it to the Central Bus Station.

Új Kelet took me back gladly, on two counts: on the one hand because they needed me and on the other because my venture into Israeliness had ended in failure. I began to work full-time while looking for a law office where I could apprentice. However, two weeks later I received a phone call from Shmuel Schnitzer, the associate editor-in-chief at *Maariv*, inviting me to meet with him.

Schnitzer was an eccentric, an outstandingly bright autodidact, tall and somber, with thick glasses that gave him an owlish look. The combination of his Dutch ancestry and his introverted nature earned him the obvious nickname "The Flying Dutchman." Other than Carlebach, he was the only senior staff member at *Maariv* who treated me warmly.

"We want you back," he said.

"What? Why?" I asked.

"Kastner's appeal is about to start and I want you to cover the trial."

I had followed Kastner's trial from afar. It angered and disgusted me, and not only because of my acquaintance with him but also because I understood that this entire affair represented the complete lack of understanding that native-born Israelis had for what happened to us during the Holocaust.

These days, as the result of decades of meticulous documentation and shock, there is general acceptance of the fact that on that other planet known as Europe during the Holocaust, the laws of existence were different from anything ever known to humankind. But back then, in the

1950s and 1960s, conventional thinkers and the general public treated us with condescension. "Why didn't you fight back?" they would ask. "Why did you go like sheep to the slaughter?" They were First-Class Jews who took up arms and fought, while we were Second-Class Yids whom the Germans could annihilate without encountering resistance.

At the time, there was a cook in the *Maariv* offices who was a survivor of Auschwitz with a number tattooed in blue on his arm. The longtime staffers called him Soap, a twisted play on the famed Nazi plan to use Jewish body fat to make soap. "Hey, Soap," they would say. "What's for lunch today?" to which Soap would chuckle uncomfortably and fill their plates.

So it was into this atmosphere that the Kastner affair shot like a poisoned arrow.

Israel Rezsö Kastner was one of the heads of the Aid and Rescue Committee for Hungarian Jewry. In early 1944, when Adolf Eichmann began implementing his plan for the extermination of Hungarian Jewry, Kastner managed to make contact with him and offer a deal: the Jews would pay with trucks and money and the Germans would let them go. After protracted negotiations, a train filled with Jews left for Switzerland, but the authorities stopped it at Bergen-Belsen. Kastner, however, would not give in and he reopened negotiations with Himmler's envoy, Kurt Becher, persuading him to let the train continue to Switzerland. One thousand six hundred and eighty-four Jews were saved.

The Israelis, however, turned up their noses. How could anyone make a deal with the Nazis? A Jerusalem right-wing activist, Malchiel Gruenwald, self-published a manifesto in which he attacked Kastner for aiding the German war effort. "My dear friends," he wrote, "the stench of a carcass reaches my nostrils. Dr. Rudolf Kastner must be eliminated."

Kastner, incensed and outraged, sued Gruenwald. What was supposed to be a swift and short libel case became, within weeks, a real imbroglio. Gruenwald hired the best-known prosecutor in the country, Shmuel Tamir, who would later become the minister of justice. It did not help that Kastner had kept the promise he made to high-ranking Nazis that he would help them after the war if they aided him in saving

Jews. He traveled to Germany during the Nuremburg trials to testify on behalf of Kurt Becher and other Nazis. Even I, who was sympathetic toward him, found it difficult to explain such a bizarre act. I tried to speak with him about it on several occasions but he always changed the subject. The only explanation that makes sense to me is that Kastner was, in his own eyes, a European gentleman, and European gentlemen always kept their promises. I cannot justify his behavior, however; it was "European gentlemen" who murdered my father and most of Europe's Jews.

The trial turned into a circus. The plaintiff became the defendant. At some point, Tamir decided to showcase the role of the Jewish paratroops sent to aid Hungarian Jews as proof that it was possible to resist the Nazis in other ways. He called Catherine Szenes, mother of Hannah Szenes—the famed Israeli paratrooper executed by the Nazis after parachuting into Hungary—to the witness stand. "Why did you not help my daughter?" Catherine Szenes cried out tearfully to the pale Kastner. "You should have tried to gain her freedom." Kastner did not reply. What could he have said? That if he had gone to Eichmann demanding the release of Hannah, the homicidal Obersturmbannführer would most likely have taken his pistol and shot him in the head instead?

It was an impossible, hopeless situation in which Kastner's supporters and detractors refused to listen to one another. As the trial dragged on, I grew angrier, and more frustrated. I could not understand how the native-born Israelis—who had come through the war without the slightest idea of the hell that was taking place in Europe—could allow themselves to put us on trial for choosing to survive in any manner we could.

In June 1955, Judge Benjamin Halevi published his verdict. "Kastner sold his soul to the devil," he claimed, and exonerated Gruenwald on every count but one, setting his punishment as the payment of a single Israeli lira.

The appeal was set for January 1957 and I started work two months before that. *Maariv* took an anti-Kastner stand throughout the trial, but they wanted someone with access to the other side. Schnitzer even asked me not to stop working for *Új Kelet*, Kastner's fortress, so that I could remain as close as possible to the story's tragic hero. When I mentioned this to Kastner, he laughed. "Better you should be a double agent," he said. "At least that way someone will hear my side of the story."

His laughter was a rare event in those dark days. He was fading away, turning gray. He would spend his days in court or with his lawyers, then at the *Új Kelet* offices at night, where he continued working as the night editor. No one ever saw him sleep, he lost weight, and his famed arrogance—which had enabled him to grapple fearlessly with the most notorious murderers—slipped away from him like an old pair of trousers.

Several days after the appeal began, we went together to a small Middle Eastern restaurant near the Central Bus Station. As we sat eating at a table on the pavement, an alley cat jumped onto a rubbish bin and knocked the metal lid to the ground. Kastner leaped from his chair, terrified. When he realized what had happened he sat down slowly. There was sweat on his upper lip. "They want to kill me, Tommy," he said. "I'm getting threats every day."

"Nobody's going to kill you, Rezsö," I told him. "It's just talk."

"I hope you're right," he said.

On 4 March 1957, three young men—members of an extreme right-wing underground organization—ambushed Kastner at the entrance to his building, and when he stepped out of his car they shot him and ran away. Kastner was taken to the hospital, where he died of his injuries. Not long after the murder, the three were captured and confessed. Fifty-two years later, one of them, Zeev Eckstein, appeared in a documentary film in which he intimated what we had always believed: that the Israeli secret service had been involved, if not actively then at least silently. Kastner had died in order to save the leaders of the country from embarrassment.

In spite of the fact that Kastner was dead, the trial continued, and in January 1958 the Supreme Court overturned the earlier verdict and cleared Kastner's name of any wrongdoing. This was paltry consolation, and far too late. No one was left unscathed. Even the Hungarian community was split in two, between those who supported Kastner and those who stood behind the Szenes family. I belonged to the first group, but my heart went out to poor Catherine Szenes, who did not realize she had been turned into a pawn by forces greater than she.

In 2003, while on a state visit to Budapest, I asked for the archives containing the protocols of Hannah Szenes' trial and execution to be opened for me. "The prisoner is twenty-three years old," wrote her murderers dryly, "and in good physical condition. She was tortured brutally but refused to hand over her comrades or request clemency. The firing squad fired inaccurately and she suffered for a long while until her heart stopped beating."

I sat alone in the cool archive, reading and crying.

CHAPTER 23

Lord Robert Boothby, who was Churchill's private secretary and later a member of Parliament for thirty-four years, once told me the following story: "In 1931 I visited the Führer in Munich. When I entered his office he jumped from his seat, stood at attention, raised his right arm in the Nazi salute and shouted, 'Heil Hitler!' I had no choice but to stand to attention as well, raise my right arm, and shout, 'Heil Boothby!'"

Several weeks after Kastner's death, I understood that it was time for me to start shouting my own name.

Public interest in the affair was beginning to wane as the appeal dragged on, and I feared that for the second time I was about to be let go from *Maariv*. I decided I was going to have to try writing differently.

Apart from journalistic superstars like Carlebach and Kishon, Israeli journalism was mainly influenced by the very pedantic German press. Everyone took excessive care with the Five Ws and punctuation, producing writing that was professional and precise, but also dry and dusty and boring as old toast.

On the other hand, the Hungarian press on which I was raised had an entire genre that was unknown in Israel—small, picturesque human anecdotes collected from the margins of interviews. It was not the headline that was important but the hidden safety pin that held together the dress of the high-society woman, the flask of gin concealed by the smiling politician, the colorful travel stickers on the case of the sleeping cello belonging to the world-class musician.

For the first time in my life, I began to write in my own voice.

At *Maariv* there were those who disapproved, but I did not care. If they were going to fire me then at least I would know I had done it my own way. And anyway, it turned out that the public liked my new style; my humble little mailbox behind the secretaries' desk began to fill up with letters.

One morning I was walking down the hall and encountered Schnitzer, who was just stepping out of the men's room, still wiping his hands on a paper towel. I nodded in greeting and continued down the hall, but his voice stopped me in my tracks.

"Tommy," he said, the look on his face that of a man preoccupied with some new idea that had just crossed his mind. "Those little pieces of yours, people seem to like them."

"So I've heard," I said.

"Why don't you make it a regular column for the Friday paper? Interview people and write anecdotes about them."

"Sounds fine to me. When should I begin?"

"Next week?"

"Sure." I continued tranquilly down the hall, my back aching with the knowledge that he was still watching me and trying to figure out if he had done the right thing. It was only when I rounded the corner that I began jumping up and down on the steps like a lunatic. My own column! Every week! One of the secretaries began climbing the stairs, caught sight of me and, with a nervous glance, turned around and went the other way.

It was only after I had calmed down that I asked myself what would have happened if Schnitzer had not had to take a piss that morning. I have no answer to that question. It is possible that the idea would have come to him anyway, and it is possible that I would, after a number of years, have become the associate editor of *Új Kelet* and ended my career near the Central Bus Station. Life is comprised of quite a number of "ifs" and it is far better to jump about on the stairs like a lunatic than to worry about them.

My column, "This Week's Newsmakers," became an instant hit.

Every week I interviewed three or four people and turned our conversations into short pieces of four to five hundred words apiece. At times it seemed there was nobody in Israel I had not interviewed at least twice. Schnizter, swollen with pride, wrote this about my column: "You may be a distinguished scientist, a flourishing tycoon, a promising artist, a young poet laureate or a master of political intrigue—if the phone hasn't rung to inform you that Lapid wants to interview you, then you still haven't reached the station called Success."

But I did not stop with Israelis; quite a few of my interviews were conducted with visitors from abroad. The young Jewish state was a world attraction at the time, and everyone who was anyone came to see this new miracle in person. We were their anecdote, and they were mine.

In the five years during which I wrote the column I interviewed Yves Montand, Simone Signoret, Rudolf Nureyev, Coco Chanel, Henry Kissinger, Willy Brandt, Igor Stravinsky, Pablo Casals, Ella Fitzgerald, Amália Rodriguez, Stanley Matthews, Arthur Rubinstein, John Gielgud, Peter Sellers and many, many others. Quite a few of them—Harry Golden and Danny Kaye being the two best examples—became my friends. They especially loved the fact that I did not ask them the same banal questions they were asked everywhere else. I talked politics with the musicians, fashion with the politicians, military history with the designers. Louis Armstrong told me about his days in prison in the Deep South, I spoke with Marcel Marceau about his upbringing in a traditional Jewish home in Strasbourg, and Helena Rubinstein told me about her collection of miniature furniture, the most valuable in the world. It was only when she rose from her chair that I understood the secret of her passion for this subject: the legendary cosmetics industrialist was herself a miniature, not even five feet tall.

CHAPTER 24

In 1999, shortly after I was elected to the Knesset, I felt that something was missing in my life. At first, I could not figure out what it was, but then I realized it was the writing. For forty-five years I had written every week, sometimes daily. Of the nine Muses of Greek mythology, my favorite was actually Meleté, the Muse of practice and repetition. Pianists play every day, painters enter their studios each morning, writers need to write. So as not to lose my touch, I occupied myself with our neglected party journal, which I wound up writing, editing, proofreading, supplying with headlines and even giving printing instructions. Other than readers, I had everything I needed there.

In one issue I interviewed Dr. Ruth Calderon, the founder and executive director of Alma College in Tel Aviv and Elul, both institutions dedicated to the study and advancement of egalitarian Hebrew culture for secular and religious women and men. Quite naturally, the conversation turned to religion.

"Freud says that religion is an expression of underlying psychological neuroses and distress," I said, taunting Ruth. "A kind of sickness."

"Tell me," she said, breaking into a smile, "didn't he say the exact same thing about love?"

In 1958, the love of my life was waiting just around the corner, but I did not know it yet.

In the meantime, I took full and unabashed pleasure in my new status. I was only twenty-seven years old, and suddenly all the politicians were pursuing me, government ministers called me by name, and women who only a year earlier walked by without even glancing in my direction were suddenly gazing longingly at me.

One morning, I was walking down the street when a beautiful girl—the type the French would call *petite*—passed by. She said a bashful hello and only then did I realize I knew who she was: Shulamit, David Giladi's daughter, whom I had met once in the *Maariv* archives but had not dared approach. I asked her how she was and she told me that her father had just been appointed as the paper's Paris correspondent and that she was heading there with her parents. I wished her luck and suddenly she said, "Why don't you write to me?" "With pleasure," I answered, and that is truly what it was—a pleasure.

During the period she lived in Paris and later in London, we corresponded once or twice, but I had the feeling that she was not taking me too seriously (not to mention the fact that, like most professional journalists, I had deep reservations about writing for free). Some two years later, the paper sent me to cover the World Bible Competition and I met her again, with her father. Standing next to her like a shadow was one of the paper's star reporters, Aharon Dolev. Dolev was serious competition, a man who was everything I was not: a native-born Tel Avivian, elegant, reserved, aware of his own self-worth (a little too aware, if you ask me), a man who got all the assignments that I wanted, from interviewing the prime minister to trips abroad. This time, I decided, I had no intention of losing out to him.

I began courting Shulamit enthusiastically, with all of *Maariv* watching the two young rivals. Tel Aviv florists felt a sudden upsurge in sales and each of us used his best maneuvers—Dolev with his exceptional manners and me in my customary noisy way. The problem was, with Shula you could never truly know—not then, not during the course of the next fifty years—what she was thinking. She was quiet and introverted and fragile as Venetian glass, and men awakened in her a touching sheepishness. It was the first time in my life that I had met a person who did not enjoy being the center of attention. Only on my twenty-eighth birthday did I get a sign that I might be the leader in the race for her heart. We met for a drink at Cassit and she handed me a gift-wrapped book. I stepped aside and tore the wrapping paper off. It was Aristotle's *Poetics*.

Several weeks later I went to interview Danny Kaye in Jerusalem. Before leaving Tel Aviv I phoned Shula to see how she was. "I'm fine," she said. "Dolev is here."

I got to the interview in very low spirits. Kaye, a warm Jew and a sensitive man, could see that I was unfocused and asked me what had happened. I told him I had met the love of my life but I feared she had given her heart to another man.

To my dying day I was grateful for his reaction. "Forget this interview," he said. "I'll make time for you tomorrow. Go to Tel Aviv and ask her to marry you."

I shot up from the chair, went outside and caught a taxi at once. "To Tel Aviv," I told the driver. "And fast."

As the Jerusalem hills flew by I could feel the anger rising in me. With all due respect to Aristotle and his poetics, it was another of his sayings that I recalled at that moment, which suited my mood far better during that painfully lengthy hour-long drive: "Anyone can become angry—that is easy, but to be angry with the right person at the right time, and for the right purpose and in the right way—that is not within everyone's power and that is not easy."

By the time I reached Tel Aviv I was in a state. I entered Shula's house and stood facing her. "I'm sick of this," I said, raising my voice. "We're getting married."

"Fine," Shula said. "But why are you shouting?"

CHAPTER 25

At eight thirty in the morning the telephone rang. I opened one eye and saw the shadows of an unfamiliar hotel room. My head hurt from excessive drinking and my mouth was dry. I fumbled around in the dark and found the receiver.

"So," my mother said cheerfully, "how was it?"

"How was what?"

"You know."

I looked to my left. A dark head and a pair of black eyes rose from the pillow next to me and gazed at me in confusion. With a slight delay I realized that this was my new wife of twelve hours.

"For the love of God, Mother, I'll call when I wake up!"

Before I could set down the receiver I could hear her laughing.

A week earlier, the wedding had nearly been called off. We had gone to register our marriage with two witnesses, Kishon and Dosh, but the moment we entered the seedy and neglected Rabbinate building, Shula panicked and said she was going home. I just stared openmouthed at her and said nothing. Luckily, Ephraim took control. "Wait here," he told me. He took her arm and led her outside for a long walk during which he explained that all brides panic just before their weddings.

"Fool!" he whispered in my ear when they returned. "Are you not aware that she's a virgin?"

I was both shocked and amused. All my life I had been surrounded by sexually open-minded women, and now I was about to marry the last virgin in Tel Aviv.

It was a minor incident, but it defined something in our relationship that did not change right up to the day I died: I was the goat with a large bell tied around his neck, loud and voracious, always engulfed in a circle of friends, quick to laugh and quick to anger, while she was—and still is—introverted and sensitive, an inward-looking artist with a poetic soul who found the encounter with everyday life to be filled with anxieties.

Our wedding was held at the Journalists' Building in Tel Aviv on 15 February 1959. The date was no coincidence; *Maariv* was founded on the same date and we hitched a ride on the paper's traditional celebratory toast in order to save on the costs of the wedding. The ceremony itself took place that morning in the garden of the home of my new in-laws on Mapu Street. Shula wore white, and anyone who tries to tell me that there was ever a more beautiful bride will have to go head to head with me one day in Heaven's court. Her mother, Helen, stood beside her casting suspicious glances at me; this daughter of a Transylvanian egg-seller did not particularly like the ambitious immigrant her own daughter had chosen for a groom. She figured I was trying to get ahead at *Maariv* by marrying the daughter of one of the paper's senior staff, and she made no attempt at keeping her opinion to herself. As for me, I figured she was acting pretty snobbishly for a woman who had begun her life in Israel as a mule driver, and, like her, I made no attempt at keeping my opinion to myself. Before I was even married five minutes I already had a true mother-in-law.

In retrospect—and what do I have now but retrospect—I treated her unfairly. Helen Giladi was a tempestuous, exceedingly funny woman with milky skin and black gypsy eyes. She had left school after only six years but loved literature and theater and could speak, read and write in Hebrew, English, French, German, Hungarian and Romanian. Even when she barely had enough money to buy food, she sent her only daughter to drawing lessons and drama classes and took twelve years to pay off in installments the piano she bought for her in Jerusalem, at Kleinman King of Pianos.

To her quiet husband's horror, Helen also had a love of practical jokes. On occasion, guests in her house would be treated to chocolate balls filled with hot pepper, or salt cubes for their tea instead of sugar. She had a biting and unbridled sense of humor, and no one was spared her sharp and witty tongue. For years I was the primary target of her lashings, and in my customary manner I gave it right back to her. It was only after she died that I realized how much I missed her.

I was tense and nervous under the wedding canopy, until I recalled a story that the renowned American opera singer, Richard Tucker (a Jew, born Rubin Ticker), had told me several weeks earlier: one day, the legendary conductor Arturo Toscanini chose him for the main role in *Aida*, which was being staged at the Metropolitan Opera. In the middle of a rehearsal of the final act, Toscanini stopped the music and asked, "Mr. Tucker, why are you so serious?" Ignoring Toscanini, Tucker continued singing with a funereal expression on his face because his character, Radames, was going to be executed at the end of the scene. Toscanini stopped the music again. "You're going to die!" he roared. "Smile!"

A smile spread across my face.

For our forty-fifth wedding anniversary we traveled to the Galilee with our children. In the evening we sat in a restaurant called, fittingly, Shulamit's Estate. After we had downed two bottles of wine, Meirav asked me, "What's the secret? How does a couple stay together for so many years?"

"There are three conditions," I said. "The first one, children—even children your age—do not wish to hear about . . ."

Glasses clinked, laughter was stifled.

"The second condition," I continued, "is shared interests. I know people who come from very different cultural backgrounds and have wonderful marriages, but it was quite a bit easier because the two of us come from similar backgrounds. We both love Chekhov and Mozart, English culture and American literature. We have both devoted our lives to words—Mother to literature and me to journalism."

For a moment I stopped talking and looked around the table. My son-in-law and daughter-in-law looked at one another and smiled. Like Yair, Lihie is a writer and a columnist. Like Meirav, Danny is a respected clinical psychologist. They understood exactly what I was talking about.

"And the third condition," I said, "is that inexplicable thing called love. It has no exact definition but it lives and beats like a heart, and if it is not present then none of the other things suffice. I have had a real, profound love for your mother for forty-five years, and it seems that in the past two weeks or so she has begun to develop some affection for me as well."

Everyone clapped. I continued, unable to contain my love of dramatic gestures: "Forty-five years ago, right after our wedding ceremony, I removed my wedding band on the claim that it was uncomfortable. The next day I realized I had lost it and since then I have never worn a wedding ring. Today, I decided to buy us wedding rings." As I spoke, I produced a small velvet box.

Shula said, "Oy, Tommy, really," as she did whenever I did something that embarrassed her in public, and we put our rings on one another.

Nearly five years later, just a few moments after my heart stopped beating, Yair gently removed the ring from my finger and since then has worn it himself. I hope that it will bring him no less good fortune than it brought me.

CHAPTER 26

When Senator Hubert Humphrey had something funny to say he would lean the top half of his body forward so that his high forehead blocked everything else from your line of vision. "The right to be heard," he once told me, "does not automatically include the right to be taken seriously."

We both laughed. It was one of the influential senator from Minnesota's favorite sayings and he shot it at me in the way that Americans have for making you feel you are their best friend just five minutes after you have met them. But it turned out days later that Humphrey, who later became vice president and very nearly president (losing to Nixon by only point seven percent of the vote), had actually taken me quite seriously.

I had been married exactly three weeks when we received a phone call from the American embassy in Israel. "Senator Humphrey was very impressed with you," said the voice on the other end of the line, "and he has arranged to make you a recipient of a State Department scholarship for young people from around the globe with great potential. We are offering you the chance to work for two months as a reporter for a local American newspaper in Lynn, Massachusetts, and then to travel around the US for another month, at our expense. Are you interested?"

Was I interested? You must be kidding.

———

Our first honeymoon was in an un-air-conditioned hotel room in Eilat, but now, just three months later, we were headed for our real honeymoon.

We spent the first ten days in New York City. Nowadays, when young people arrive for the first time in New York, they experience a feeling of déjà vu: they have seen so many films and television shows featuring Times Square and Madison Avenue that it sometimes feels as if they have actually been there before. But back then, in the late 1950s, the effervescent power of America was like an electric shock that struck all my senses. I had come from a country where ice was sold on horse-drawn wagons and meat and eggs were still rationed, while in America it seemed that every family had two cars, a double-door refrigerator and men wore a different suit every day of the week. The abundance was dizzying.

But New York—as every American who does not live there will only be too happy to tell you—is not America. New York is the Big Apple while America is a land of small cities. New York is cosmopolitan while America is rustic. New York never sleeps while America turns out the lights at nine thirty. New York is spendthrift and bohemian while America is based on the puritanical ideals of work ethic and family. In short, New York is New York while America is Lynn, Massachusetts.

The first settlers arrived in Lynn in 1629, and nothing much has happened since then. The main source of pride for residents of Lynn was that soldiers in the Continental Army wore Lynn-made boots when they went to war against the British. By the twentieth century, the boot industry had given way to electronics, but most of Lynn's 80,000 residents worked in nearby Boston, making Lynn a rather sleepy community. When we first arrived, as the taxi passed through the streets, Shula noted that while there were lots of cars parked on the streets there were no people to be seen anywhere.

The largest hotel in town was called Ocean House, but we could not stay there because everyone knew that the management was not willing to rent rooms to Jews. It was not official policy, of course, but any time a Jew wished to rent a room it was explained to him politely but firmly that there was no occupancy. Ten years later I received a one-line postcard from a friend living in Lynn, which said, "Tommy, you'll surely be happy to hear that the Ocean House burnt to the ground."

I worked for the *Lynn Daily Times* and we lived with a warm and welcoming local Jewish family, the Turneys, who refused to take any money from us and even gave us an extra car of theirs to use—a beat-up Volkswagen from the 1940s. One evening (or, as Kishon called them, "one last-night"), Shula and I took a bus to a Boston jazz club. At two in the morning we discovered that we had missed the last bus back to Lynn. We went back into the nightclub and began asking around to see if anyone was headed that way. Four young black guys sitting at the table next to ours said that they were traveling in that direction and would be happy to take us. We all crammed into their big Chevy and chatted amicably all the way home about the performance we had seen. In the morning, Mrs. Turney said, "You got home a little late last night." We told her how we had very nearly got stuck in Boston overnight, but had been lucky enough to find a ride home. She nearly fainted. "You got into a car with four black men at two in the morning?" she asked. "Are you out of your minds? It's a miracle they didn't kill you!" We both looked at her, utterly perplexed. Why? What exactly was the problem?

Many years later, I had the opportunity to tell that story to my lunch companion at Raphael restaurant in Tel Aviv. He was a handsome, self-assured African American who laughed at the story. His name was Barack Obama.

After two months in Lynn, we set out on our long journey, traveling America crosswise and up and down for a month in tiny airplanes and huge cars, watching from up close—without knowing it—an America that was about to become extinct. America before the Vietnam War, before flower children, before Martin Luther King's march on Washington. An innocent, conservative America whose biggest rock star, Elvis Presley, stopped his career midstream to join the army.

In each city we visited we were hosted by friendly local families arranged for us by the State Department. We stayed with Mormons in Salt Lake City. We were entertained poolside in Hollywood by Joe Pasternak, the legendary Hungarian-Jewish director, while a bevy of long-legged girls in bathing suits paraded around trying to catch his attention. We stopped at Niagara Falls, San Francisco, Chicago, Dallas, San Antonio, Charlotte, the Grand Canyon. I cannot explain exactly why, but I felt an immediate click with the Americans—me, an Old World European to the core. I liked them and they liked me, and even before my English became fluent we were speaking the same language.

In Las Vegas, our host was Abe Greenspan, the Jewish editor of a local paper with ties to the Mafia. For three days, no one would take a cent from us; we were so drunk on the unexpected savings that we spent all our money at a roulette table until we were down to our last dollar. Shula, in an act of desperation, put it on zero. The roulette wheel went round and round, stopped, and we won back everything we had lost. A purple-haired old Jewish woman sitting next to us raised her head and said to us in Yiddish, "Now get out of here and don't come back." And that is exactly what we did.

We strayed from our travel agenda only once, to visit my friend Harry in Charlotte, North Carolina.

Harry Golden, né Herschel Goldhirsch, was a fat little Jewish guy, smart and funny. The world is full of fat, little, smart, funny Jewish guys, but Harry turned it into a profession. He had grown up on the Lower East Side of New York, worked nights in a hat factory to finance his studies, became a teacher, then a journalist and finally a failed businessman who got caught up in a case of stock fraud and spent five years in federal prison. Upon his release he left New York and settled in Charlotte, where most people had never seen a Jew in their lives.

He started writing a column for the largest newspaper in town and became a leading voice in the desegregation movement (and undoubtedly its funniest). In 1942 he began publishing his own newspaper, the *Charlotte Israelite*. The paper had no publication date or schedule; each time Harry finished writing enough pages of his shrewd and witty reflections he would simply print it and send it out to his fifty thousand subscribers, among them many of America's movers and shakers, including seventy-five senators. His first book, *Only in America*, was a huge bestseller and was made into a play as well. The former prisoner had become a wealthy and famous man and began smoking fat Cuban cigars and enjoying every moment of it.

We had first met in Tel Aviv, when Harry was there to write about Israel and I came to interview him. We became friends at once. At the time he was sixty-one years old and I was twenty-seven, but he apparently recognized my potential for one day becoming a smart, fat Jew. After the interview he hired me as a researcher for a series of articles he was writing about Israel, and we roamed about the country together. On his last day in the country, I came to his hotel to say goodbye and I was standing next to him when he went to the front desk to settle his account. The hotel manager came out of his office smiling profusely and handed back Harry's stuffed envelope of bills. "Mr. Golden," he said, "we're proud that such a famous man as yourself chose our hotel, and the management has decided not to charge you for your stay."

Harry took the envelope, wadded it into a ball, and stuffed it into my hands. "That's life, Tommy," he said. "When I was poor, I couldn't afford to stay in a place like this. Now that I'm rich and can afford it, they don't want my money."

The day that Shula and I spent with him in Charlotte was etched in my memory more than all the rest of the trip. Harry was overflowing with charm and anecdotes and even managed to break through Shula's natural shyness while regaling us with stories of his favorite topic: the Jews of the United States.

"You Israelis," he said, "have a big advantage. In spite of the Arabs, you live free from fear. The American Jew is afraid, even though he has nothing to fear. The thick shadow of the past chases after him. Listen, I get invited to speak in some city and afterwards I'm the guest of the rich local Jew. He drives me in his Cadillac to his mansion, his elegant wife has a maid and she lives like a queen. He employs three hundred people and travels to Europe every year. People respect him, flatter him; life is good. We eat, we drink whisky. After the fifth glass, around midnight, this Jew stands up, comes and sits right up close to me, and in a near whisper says, 'Golden, you're a smart Jew. Tell me, Golden, what's gonna become of us Jews here?'"

———

Two years later, Harry and I met up again when he came to cover the Eichmann trial for *Life* magazine. We remained close to his dying day, in 1981. He was seventy-nine years old when he died. All his life he ate too much, drank too much, smoked too much. But he always lived according to Hubert Humphrey's principle: he never took anything too seriously.

CHAPTER 27

My friend Jennie Lebel once quoted me in one of her books saying that life is not "either/or" but "this and that." Life is built upon parallel lines that do not cross or contradict one another, moving ceaselessly between the private and the national, the general and the intimate, the individual and the communal. May 1960, for example, was a month comprised of robbers, monkeys and Nazi criminals.

The month began when, one afternoon, we returned home and as soon as I opened the door I understood that robbers had broken into our apartment. The foyer was a complete mess—drawers pulled out, furniture overturned.

"Maybe he's still inside," I whispered to Shula. "Wait here." I entered one of the bedrooms, which looked as though a tornado had passed through. I opened other doors but no one was there. All that was left to check was the living room.

"Forget it," Shula whispered. "Let's call the police."

At that moment we heard a crash in the living room. I was terrified, but as a retired IDF corporal I could not think of embarrassing my unit, my army and my country. I took a broom from the kitchen and threw open the living room door, breaking into the room with my weapon flailing in all directions. But the living room was empty, not a soul in sight. I stood confused for a moment, and then suddenly a terrible scream came from behind me. I whirled about: Shula was standing in the middle of the room, pointing upward. On the top shelf of our bookshelves was a monkey watching us with blinking eyes. He was small and hairy, with a pale belly and the face of a naughty old man. The sound we had heard was a book he had hurled to the floor.

We were absolutely at a loss. What does one do when one discovers that a monkey has broken into one's house?

"He probably ran away from the zoo," Shula said. That made sense, since at the time the city zoo was in the middle of Tel Aviv, some two hundred meters from our flat.

I phoned the zoo and asked if they were missing a monkey. The man who answered sounded utterly unsurprised by my question. "I'll just go check," he said. A few moments later he returned to the line. All the monkeys were accounted for, but he told me that the Circus Medrano was in town and that I should check whether they had lost a monkey.

I phoned Circus Medrano.

"Are you missing a monkey?" I asked.

"Yes! Have you found him?" came the reply.

Half an hour later, a monkey tamer arrived at the apartment, lowered the monkey from the shelf and gave him two smacks on his bottom. They left without apologizing. It was only then that Shula picked up the book that the monkey had thrown to the floor. You may think I'm making this up, but Shula can attest that it was Shmuel Joseph Agnon's *A Guest for the Night*!

Several days later, I returned home from work and found Shula gazing out of the open window and smiling like the Mona Lisa at a few eucalyptus trees on the street. I asked if she was okay. "I'm pregnant," she said.

Was I able to hide from her the fact that the tears that flooded my eyes were both tears of joy and pain? I cried with happiness about becoming a father and I cried from grief that my father would not be there to watch me become a father.

Another few days passed, but the wonders of May did not. On the twenty-third of the month I was sitting looking out that same window, but since I did not tend to smile mysteriously at trees, I was listening to the radio. Prime Minister Ben Gurion was about to speak in the Knesset. The speaker of the Knesset rapped his gavel and the prime minister cleared his throat. He sounded more emotional than usual.

"It is my duty to inform the Knesset," he said, "that a short while ago, Israeli security services located one of the most notorious Nazi criminals, Adolf Eichmann . . ."

I dashed from the house, running and skipping like a madman and trying to hug passers-by (who recoiled in fear). I skipped all the way to the *Maariv* offices, where I burst in shouting, "Eichmann's been captured, they've got Eichmann!"

"We know," people around me said consolingly. "Don't worry, it's already been decided that you will be on the team covering the trial."

These days it is hard to imagine, but until the Kastner trial that had taken place only five years earlier, few Israelis had ever heard of Adolf Eichmann, while for me his name carried chilling personal meaning: Eichmann had signed the order carried by the SS man who came for my father on 19 March 1944 and was the man who sent my grandmother Hermina to Auschwitz and my uncle Irwin to Dachau. Hitler was a faraway demon who gave angry speeches from his bunker in Berlin. Eichmann was the devil we knew.

His capture signified the end of the period of silence. This was a collective earthquake, the eruption of a volcano of emotions and flowing lava of memories. It was a change in the map of our consciousness. Fifteen years of mute silence had ended. The survivors began to speak out, at first hesitantly and then in an unstoppable flood. Even the arrogance of the native-born Israelis disappeared as if it had never existed. At first it was replaced with shock, then understanding, and finally the mute acknowledgment that there was no difference between us and them, the survivors and the native-born. For the first time, people asked me questions about what had transpired there, and for the first time, I answered.

However, it was only forty-seven years later that I was able to express to myself what we were all feeling back then. At the main *Yad Vashem* event on Holocaust Remembrance Day, I stood on the stage and told the audience, "We are all refugees of the Holocaust. Even those who were not there. And those who were not yet born. Every person, each one of us, is a refugee of the Holocaust."

Life is "this and that."

On 5 November 1960 our first daughter, Michal, was born.

On 11 April 1961, I sat in the Jerusalem Community Centre and watched them seat Eichmann in a glass booth. I was surprised, as were so many others in the auditorium, at how small he was. How had this nondescript, bespectacled clerk murdered a man so passionate for life as my father?

The prosecutor, Attorney General Gideon Hausner, rose from his chair. His opening remarks at the trial are among the most famous in Hebrew jurisprudence. That evening I sat with him and with the other prosecutor, Gabriel Bach (later Judge Bach), and they told me how they had worked together back and forth on that speech until they understood, in a kind of epiphany, that unlike any other trial, they were not speaking on behalf of the State of Israel but on behalf of the victims.

"When I stand before you, oh judges of Israel, to lead the prosecution of Adolf Eichmann," Hausner began, "I do not stand alone. With me here are six million accusers. But they cannot rise to their feet and point their finger at the man in the dock with the cry *'J'accuse!'* on their lips. For they are now only ashes—ashes piled high on the hills of Auschwitz and the fields of Treblinka and strewn in the forests of Poland. Their graves are scattered throughout Europe. Their blood cries out, but their voice is stilled. Therefore will I be their spokesman. In their name will I unfold this terrible indictment."

I do not know why, but during his speech there was one particular gesture that stood out for me more than any other. When he said the words "point their finger" he raised his own hand and pointed at Eichmann. If I have to choose a single moment, the exact point, at which my act of becoming an Israeli was complete, in which my journey from the prow of a rickety ship to being a part of the state as much as the state had become part of me, it was at that moment, in that gesture, in Hausner's fearless finger.

The trial lasted for eight long months and it frayed my nerves. I spent most of my days in Jerusalem listening to testimony from that other planet, and sometimes, when I could not stomach it any longer, I would run off to Tel Aviv to see my wife and our new baby. I am not a big fan of babies (they do not know how to play chess), but I could not get enough of her tiny fingers and the smile that showed off her first tooth.

These, however, were stolen compensations; at night I slept fitfully, racked with nightmares from the war, memories now reawakened by what I was hearing daily at the trial. Whoever watched Yehiel Dinur (the writer K. Tzetnik) give testimony in his white suit, heard him say, about the daily parade of inmates going to their deaths, "For close on two years they kept on taking leave of me and they always left me behind. I see them, they are staring at me, I see them, I saw them standing in the queue . . ." and then fainting on the witness stand, could never, ever forget it.

One evening, in the darkened bar of the King David Hotel and under heavy security, I conducted an exclusive interview with Dr. Robert Servatius, Eichmann's German defense lawyer. He was a fat, white-haired and energetic gentleman who, apart from his cold blue eyes, could have been mistaken for a bartender in a Munich beer hall.

"Why did you agree to defend him?" I asked.

Servatius sighed. "His friends could not serve in his defense and his enemies were not willing," he said. When he saw that the answer did not satisfy me, he added, "I wished to see with my own eyes and ears what it was that the Nazis really did. Yes, I know they exterminated European Jewry, but I want to know who was responsible. If they prove it was Eichmann, I will have no trouble hanging him. But this needs to be proven."

One part of me wished to strike him, but I knew that Servatius was walking proof that life was "this and that." He had been identified by the Nazis as someone not to be trusted because he had once defended the famed Jewish crook Ignatius Timothy Trebitsch-Lincoln in a fraud trial. For Jews, he was the Nazi's defense lawyer but for the Nazis he was the Jew's defense lawyer.

The verdict in the Eichmann trial, which comprised hundreds of pages, was read aloud over a period of three straight days. On 13 December 1961, just two weeks before my thirtieth birthday, the court condemned Eichmann to death. I could not have wished for a more perfect birthday gift for myself.

And here is one last "this and that," a sad one: Gideon Hausner and I remained close until his death. We had a lot in common: we were both jurists, both members of the Knesset, both government ministers, both chairmen of *Yad Vashem*. He died on 15 November 1990, but I did not attend his funeral because that date is also the anniversary of my daughter Michal's death, and we were at her memorial service.

CHAPTER 28

We are waiting at a red light, Shula and I. Waiting and waiting. Finally, I turn to her and shout, "Damn it! This light isn't working."

She bursts out laughing.

"What's so funny?" I ask, furious.

"For thirty years, every time the light is red you tell me it isn't working."

I want to say something, but the light changes and we continue on our way.

I was an angry man my entire life.

My close friends and relatives spoke often about the difference between my public persona (impatient, militant) and my private persona (easygoing, bear-like, appeasable with a fine sausage or a calorie-rich slice of cake). In fact, both are true. Even they knew that under the pleasantness there was the sizzle of a red-hot ember that could ignite at any moment. Once, at a party, the writer Eleanora Lev told me she had no idea why she liked me. "That's true," *Haaretz* journalist Gideon Samet chipped in. "That's what people always ask themselves: Tommy Lapid is such an insufferable person in every respect, why do we like him?"

"That's right," I said. "And about you, people always ask each other:

Gideon Samet is such a great guy in every respect, why can't we stand him?"

Shortly after I left politics—or to put it more correctly, after politics left me—my daughter Meirav, the psychoanalyst, sent me a letter trying to explain that aspect of my character.

"It's the mark of the Holocaust," she wrote. "Not in the sense that it was victorious over you but that it has left you with the sense that you cannot stand even a single moment of feeling impotent. All your battles are characterized by this 'life or death' drama. 'They' are the winners. 'They' are Nazis. 'They' (sorry to mention this in the same breath) are native-born, left-wing Israelis calling you a new immigrant—all these 'they's wish to destroy you and you fight like a lion and you attack them fearlessly because if you let your guard down even for a moment you will lose everything."

I have a very intelligent daughter. Far more intelligent than her father.

In December 1961, three lucky journalists—myself included—won the chance to fly to Burma with Prime Minister Ben Gurion, his son, Amos, his secretary, Yitzhak Navon (who would later become president of Israel), and a gnomish, bespectacled, smiling representative of Mossad named Rafi Eitan, known as Stinky Rafi. Back then, no one knew that Rafi, who would one day become a member of the Knesset and a government minister, had headed the team that captured Eichmann.

This was my first encounter with Ben Gurion and I was very excited, but this tiny giant did not even glance at me. He was engaged in an ongoing quarrel with *Maariv*—which was systematically, aggressively anti–Ben Gurion—and he seemed quite pleased to chat with the other journalists while ignoring me entirely.

The plane took off toward the east but suddenly landed after two and a half hours, and we discovered we were in Tehran. It turned out that the prime minister had a secret meeting with the shah.

We were taken off the plane and locked inside the shah's personal bungalow adjacent to the terminal so that we could not report this news.

I have never been in a more beautiful waiting room (tiled with marble, adorned in gold), or a more frustrating one. Ben Gurion was in a secret political meeting that no one knew about and we were stuck in a golden cage.

Several minutes after Ben Gurion disappeared, we were joined by the Israeli military attaché in Tehran, a heavyset and affable man named Yaacov Nimrodi, who would, thirty-seven years later, become the owner of *Maariv*. I asked if he could spare me a few Persian lira and he was only too happy to oblige. Armed with a bit of money, I tried to bribe the guards to let me out to phone, but the SAVAK men from the shah's National Intelligence and Security Organization (each one of whom was a head taller than me and as broad as a bank safe) pushed me brusquely back into the room.

I sat there seething until, after half an hour, I had an idea. I approached the El Al pilot, who was also in the room with us, and said, "Listen, my mother doesn't know we've stopped here and if I don't let her know we've arrived safely in Burma she'll die of fright. You've got to help me inform her."

"What's her number?" the pilot asked.

"She doesn't have a phone," I said. "Just let Chick, the editor of *Maariv*, know, and he'll get in touch with her."

A worried Jewish mother is always a winning excuse. The pilot told the guards that he had to check something in the plane and from the emergency phone in the cockpit he left the following message for Chick: "Lapid is stuck in Tehran, he asks you to let his mother know he's fine."

I had many confrontations with Chick in my lifetime, but his journalistic instincts were fine-tuned, and he understood at once the meaning of this odd message. The next day, *Maariv* was the only paper that printed a headline informing its readers that "Ben Gurion in Secret Meetings in Tehran."

My scoop did nothing to improve my relations with Ben Gurion (or with the other journalists, for that matter), but since it was impossible to leave me in Tehran we continued to Burma.

After many months of stress and pressure, Burma had the effect of an Asiatic wonder drug on me: it was a distant, Oriental paradise with a pace that was as soft as the footsteps of a tiger padding slowly through the jungle. Upon arrival in the capital, Rangoon, we were met by an official delegation headed by Prime Minister U Nu (who would be deposed the following year in a military coup). In those days, Israel was helping Burma establish a system of modern farms, and everyone we met there was very friendly toward us, and grateful. Speeches were made, glasses raised in toasts, and the next morning Ben Gurion disappeared.

We were beside ourselves. What was going on? Where was the prime minister? Was this another secret meeting? Each of us had a different scenario, each one crazier than the last. In the afternoon, Yitzhak Navon appeared in the lobby of the hotel and we all stormed him with questions. "You won't believe me anyway," he said with an embarrassed smile, "so why should I tell you?" We promised we would believe him. "Well," he said, "the prime minister decided to close himself off for three days in a Buddhist monastery to meditate."

We gaped. Buddhist theories and practice had yet to catch on in the West and none of us knew at the time what exactly this meant. In today's terms, it was like saying that the prime minister of Israel had decided to join a rap group, or climb Mount Everest. Three days later, Ben Gurion reappeared, more relaxed and at peace with the world than ever. Even his behavior toward me improved. I took the opportunity to ask him about his strange disappearance.

"Tommy," he said, "I am the prime minister of the most complicated nation on earth. I am responsible for all of it: Jews and Arabs and the memory of the Holocaust and waves of immigration, coalitions and opposition parties, the poor and the rich. When you are the prime minister of such a complex country you need to think. Politicians tend to forget that a large part of their job is to stop on occasion to think. If I don't take a break to think about everything, how can I act?"

Years later, when I worked closely with other prime ministers, I looked on as they were crushed beneath the burden of unfolding, hectic events. People coming and going, secretaries juggling intense schedules, every moment someone needing an urgent answer and explaining excitedly that the fate of the nation was dependent upon the speed of the response. They woke up before everyone else, went to sleep later than everyone else, and when they finally had a moment to look at the paper all they saw were more reports about how they were not achieving a thing. Only then did I understand how right Ben Gurion had been. A prime minister is subject to what philosopher John Ruskin called the moral obligation to be intelligent. It would benefit us all if they were to act less and think more.

CHAPTER 29

During my childhood in Novi Sad, we all had two football clubs we supported. The first was the local Vojvodina club and the second was an English team. I was a fan of Aston Villa while my good friend Sasha Yvoni was an Arsenal fan. As boys will do, we held never-ending debates about which clubs were better, but like every football fan in those times, we were forced to admit that there was no question at all about who was the best player in England (and thus in the world): Stanley "The Magician" Matthews, right wing for Blackpool.

Matthews wore the national uniform fifty-four times, was knighted by the Queen and was the first winner of the European Footballer of the Year award. When I met him he was forty-eight years old and still an active player with Stoke City. His hair was gray and thin but his body was as lithe and sprightly as a young man's. It was as though the wrong head had been grafted onto his body.

I asked him the question that every fan wants to ask his favorite player: what was the most unforgettable game in his career? To my surprise, Matthews burst out laughing.

"In 1945," he told me, "when Dinamo Moskva came to London to play Arsenal, there was such heavy fog that from the middle of the field you couldn't see the goalposts. One of our players, Jerry, gave a rough hit to the Dinamo goalkeeper and the referee sent him off. We continued playing with ten players. We played and played and suddenly Jerry ran past me with the ball. 'Shhhh,' he said to me, 'I'm back in on the sly, don't tell the ref.' Jerry played right to the final whistle without the referee ever noticing him. All because of the fog."

In the spring of 1963, Shula informed me that she was once again pregnant. This time I did not cry, I simply hugged her, overjoyed. After years of compressed living, with events piling up one after another at a dizzying pace, I felt that I had found my place in the world. And that place—home—was definitely in Israel. Sure, my rolling Hungarian "r" was as prominent as ever and would remain so to the end of my life, but I was what the author Tom Wolfe called "A Man in Full." Israel was my nation, Hebrew was my language, my career was flourishing and my wife had spun a life for us in her own gentle fashion, a warm and comfortable home where I could relax with her and with our daughter.

On 5 November 1963—the same day his older sister Michal was born three years earlier—Yair came into the world.

The biography you are now reading is, like every biography, a sort of deceit, a delusion, because the happiest events of our lives are the ones about which there is nothing to write. They are events shared by all of us and are not unique. I once read a long article about General Charles de Gaulle's infinite devotion to his young daughter, Anne, who had Down's syndrome. There was no end to the pain he experienced at her death in 1948, but for the history books it is merely a footnote during the year he tried, unsuccessfully, to return to the center of French politics. Is there any doubt that his daughter preoccupied him at that time more than the intrigues involving petty politicians and angry generals written about at length by his biographers? Is it not clear what would have made the proud de Gaulle weep in his bed at night?

I am not, of course, comparing myself to de Gaulle (I always loved the phrase Churchill used to describe his flight from Occupied France: "That small aircraft carries the honor of France"), but my private life, like his, was full of moments about which there is nothing to write, like watching my daughter approach her brother's crib with the hesitant steps of a three-year-old, hold out her hand, and her brother of two weeks taking her finger and trying to pull it to his mouth. She laughs, we laugh. Tolstoy got it wrong: even the happiest families are all happy in their own ways.

Several weeks after Yair's birth, Aryeh Disenchick informed me that he was appointing me to be the paper's London correspondent. I had never visited the UK, but long before I ever set foot there it was my intellectual and spiritual capital. The voice that burst forth from the improvised radio we had in the ghetto (always tuned to the BBC) was our lone beacon of humanity and valor, and I admired everything associated with it: the plays of Shakespeare, the poems of W.B. Yeats and Elizabeth Barrett Browning, the films of Hitchcock, the works of Dickens. The globe had spun and spun and in the end I had miraculously succeeded in fulfilling the childhood prophecy I had made to Sasha on the banks of the Danube: that I would become a journalist in London.

I arrived in London in January 1964—alone; Shula preferred to wait several months until she could wean Yair—and found a Tudor-style flat at Clifton Court with wooden crossbeams and a glass ceiling that dripped rain in the summer and was covered with a thick layer of snow in the winter, leaving us in a permanent state of darkness.

I worked from a small office in the *Daily Telegraph* building which I shared with a dark-cheeked, good-natured Greek journalist. From the first day, he explained that the main focus of our work as foreign correspondents was to maintain good relations with Mr. George.

"Who is Mr. George?" I asked.

"Mr. George," said my Greek colleague, "is a thief."

Several hours later, he introduced me to George, a short, red-nosed, loudmouthed Cockney whose expertise was in going from one newspaper headquarters to the next throughout London in the wee hours of the night and stealing the first papers off the press. These papers, which would hit the streets only hours later, first thing in the morning, enabled us to send home the most up-to-date news, so that the headlines in Tel Aviv and Athens appeared at the same time they came out in London. On second thought, George was not the only thief: we were as well.

A few days later, someone at the *Daily Telegraph* informed me that Churchill was going to make a rare appearance in Parliament. I raced over there and grabbed a seat in the press galley. He entered a few minutes later and made his way slowly through the hall leaning on the arm of his successor, Harold Macmillan. His head was as smooth as a billiard ball, his gaze muddled; he looked terribly old at ninety. To the surprise and dismay of the British journalists sitting near me, I burst into tears.

CHAPTER 30

"I have a scoop for you," whispered one of my sources at the Israeli embassy in London.

"Yeah, what is it?" I asked.

"Abba Eban is going on a secret diplomatic mission to Buenos Aires in order to improve our relations with Argentina."

At the time, Argentina was still furious with Israel over the kidnapping of Eichmann and had even threatened to sever diplomatic relations with us. Eban, at the time Israel's deputy prime minister, was expected to use his renowned international status to solve the crisis. I phoned Israel to ask Eban if the story were true, but I was told he had already left for Washington and would be continuing his mission from there. After a lot of pestering on my part, the secretary finally agreed to give me the name of his hotel. I phoned Eban there late in the evening but he was out at a meeting. I left a message asking him to return my call and fell asleep.

At two o'clock in the morning I was awakened by the phone and an operator informed me that she had Abba Eban on the line. Apparently I was so deep in slumber that I could not for the life of me recall why I had wanted to speak with him. In order to stall for time I asked him about the weather in Washington.

Eban was rather surprised by the question. "It's snowing," he told me.

"Heavily?" I asked in a panic, still unable to remember what I wanted to ask him.

"Yes," said Eban.

"Must be pretty cold then."

"It certainly is."

"So make sure to wear an overcoat, Mr. Eban."

"That's a fine idea."

"So, good night," I said.

"Good night to you, too," concluded the legendary diplomat.

I was awakened again in the morning by the telephone. This time it was Aryeh Disenchick. "Tommy, are you all right?" he asked, worried.

"I'm fine," I said. "Why do you ask?"

"Because Abba Eban phoned me from Washington," he said. "He told me you'd called him to ask if he was wearing an overcoat. He wanted me to make sure you hadn't lost your mind."

I had not lost my mind, but London had.

It was gay London, frivolous London, where the 1960s had most definitely arrived. Three weeks after my arrival, four young men from Liverpool calling themselves the Beatles had entered a recording studio and within ten hours had recorded their first album, *Love Me Do*. Already that summer they had broken all sales and listening records with "She Loves You." Their more rambunctious rivals were the Rolling Stones, but for those who preferred something sweeter, there was Cliff Richard and his saccharine ballads.

London theater was experiencing a golden era under the leadership of Laurence Olivier, John Gielgud, Maggie Smith, the Redgrave family. Writers and playwrights like Harold Pinter, Alan Sillitoe, Arnold Wesker and John Osborne created a new school of drama called Kitchen Sink Realism. Stanley Kubrick had just brought the unforgettable *Dr. Strangelove* to the screen, the young Francis Bacon and Lucien Freud were changing modern painting, Twiggy's ultra-thin legs adorned billboards the length of Carnaby Street, where girls in miniskirts and boys in flowered shirts carrying guitars hanging from their shoulders ran into businessmen emerging from nearby Oxford Street embalmed in their suits and bowler hats and carrying umbrellas. We were living in the midst of a colorful, noisy, exciting revolution and we loved every minute of it.

At *Maariv*, however, they did not always understand what I was going on about in my articles. For example, in 1964 the Beatles decided to make their first American tour. Two seats on the plane were reserved for foreign journalists wanting to cover the event, and I won one of them. Woozy with joy, I cabled *Maariv* to let them know I would be gone for about two weeks. I received a ten-word response from the editor: "Who cares about four dirtbags from Liverpool. Stay in London." To this day I am sorry I obeyed the order.

At the same time, as though completely disconnected, a different England was continuing on its path, an England of tradition, ceremony, seriousness of purpose. An England where a woman could spend weeks picking a hat to wear at Ascot, where gentlemen with bloated bellies drowsed at their clubs and where Parliament was still debating issues as though the sun had not already set on the Empire.

At the Queen's annual Diplomatic Reception, I was one of 5,000 guests sitting in large tents on the grass of Buckingham Palace. Suddenly, a murmur passed through the crowd—the Queen had begun passing down the line of guests and shaking hands with those in the first row. All at once it dawned on me that my mother would never forgive me if she understood that I had missed the chance to shake the hand of the Queen of England, so I jumped into action and, after five minutes and much blatant Israeli pushing and shoving, I found myself right up front, ahead of a trail of plowed-over Englishmen with offended looks on their faces. The Queen shook my hand warmly and continued onward. What a man won't do for his mother . . .

I actually made a friend or two in London, people who enjoyed meeting someone who spoke his mind and discussed his feelings. One of them was Nigel Judah, a senior staff member at Reuters. He was a tall, dark Englishman of Jewish extraction whose looks—that of a melancholy prince—caused women to fall in love with him all the time. Every time we met, I insisted that we speak "Israeli," that is to say, openly. We talked about his frequent love affairs, our careers, our obstinate rivals and our hidden fears; in short, all the things that trouble young men at the start of their adult lives.

Years later, Nigel became the general manager of Reuters and we always kept in touch. When he passed away, his family found a stipulation in his will asking that Tommy Lapid, "my best friend," deliver the eulogy at the St. Bride's Fleet Street church.

I was very fond of Nigel, but until that moment I had no idea that I was his best friend. His widow, Phoebe, told me, "You were the only person who spoke with him about the things that really troubled him. In England, no one talks about those things."

Obviously, I flew to London and delivered the eulogy in the church packed with people who never bothered to understand him while he was alive.

After several months in England I bought a car—for the first time in my life. It was a cute, compact Ford Anglia outfitted with an exciting innovation: electric windshield wipers. We used the car to set out on long journeys: we saw Olivier play Othello at Chichester, we sat on the grass to watch Shakespeare at Stratford-upon-Avon, we looked down at the English Channel from the white cliffs of Dover and we walked the green hills of Cornwall. With time we came to know rural England, slow-paced and mellow, so different from dusty Israel, an England where people lived in utter tranquility surrounded by cows and sheep and evergreen vegetation, people who knew exactly when they would rise each morning and go to sleep each night, when they would work and when they would rest, when they would live and when they would die—of boredom, of course.

I spent no small amount of my time hosting Israelis visiting England. I traveled with Ben Gurion to Oxford and we browsed the small and crowded bookstores together, the prime minister openly enjoying the fact that no one recognized him. With Abba Eban—who apparently had been persuaded that I had returned to sanity—I went to the House of Lords, where he entertained some thirty peers with anecdotes as they sat listening to him, enthralled. (And they were not his only admirers: from the place where I was sitting, off to the side, I could see that Eban could not stop secretly watching himself in the mirror behind the peers, clearly pleased with what he saw.) When Prime Minister Levi Eshkol made a state visit to London, I accompanied him to 10 Downing Street. While the prime minister was swallowed into the building, I was detained by the security detail and remained outside, behind the rope. That was the first time I told myself that there would come a day when that scene would reverse itself: I would enter the building while the journalists stayed outside.

One morning, the director of the Cameri Theater in Israel phoned to tell me that the poet Avraham Shlonsky was coming to London. Shlonsky had translated more of Shakespeare's plays into Hebrew than anyone else, and I prepared myself for a particularly cultured and cultural visit. The day following his arrival, his wife phoned from their hotel. "Avraham is standing dripping wet in the shower and there are no towels," she told me. "He wants me to ask you how to say 'towel' in English." It turned out that this renowned translator of Shakespeare did not know a word of English. He had translated the plays from Russian.

Lord Byron once wrote that "the memory of joy is no longer joy; the memory of pain is pain still." Which might explain why the strongest memory I have of this joyous period in my life is actually a sad one: the funeral of the only man I had admired for as long as I could remember, Winston Churchill.

On 24 January 1965, the various news agencies announced that Churchill was dying. I went to his home, where hundreds of journalists and curious onlookers had gathered. Once in a while, someone would step out of the house to brief us on his condition. It was a rainy evening and the crowd was hushed, withdrawn, British. I was riveted, though it was not a matter of reporting for me; rather, it was something between Churchill and the boy listening to him on the radio in the ghetto. At three o'clock in the morning, Churchill's private physician, Dr. Moran, appeared in the doorway. "Winston Churchill is no longer," he announced.

The Foreign Press Association of Britain, which numbered some two thousand members, received just two tickets to the funeral service at St. Paul's cathedral. This time, like before—I do not know how or why—I won one of them. The service took place on a Saturday, and I was accompanying Ben Gurion and President Zalman Shazar who, in order not to desecrate the Jewish Sabbath, went on foot from the Savoy Hotel to the cathedral via The Strand, in the rain. The hundreds of thousands of British citizens who lined the pavement were astonished at the sight of the two diminutive old men wearing top hats and surrounded by bodyguards marching proudly down the middle of the street.

The atmosphere in the cathedral was grand and solemn. The Duke of Norfolk, hat in hand, led the honor guard that carried Churchill's coffin to the sounds of Handel's "Dead March," and there were few dry eyes in the cathedral. There was only one detail that took away from the feeling of majesty: Ben Gurion had been placed next to Charles de Gaulle. The very tall Frenchman looked like Jacob's ladder next to "Old Man" Ben Gurion, who barely reached his belly. Even the Queen of England smiled.

CHAPTER 31

In the middle of the 1980s, Prime Minister Yitzhak Shamir made a state visit to Africa. Several days after his return we met by chance at the Knesset.

"You have regards from Togo," Shamir told me.

"Togo?" I asked, surprised.

Shamir laughed under his mustache. "I was at a reception at President Eyadéma's palace," he said, "and a tall, nice-looking diplomat came up to me and asked me, in fluent Hebrew, 'How is Tommy Lapid?' I asked him where he knew you from and he told me he had once acted in a play of yours."

A smile spread across my face. "Amdos," I said. "You met Amdos."

During the year before our return to Israel from London, I began writing my first play, a comedy. Under the tutelage of Israeli director Shmuel Bonim I learned that, unlike literature, a good play has to be a bad text, that you need to leave huge spaces between lines so that the actors can create their characters and bring something of themselves to the stage.

By the time of our return to Israel in January 1967, I was putting the finishing touches to the play, still working on dialogue, adding lines and taking others out, as we flew from London to Tel Aviv. Several days later, Bonim and I had a meeting with the director of the Cameri Theater, and

I began reading aloud from the text as was done back then. After only a few minutes, Bonim shut his eyes and appeared to be sleeping. I thought I would explode. If this man—who was supposed to be my partner and director—was openly bored with my text then what would the people who were considering acquiring it think?

Before we had even left the building I began shouting at him. "How could you do such a thing to me?!" I roared. "What will they think of us?"

"What's your problem, Tommy?" Bonim said levelly. "Couldn't you see they loved it?"

This comedy, called *Black Man's Burden*, told the story of an Israeli family that invites an African businessman named Ombuko to their home. They go out of their way to show him how enlightened and progressive they are, explaining again and again how they have no preconceived notions or prejudices against black people. But then their daughter falls in love with the charismatic visitor and decides to share her life with him. All at once, their enlightenment vanishes and the shocked parents do everything in their power to separate her from her new beloved.

The film buffs among you will note that the plot resembles that of Sidney Poitier's classic film *Guess Who's Coming to Dinner*, which also starred Katharine Hepburn and Spencer Tracy. In my defense, I would like to point out that my play was staged six months before the film was released. Maybe they even stole the idea from me . . .

During rehearsals, news of the play I was staging reached the ears of people in the Foreign Ministry, and there were fears that it would offend our African friends. They appealed to the management of the theater and asked them to cancel the show or at least drop any offensive lines. It was not called censorship back then, or "the insufferable meddling of the authorities," only "a friendly appeal from above."

What were we supposed to do? Cameri director Shaike Weinberg asked a foreign student of physical education from Togo named Amdos, who was known to be both intelligent and quite fluent in Hebrew, to come and watch rehearsals. We nervously awaited his opinion at the end of the show.

With some hesitation, Amdos said, "I would like to play the part of Ombuko's brother Yehonatan."

"So you weren't offended?" one of us asked.

"The play makes fun of Israelis, not Africans," Amdos said, proving himself quite a bit more clever than the folks from the Foreign Ministry.

We breathed with relief. Several weeks later, the play was staged and it was a big hit, with audiences filling the theater night after night. Even the critics were unusually complimentary toward me. "The famed humor of Hungary has finally reached the Hebrew stage," one crowed.

And each night, in the final scene, Amdos took the stage in the role of Yehonatan. His only line was "Shalom," but thanks to that one-word line he appeared on stages throughout the country as a regular member of the Hebrew theater.

Incidentally, the key line of the play—"The black guy has done his work, the black guy may go"—became a popular phrase. Even the famed critic Michael Handelzalts, a man of great erudition, once wrote that this was one of my most important contributions to the Hebrew language. I did not tell him the truth: that of the entire play, it was the only line that was not actually mine. I had lifted it from *Fiesco's Conspiracy at Genoa* written by the German playwright Friedrich Schiller in 1783 ("The Moor has done his work—the Moor may go").

While rehearsals were taking place, I was invited to a meeting in the office of *Maariv* editor-in-chief, Aryeh Disenchick. "I want you to set up a women's magazine," he said.

"Me?"

"We have a budget for Israel's first glossy magazine. It's going to be a revolution."

"But why me?"

"Tommy, I've given it a lot of thought and you're the person best suited to the job."

When I left his office, I went to the men's room and looked at myself in the mirror. Looking back at me was a thirty-six-year-old potbellied male with a cigarette between his fingers, wearing a suit and tie with spots from the meat sauce I had eaten for lunch. The person best suited to the job? Not only had I never edited a women's magazine before, I had never even read one. I went straight out and bought the first copy of

Cosmopolitan I could get my hands on. Three years earlier, the magazine had been taken over by the legendary editor Helen Gurley Brown, author of the bestselling and scandalous *Sex and the Single Girl*, and she had turned it within months into the most widely read and widely discussed magazine among American women.

I must be the first and only person alive to have found the g-spot while sitting with his feet up on a chair in an empty office, eating peanuts from a bowl. Whole new worlds opened up before me with every page I flipped: it turned out that women liked to look at men's butts; that some women had multiple orgasms while others faked them; that there were women who worked not to supplement their husband's income but because they wanted a career; that women related to something mysterious called "mascara" with deadly seriousness: and that hemlines would be dipping once again below the knee that year.

I decided to call the magazine *At*, the feminine form of "you."

In order to understand who our potential readers would be, I gathered a group of women together and described our ideal reader to them as "about thirty-five, with a bachelor's degree, two kids, a husband serving as a career officer in the military. She wants to replace her fridge and get out to a cinema or theater at least once a week."

They looked at one another, perplexed. One of them said, "Why don't we just find her?"

I jumped at the idea like someone finding buried treasure, and a few days later we announced in *Maariv* that a new monthly magazine was looking for its ideal reader. The paper was flooded with hundreds of letters from women who claimed that they—and only they—fit the profile we had presented. In the end, we did not find one woman who suited every aspect, but at least we had a clear picture of the new bourgeois Israeli woman.

The first issue reached the stands in April 1967 with a star-studded lineup of contributors, including singing idol Yehoram Gaon; Yael Dayan, the daughter of Moshe Dayan, who would go on to become a member of the Knesset; and even a scoop: we exposed astonished readers to the secrets of a new and unknown tropical fruit called the avocado.

For the second time in a single month, I had a hit on my hands.

CHAPTER 32

Two weeks before the Six Day War, the phone rang at our house. Shula answered. "Hello, Mother," she said, pleased to hear from her. Shula's father had been appointed Israel's ambassador to Hungary the previous year and it was rare that she got to speak with her parents. A few seconds later her face grew serious and she motioned me to the phone. I took the receiver from her hand.

"You've all got to come here," Helen said without preamble.

"What? Why?"

"War is about to break out."

"We'll be fine."

Her voice lost its hard edge. "Tommy," she said. "The country may not hold its own. If you two won't come, send the children so at least they'll survive."

I exploded. "I'm not sending my children anywhere!" I shouted. "I'm done running. I wasn't saved from the Holocaust for this. I didn't move to Israel for this. We live here and if need be, we'll die here."

Helen was silent.

Three months earlier, in February 1967, our daughter Meirav was born.

The family photograph was now complete; we had become a Norman Rockwell picture of sweetness: Mother, Father, three children, a white Contessa parked outside. Two months after Meirav's birth we moved into a new home. A group of journalists had banded together and built two buildings on a quarter acre in the Yad Eliahu neighborhood of south Tel Aviv. Shula and I scraped together all our savings to join the project, but there still was not enough money. One evening I recounted my woes to Kishon. He was silent for a moment, then said, "I'll loan you the money, but on one condition."

"What's the condition?" I asked.

"That you won't tell a soul—not your wife and most especially not *my* wife—that the money came from me."

"No problem," I said. "But why?"

"Because everyone knows I'm a miser," Kishon said, "so they don't expect any help from me. If they think I'm a nice guy then they'll all want loans."

I burst out laughing.

It was a white, four-story building. We lived on the top floor, in a seventy-square-meter apartment. It took me more than ten years to pay it off, but after living for years in that pint-sized flat in King Solomon Street, it seemed like a palace to me. At last we had a living room, the children had a room of their own, and I even had a study with a window overlooking the back garden.

For several months everything seemed perfect, but it did not take long before the clouds of war began to gather and cast a shadow over our family idyll. The day after Helen's worried phone call we practiced getting the children down to the shelter. Shula spread a pink piqué blanket on the dusty cement floor and placed a few toys there. Michal and Yair sat on the blanket and rolled a brightly colored ball between them while Meirav drowsed in her cot. I looked at them, full of doubt. Did I have the right to endanger my children's lives in the name of principles they didn't even know existed?

Adults remember the Six Day War thanks to the incomprehensible victory, and the voice of Motta Gur, commander of the Paratroopers Brigade at the time, over the radio: "The Temple Mount is in our hands!"

Younger people remember the war because it was to blame (or to thank, depending on whom you ask) for the fact that Judea and Samaria

were now in Israeli lands. This changed the face of the nation and created the main political point of contention between left and right that
we are still grappling with to this very day.

I, however, recall best the weeks leading up to the war. This was the
last time the very existence of the State of Israel was called into question.
The numbers showed an invincible situation: 2.5 million Jews surrounded
by 500 million enemy Arabs; an embargo on weapon imports; an econ-
omy that had not yet emerged from two years of recession; frightened
phone calls from abroad. The seven divisions that Nasser sent to the
Sinai alone numbered some 130,000 troops, more than the entire Israel
Defence Forces. Gloomy people walked about Tel Aviv talking in whispers, asking themselves if this was how it was going to end once again:
with foreigners flooding the streets and the last Jew barricaded on the
roof of his home, armed with a gun holding a single bullet.

On 28 May, Prime Minister Levi Eshkol addressed the nation and I was
glued to the radio along with everyone else. Eshkol began to speak and
then, to our dismay, choked, grew confused, fell silent and then only after great effort began his speech again. Only later did it turn out that
his military attaché had changed "withdrawing troops" to "moving
troops" without saying a word about it to him, and Eshkol, who had noticed the change, could not decide which of the two expressions was
more fitting.

It did not matter. We were hysterical. If our prime minister was that
terrified, what could any of us say or do?

Four days later, I was summoned to Sokolov House, where the journalists gathered before being dispatched to various units. The recruit-
ment officer was a sloppy reservist with unusual eyes, slanted almost like
a Tatar's. "I'm sending you to the navy," he told me. The silhouette of
the rickety *Cephalus* that had brought me to Israel floated (or, rather, sank)
before my eyes. "No chance," I said. "I'm willing to die for my country
but not to vomit for it." He thought for a moment, then assigned me to
the division being formed by Brigadier General Elad Peled in Tiberias.
Along with me were two young journalists from the Voice of Israel.

We made our frightened way to Tiberias, but after a few hours with the troops the color returned to our faces. They were cheerful, self-assured, ready for battle. That day the prime minister had given in to pressure by the opposition leader, Menahem Begin, and appointed Moshe Dayan as defense minister. The soldiers believed in Dayan and believed even more in their stoic chief of staff, Yitzhak Rabin.

War broke out on 5 June. Peled's division raced toward the Jordanian border and we three brave journalists found ourselves under heavy crossfire during the campaign to take Jenin. I tend to believe to this very day that the Jordanians surrendered because they could no longer stand the sight of the three of us cowering behind the hill, our heads buried deep in the sand, doing our best to keep our asses from sticking out from behind the rampart.

The war came and went so quickly that no one could quite grasp its significance. In the space of three days, Israel had tripled (!) in size, and hundreds of thousands of Palestinians had passed into our jurisdiction. The country was drunk with power, we were the best army in the world, historians and military experts the world over sat to study how we had accomplished it, victory albums were printed and sold out in no time. When someone told Dayan that these territories would one day become a yoke around our necks, he replied haughtily, "Better Sharm-a-Sheikh without peace than peace without Sharm-a-Sheikh."

The war had one more result whose might no one then could understand: Israel Television was established.

Several months after the public television station had begun broadcasting, I received an offer to host a new interview program. I said I would be happy to; I had discovered television during our time in London and I loved David Frost's interviews. I suggested doing something similar in Israel.

I called my new program *I Have a Guest*, a talk show focused on a main interviewee and padded with "items," some more successful than others. In retrospect, it was not a particularly good show. I was too formal and reserved. There was nothing yet of the fire that would one day make me a television star.

Already by the third or fourth program I missed a big cultural scoop:

the guest that evening was the composer Naomi Shemer, whose song "Je-rusalem of Gold" had become the unofficial anthem of the war. Several hours before we were due to go to air, someone phoned and told me, "You should know, the song isn't original. It's a well-known Basque folk song and she stole it." During the interview I asked Naomi about it. She raised her eyebrows in anger. "What are you talking about?" she said. "Do you think I would dare steal a song from someone?" Naomi She-mer could be very persuasive when she wanted to be, and I apologized sheepishly and let the matter go.

It was only in May 2005, about a year after Naomi's death, that *Haaretz* newspaper published a letter she wrote to the composer Gil Al-meda on her deathbed, in which she confessed to having been influenced by the Basque song while writing "Jerusalem of Gold."

My show lasted only a few months, but for the first time in my life peo-ple recognized me on the street. "That's Lapid," they would whisper as I passed by on the street. "Lapid from television." I pretended not to hear but I enjoyed every minute of it.

The program had another, more marginal result: we bought a tele-vision set. It was a square Zenith the size of a chest of drawers, made of wood, with metal buttons for the different stations. The technician who came to install it spent an hour adjusting the antenna until the picture was clear. Shula and I sat in our armchairs and he pulled up a third and sat between us. Five minutes later he fell asleep. We sat like that for an hour. "Wake him up," Shula whispered. "You wake him up," I whis-pered back. It was only at around midnight, when we were certain he was planning to move in with us, that he woke up, gathered his tools, and went on his way. I learned my first lesson of the profession: viewers take the whole matter far less seriously than the people featured there.

CHAPTER 33

It is one o'clock in the morning. I am stuffed into my armchair like a whale in a checkered bathrobe but my eyelids refuse to shut. From the other room I can hear Shula typing away at her computer and I wonder whether she is writing a new book or playing mahjong again. I remove *Coffee in Bed*—a collection of humorous essays I wrote thirty-five years ago, during my days at *At* magazine—from the bookshelf behind me and open it to a piece called "A Simple Man." I read it and smile. My hand extends as if of its own will and takes up a pen from the desk, and I begin to edit it. I remove a line, correct an expression, change the Vietnam War to the Iraqi War. Young Tommy Lapid was not a bad writer, but it's a shame he didn't have an editor like old Tommy Lapid.

Half an hour later, I close the book and go to bed. Perhaps one day Yair will find the corrected version and understand that his father believed it was never too late to improve.

I am a simple man: my favourite colour is red; favourite flower, the rose. I prefer a bright, sunny, blue-sky day to one that's dark and rainy and moody. I'm capable of making use of Sartre even if I haven't actually read his books.

I'd rather spend the weekend in bed than among the thorns in the bosom of nature. I like to eat hot soups: potato, bean, because I am a simple man. In the winter I sleep with the window closed and in summer I hate bathing in the sea because of the tar that sticks to your feet. In shops I am adamant about buying what I came to buy and not what the sales clerk wants to push on me. I do not leave a tip for the waiter who forgot to bring my glass of water.

I am a simple man: I like a few friends and hate several select people, it helps my digestion. I do not believe that every rich person is a cheat because I would like to be rich, too. I believe that old people are generally smarter than young ones.

I am a simple man: I like my own children better than others' and children better than adults and Jews better than Gentiles. I do not believe we are all equal; some are more equal than others.

I am a simple man: I would like to believe the nice things other people say about me, I can't stand criticism. I like talking about people and still claim every once in a while that I never gossip. I support America in Iraq and I would like to hang onto the territories, without the Arabs, of course, just like everyone else. And I know that's impossible, just like everyone else knows it.

Like all simple people, I hope that doctors will find a cure for cancer before my number comes up, and I tend to forget that there are people who travel in buses. I eat too much, get angry at myself too often for eating too much, and make fun of people who do their morning exercises. I used to attend birthday parties, then bar mitzvah celebrations, then weddings and circumcisions and now bar mitzvahs again, this time those of my own grandchildren.

I am not superstitious but I get slightly worried when a black cat crosses my path and I never know how much to give children who ring the bell asking for contributions to this cause or that.

Because I am a simple man, a man for all seasons, a card-carrying member of the biggest party in the world.

It was not always easy to be a simple man, but with the years it became my principal weapon. Most intelligent people, especially intellectuals, tend to trip themselves up. They are preoccupied with their feelings, with their attempts at examining every problem from every side, with repeat excursions to the darkest corners of their personality. I was never that type. The world is black and white as far as I am concerned, and I am content with the fact that I can discern a little more black and a little more white than most people.

Still, as the 1970s drew near, I was faced with a very different dilemma:

what does a simple man do when his life becomes too simple? The answer? He is bored to death.

The main problem was that everything was just fine.

I continued my successful run as editor-in-chief of *At* magazine, I had a beautiful office with a beautiful desk and a beautiful secretary who had a beautiful secretary of her own. My essays were gathered into three collections that became bestsellers, my marriage was a happy one, my three children brought me tremendous joy. I imagine that there are quite a few people who would have been content with that and even pleased with their success, but I was slowly going mad. I had had goals my entire life but during that period of time I was preoccupied with lipstick.

Furthermore, I was cursed with a particularly successful assistant editor, Sara Rippin, who later became a writer and a translator; she introduced a whole generation of Israelis to Philip Roth. In no time she took over the magazine and rendered me obsolete, or nearly so.

Shula, on the other hand, was blossoming.

Several months after we married, I noticed that she was writing at night. "Let me read what you're writing," I would ask. She always refused. Only after much begging and cajoling did she let me read her first stories. There was something wild in them, anarchistic and sexy, which was completely at odds with her introverted personality. The new immigrant in me was slightly jealous of her absolute command of the Hebrew language, the way she bent and rounded and kneaded it according to her needs like potter's clay. By this time I was already an experienced enough editor to know I was looking at a diamond in the rough. "This is what you should be doing with your life," I proclaimed. "Anything else is a waste of time."

She protested mightily. In those days we were overwhelmed with a mortgage and the costs of raising children, and she thought it was her duty to get a job. In response, I threw the nineteenth-century British poet Robert Browning at her, who knew his entire life that his wife Elizabeth Barrett-Browning was the real talent of the family. "One day," I told her, "I'll only be remembered as the husband of the writer Shulamit Lapid. That will have been my true contribution to Israeli culture."

Toward the end of 1969, Shula's first book, *Pisces*, came out.

It was a collection of stories that were short and surrealistic and contained an element of repressed violence that very nearly frightened me. Later, Shula would become the biggest selling author in the history of the nation, but *Pisces* did not enjoy commercial success. The critics, unlike the public, immediately identified a new and unique creature and they praised her wildly. Even the snobbish literary establishment embraced her warmly. The only thing that bothered them was what this delicate writer was doing with the wild Hungarian sprawled out next to her.

The fact that my wife had finally found her place in life only worsened my own sense of feeling lost. In my misery, I went to Aryeh Disenchick and asked for more work. He thought about it for a few days, then appointed me to be the paper's Knesset correspondent.

Several months after I began working in the Knesset, the political bug took hold of me. Whatever that band of fighting roosters could do, I concluded, I could do too. Of all the parties in the Knesset, I was closest to the Independent Liberals, whose head was Tourism Minister Moshe Kol. They were well educated and broad-minded, and, most importantly, they hated socialism just as much as I did.

It did not take long before Moshe Kol persuaded me to join the newly forming youth wing of the party, which never got off the ground. When my boss at *Maariv* got wind of this news he announced he was coming to visit me on the job at the Knesset. I was a bit worried that he intended to scold me, but he never brought up the subject.

"Come on," he said. "Let's go sit in the Knesset cafeteria."

At the time, *Maariv* was at the peak of its public power, and the moment we sat down at one of the scratched-up wooden tables, a wave of sycophants began making its way over. Government ministers and members of the Knesset who heard that the editor-in-chief of *Maariv* was in the building crowded around the table, flattering Disenchick, quoting from his articles, offering interviews with themselves and scoops they were saving only for him. If it had not been so funny it would have been pathetic.

Disenchick answered everyone with a pleasant expression and occasionally pretended to write something in his notepad. When we were alone he turned to me and said, "You've got to decide, Tommy. Which do you prefer? Pandering to others or being someone who gets pandered to?"

"I'd rather be the one who gets pandered to," I said hesitantly.

"Then choose. Politics or journalism. You can't do both."

I chose journalism, but to myself I said, in the words of General Douglas MacArthur during the withdrawal from the Philippines, "I shall return."

CHAPTER 34

One summer day in 2007, Shula sent me out to buy sausages. It was a pleasant walk to the grocery store nearest our house, where I picked up a package of meaty franks. On my way back home I noticed a colorful and noisy wave of human beings marching toward me down the middle of Ben Yehuda Street accompanied by music bursting from huge amplifiers placed on a truck. The odd procession was headed by half-naked dancers, most of them men. Slightly curious, I stood at the side to watch. The first row of the marchers reached me and at once surrounded me, excited. "Mr. Lapid," said one man, pumping my hand, "you have no idea how much it means to us that someone like you has come to support us." Another young man, for some reason dressed in a skirt, slapped me on the back and kept shouting into a megaphone, "Lapid is marching with us! Lapid is marching with us!"

Far too late, I understood that I had stumbled onto the annual Pride Parade sponsored by the Tel Aviv gay and lesbian community. They were so happy to see me that I did not feel comfortable telling them I had only been passing by, and a few minutes later I found myself proudly leading this procession of thousands of dancing homosexuals and lesbians behind me, one hand holding a megaphone and shouting slogans of support, the other hanging onto my bag of sausages for dear life.

The Pride Parade is one of the indicators—though by no means the only one—that we are marching in the right direction. Despite geography and perhaps also despite history, we have been lucky not to fit in nicely in the Levant. We have been conquered neither by the trilling sounds of Oriental music nor by the twirling sidelocks of Hasidic Judaism. With all its many tribes, Israel is in fact a developed, Western, liberal hi-tech nation with an uncontestable tradition of democracy.

Naturally, every human being is entitled to cling to the folklore he brings from his home, but I always believed our existence depended on being part of the European Union and not the United Arab Emirates. My biggest contribution to this issue was not in the articles I wrote or the legislation I promoted, but rather in a project behind which there were no ideological intentions whatsoever: the *Lapid Guide to Europe.*

The idea had already taken hold of me during our merry days in London, when *Maariv* flew me back to Israel for two weeks to edit a special travel supplement. I began looking for material and discovered there was essentially nothing available specifically for the Israeli traveler. The American and British guides that most people used were very professional, and dry as stale bread, and they never bothered to note Jewish points of interest: they did not provide the address of Chez Gilles, the only kosher restaurant in Brussels; they did not explain why one should not miss the Jewish Museum of Berlin; why one should make a special effort to see Rembrandt's *The Jewish Bride* at the Rijksmuseum in Amsterdam; what national tragedy was hidden in the folds of marble of the Arch of Titus in Rome; and they did not even mention the fact that at the Hotel Castille in Paris, a bearded Jew named Theodore Herzl once sat and wrote a pamphlet called *The Jewish State.*

For three months in 1969, I wandered around Europe at the expense of my publishers. I saw nearly everything and wrote down everything I saw. The writer of a travel guide is a mix of pest, author, consumer affairs expert, culture maven and army commander shouting, "This way, follow me!" all the time. In all my days I never invested as much time or attention to anything. There is no tourist bureau I did not visit, no trail I did not hike with my own two legs, no map I did not study until I had learned it by heart. I kept in mind at all times the fact that a traveler holding my book is a sort of captive; if you tell him to step out of a building, walk ten steps to the left and then drink kiwi juice at the kiosk

under the poplar tree, there had better be a kiosk, and kiwi juice, because otherwise he will stop believing in you.

The first edition came out in 1970 and almost immediately became
one of the biggest publishing success stories of all time. New and updated
versions appeared almost annually for the next thirty years. One of the
things that made it unique among travel guides was the offer I made to
readers: whoever sent me an update or a suggestion that made it into
the book would receive a free copy of the next updated version and his
or her name would be mentioned in it. In the thirty years I worked on
the *Lapid Guide* I received some twelve thousand letters. I read them all
and answered them all, even the pest who threatened to sue me because
I did not inform readers that people traveling on the ferry from Copen-
hagen to Göteborg need their passports or they will not be permitted to
enter Sweden.

When I read the first edition now, with a nostalgic smile, I discover
that Europe has remained Europe but we have changed quite a bit.

Who would believe that when I described the Italian kitchen I would
devote several lines to explaining that pizza is not made solely of dough
and tomato paste but that Italians add anchovies, mushrooms or sliced
pepperoni. In the chapter on Belgium I inform readers that in the main
square of Brussels they can eat at a clean and inexpensive American eat-
ery, the oddly named "McDonald's." And when I describe Copenha-
gen's Stroget pedestrian mall I am forced to explain that "it is unique
because no vehicles are allowed so one can walk quietly down the middle
of the street looking in the shop windows on both sides of the street"
because the Hebrew word for "pedestrian mall" had not yet been coined.
But perhaps funniest of all were my contortions to explain to the naïve
Israeli reader that in Europe there were shops that sold—right out where
everyone could see—sex toys! Back then, even the term "sex shop" did
not yet exist in Hebrew.

Competitors to the *Guide* appeared over the years, but none made the
slightest headway against it. Israelis grew accustomed to traveling with
Lapid and selecting a hotel recommended by *Lapid* (getting a ten percent
discount by showing their copy of the *Guide* to the desk clerk) and eating
with *Lapid* next to their plate telling them not to order the nauseating
octopus soup offered to all naïve tourists in Naples.

Once, as I was strolling around Venice with the *Guide* in my hand, an Arab-Israeli sailor approached me and said, "I don't know this city and I see you've got the *Lapid*. Could I walk around with you?" I told him I would be happy for his company and we spent half a day together touring the city of canals without him ever knowing that the "Yussef" he was walking about with was Lapid himself. Another time, someone sent me an article from *The Times* describing how a drunk Israeli had tried to break into 10 Downing Street holding the *Lapid Guide to Europe* and claiming vehemently that Lapid told him it was a tourist site worth visiting.

CHAPTER 35

Mother died on 7 July 1973.

Two days earlier, her doctor informed her that the cancer had spread to her liver and she would need to begin chemotherapy. She listened patiently and asked several questions in her broken Hebrew, most of which had to do with hair loss. After that she went home to her large, empty apartment (her husband, Nakhumi the psychiatrist, had died two years earlier), and phoned me. "It'll be fine, Mother. We'll survive this together." Just as we had survived the ghetto and the communists and the cancer that had killed Rudy. She cried, but not too much. In the end, as often happens in such situations, she was the one comforting me.

She had no fear. People who have died more than once are not afraid. By the standards of World War Two, she was among the lucky. The Nazis had not murdered her, they had merely taken her life.

The script of her life had been written: an intelligent husband, a lone son, a spacious villa with a mahogany dining table, high-heeled shoes which she would buy for the new year and which would tap on marble floors while sounds of hushed gossip and the clinking of champagne glasses played in the background. She was meant to grow old at Father's side, who, as men do, would continue to see her as the young beauty he had married, oblivious to the wrinkles gathering at the corners of her eyes and to the age spots hidden well by makeup.

We always speak of the 6 million Jews who perished in the Holocaust, but what we do not mention are the millions of others who survived, but whose world—the only world they knew—was shattered. My mother had been taught only one thing all her life: to behave well. To accept compliments graciously, to continue smiling at a concert even when one's eyes droop, to read books in the garden and quickly remove one's reading glasses when someone draws near. She never even got the slightest hint that things were liable to change. Cultured people, she was told, do not murder one another without cause.

She was mistaken. Cultured people murder one another every day. When she discovered her mistake she turned—in a single dramatic moment—into a roaring tigress who would do anything to save her cub. By the end of the war she had no more strength. She bolted the latches on the windows of her apartment and lived out the rest of her days pretending nothing had changed.

Outside, beyond the lace curtains, the State of Israel continued in its usual restless, irritable way. Her only son became a journalist in that impossible language. Her grandchildren shockingly went about as suntanned as peasants and wearing sockless sandals. When they came to visit, she would take her grandchildren and a bottle of orange juice and a bag of toffees down to Dubnov park, facing her apartment, so that they would not run about her living room among the porcelain.

Once or twice a week, women just like her would come to visit, wearing dresses with cinched waistlines and pearls. They would spread a cloth of green felt over a round table and play bridge. After an hour she would fetch from the kitchen a patterned Rosenthal china teapot from Germany, along with a matching sugar bowl and milk pitcher, and, with a silver tea strainer she would strain the English Breakfast tea—English Breakfast because when it came to tea, the English knew best. The women would drink slowly and play even more slowly. They made their bids in an impossible mix of Hebrew, German and Hungarian.

That evening, after speaking with me, Mother moved about her apartment for a while longer, enjoyed a cup of coffee at the round table, where she could enjoy her reflection in the glass door. Afterward, she showered, put on her best dress and her makeup, took a bottle of cognac and a crystal glass from the bar and went to her bedroom. From a small drawer beneath the mirror on her vanity she removed two packets of sleeping pills, swallowed them all, drank the cognac slowly until her consciousness dimmed and she fell to the pillow. And that is how we found her: beautiful, pale, the blonde hair that had always been her pride and joy spread out on the pillow like a golden fan.

Several years after her death, I read a poem by the Jewish Hungarian poet Sándor Mázai that made my eyes tear up. I translated it for one of the literary supplements and devoted it to Mother. It is called "After the Holocaust":

> *To die in bed was not death for Aunt Neuman*
> *But a different, strange ending*
> *That fate granted her*
> *As if she had died as a Christian*

CHAPTER 36

I knew that war had broken out when on Yom Kippur, the holiest day of the year, I saw a Jew dressed in full Hasidic garb and long sidelocks emerge from one car and wait for another. He was clutching the velvet sack that held his *tallit*, which would become a pillow somewhere that night. If there is indeed a God then he was certainly smiling at the sight of this Jew of his riding in a car to go to war on Yom Kippur armed with his prayer shawl.

Two days earlier I had run into Yaacov Erez, the military correspondent of *Maariv* and later its editor-in-chief, a small man with a big temper. He was holding a sheet of paper. "Look at this," he said. "They're crazy."

It was an article he had written that morning about how the Egyptians were amassing forces in the Sinai in preparation for war. The military censor had deleted every word in the article apart from his byline. "They're crazy," he repeated. "I'm telling you: there's about to be a war."

However, "they" were not crazy, they were just like the rest of us: at times arrogant and at times foolish, overwhelmed or mistaken or simply preferring to close our eyes in the face of bad news. The Yom Kippur War was the moment at which the relationship between the government and the Israeli public changed forever: after the war we were no longer willing to believe that unerring children of the gods were sitting in the corridors of the Knesset and the government.

When Israeli politicians complain about the aggressiveness of the Israeli media they do not remember—or prefer to forget—how we were on the brink of destruction simply because we put our blind faith in them. These days, a Yaacov Erez would run to the High Court of Appeals with his exclusive, or leak it to the Internet and from there to the international media. Our leaders would no doubt complain bitterly that the media is not patriotic enough or would accuse it of being irresponsible, but the lives of thousands of Israeli soldiers would be spared. It sure seems to me to be the better option.

At the end of the Yom Kippur holiday of 1973, I was overwhelmed by a strong feeling of déjà vu. I had already seen and heard it all before: reserve soldiers leaving their homes with large packs strapped to their backs; the announcement on the radio; drivers suddenly stopping for every hitchhiker; at gathering points, veteran soldiers greeting one another with slightly weary, slightly knowledgeable smiles. An overweight soldier tries on a pair of narrow army pants behind a bus. Another says, "I want to phone my wife." This is the identifying remark of every Israeli war, the true password of every reserve soldier of every generation: "I want to phone my wife."

The next morning, *Maariv* phoned to let me know I should attend a press conference with Defence Minister Moshe Dayan. Dayan was focused, relaxed, his black eye patch shone in the light. Standing in front of dozens of microphones and television cameras, he opened in Hebrew then switched to English. "Israel will not rest until it has removed the last invader from its soil," he said with confidence.

Something in me was inspired, stood proud. Years later, I learned that only a few hours earlier, in an attack of anxiety and desperation, Dayan told the top brass at the General Staff that this was the "destruction of the Third Temple" and he doubted whether the country would pull through.

That evening when I returned home, Shula and the children were in the shelter, but I went up to our fourth-floor flat and stood on a small stool in the kitchen and taped black cardboard to the window. Civil Defence had posted blackout information instructing citizens to ensure that no light would let enemy aircraft know where there were heavy population concentrations. I climbed down from the stool to regard my handiwork. The kitchen was dark and stuffy and reminded me of a bomb shelter. Was I really hearing airplane engines, or were those my memories? I was gripped with hunger—or perhaps the hunger never left me—and I removed a sausage from the refrigerator and took two thick slices of bread. I sat alone at the blue-and-white checked Formica kitchen table and ate in the darkness.

The war lasted three weeks, and we won, but as King Pyrrhus of Epirus said, "One more such victory will undo me!" A total of 2,656 Israelis were killed in battle, and along with them our self-assurance disappeared. War—any war—is a mosaic of "What if?" and every "What if?" contains chilling ramifications. What if Division 7, under the command of Avigdor Kahalani, had not stopped a Syrian tank brigade three times larger than ours in the famous battle at the Valley of Tears? What if Prime Minister Golda Meir had not allowed the chief of staff to mobilize reserve units against Dayan's position? If Ariel Sharon had not succeeded in his mission at the Suez Canal? If the Americans had not decided to airlift military equipment that saved us from defeat? (Chief of Staff David "Dado" Elazar said, "Each morning we fire what the Americans sent us the night before. We used up our supply a long time ago.")

My mood was no better than that of most of the population. For the first time since I had come to Israel, I did not feel I was a full participant in what was happening. I was forty-two years old, too old to fight (or even fix broken vehicles) and too young to voice an opinion that would change anything. During the war I penned a few ardent articles designed mainly to encourage myself, but my voice was lost in the general uproar.

Even my new play, *Catch the Thief*, which premiered at the start of the year, did not fare well. The critics panned it and it ran for only eighty-four performances then disappeared—like a thief in the night. I never wrote for the stage again.

A strange silence took hold. People returned from the war and went back to work, all the while aware that what had been broken could not be fixed. There was no explosive anger; instead, it dripped slowly like a poison. The Agranat Commission of Inquiry was formed, then the grave conclusions and the dismissal of the chief of staff. I felt bad for Dado; like me, he was a refugee from Yugoslavia who had escaped the Holocaust, and when we met we tended to chat in Serbian.

In May 1974, Golda Meir resigned and a young Yitzhak Rabin was appointed in her place. Perhaps it was egotistical of me to feel as though matters related to me personally, but I could not help it—people of my generation (Rabin was only nine years older than me) were taking the reins of power while I was stuck at a women's magazine, among recipes that had lost their flavor and gaunt models who minced past me on their way to be photographed. I was waiting without knowing what for.

CHAPTER 37

Sometimes I asked myself, through the long months during which I worked on this biography, whether I was giving enough attention to the fact that I am dead.

Frankly, my death was meant to be something more than just a publicity stunt or a way of freeing Yair from the very heavy shadow of a dominant father. My son is already a grown man with graying hair who sits in his study and cries in silence. Unlike his father, who never hesitated from bursting into tears around other people, Yair tends to cry only when he is alone. Like other members of our family, he is well versed and experienced in matters of death. My Michal (oh, my daughter, my darling daughter, would that I had died in your place; no person should ever have to bury his own child) taught us how to cope with bereavement and taught us also that in fact there is no coping with it.

"O grave, where is thy victory?" sings the choir in Brahms' "A German Requiem" playing now in the background. Yair downloaded all my old classical recordings onto his computer and now this rock 'n' roll boy listens to them again and again until their sounds overtake him and his hands drop from the keyboard as he stares into a dimming screen.

What has death taught me that I did not already know in life? What lesson in perspective has it given me? What did I understand during a month and a half of dying—in a surprising state of tranquility—in Room

84 of the Ichilov Hospital tower in Tel Aviv that I did not already know beforehand?

I can only speak from my own experience, I have no other. I sink under the weight of the hundreds of letters, thousands of documents and millions of printed words that comprised my life only to discover, to my embarrassment, that time and again I was convinced that my life was over. "I'm afraid I have become someone who was," I wrote at the ridiculous age of thirty-three; "It seems as though my career has nowhere to go," I wrote at forty-two, just before finishing my tenure as editor of *At*. "It's apparently over," I wrote at fifty-two, when I was not reappointed to head the Israel Broadcasting Authority and suffered a minor heart attack. "I have had a beautiful life and I have nothing to complain about," I declaimed before a group of friends on my sixty-eighth birthday, convinced that as a realistic and rational pensioner it was time to pass along the torch to the next generation. (That was before I knew that two months later I would take the leadership of the Shinui party and start all over— once again.)

Death has not made me more clever (I was clever enough in life), but at least thanks to death I can understand this wonderful sentiment expressed by the singer and actor Jimmy Dean: "You gotta try your luck at least once a day, because you could be going around lucky all day and not even know it."

My fate was determined by the fact that I never missed an opportunity to reinvent myself. The years taught me that the people who fear change the most are the ones least satisfied with their lives. I am no great psychologist but that fact astonishes me: what exactly do they have to fear from change? If you do not like your life then go and do something about it. From experience, I can tell you that it will improve not only your own life but your death as well. There are few gifts a person can grant himself more valuable than a death without regrets.

Yair, can you feel my hand on your head right now, a warm hand, soft and chubby, caressing you until your shoulders stop shaking and you are at peace? Do you remember the letter I wrote you for your bar mitzvah? "You are my private response to my own bar mitzvah, to the Nazis, to the fate of the Jews in the Diaspora, to my father's death." Keep writing, my son. Let me continue to tell you the story of my life. I tried to teach you everything while I was still alive and we were together, but we cannot give up now, during this final lesson: Even when we do not know what to do we continue to do. There is no other solution.

The spring of 1977 brought with it a sprinkling of change.

In early March, journalist Dan Margalit exposed the news about Prime Minister Yitzhak Rabin's forbidden dollar account in the United States, which led to Rabin's resignation. Two days later, another national disaster took place when I discovered I weighed nearly 230 pounds. I began a diet.

Elections were held on 17 May. At ten o'clock that evening, anchorman Haim Yavin broadcast the results: "Ladies and gentlemen," he said, "it's an upset!" For the first time in the history of the State of Israel, the right-leaning Likud party would lead the country.

I sat at home watching the election results and feeling a gnawing sense of frustration. On the Likud list there were people like the younger members of the Independent Liberals I had been a part of in my distant past, and now those people were going to become government ministers while I was resigned to watching them on television. Had I missed the train without noticing it, or was I just not fit for politics? I stopped dieting.

On 9 November, Shula celebrated her forty-third birthday. As usual, I wanted to fill the house with friends and balloons and dance the night away; as usual, she refused. In the end we went out for a meal with the children and raised a toast in her honor. I regarded her through the gleaming red of the wine and was filled with joy. She was more beautiful than ever, still thin after three births, intelligent, fascinating, the best partner a man could ever hope for.

I turned to the children. Michal was seventeen, the light of my life: clever, sociable, an outstanding student, always surrounded by friends and suitors, a beloved elder daughter who identified with her parents and was involved in educating—and worrying about—her younger brother and sister as much as we were.

This source of worry was sitting to her right, melancholy and introverted. At fourteen, the boy who had gone everywhere with me and imitated my every gesture had turned into a classic adolescent. He wore his hair at shoulder length, bought a guitar and stopped talking to me. His marks went down, and I scolded him and shouted at him to no avail. Several weeks earlier, when I caught him trying to hide his trimester report from us (after seeing it I was a little sorry that he was not a better liar), I stunned him with blows. There are few things in life I regret more, but in my defense I will say that I was raised in a generation and a time in which corporal punishment was an obvious part of one's education. Years later, when he was a father himself, we spoke about that openly. "You knew how to raise me until I was thirteen because that's exactly the age you lost your father," Yair told me. "We raise children according to the model we knew and experienced when we were children ourselves, and as soon as you didn't have a model any more, you sort of got lost." I thought maybe he was letting me off the hook (I didn't deserve it), but I was happy to adopt his version of events.

And Meirav was Meirav. Our wise one, whole and self-sufficient at age eleven, a little autarchy that looked after herself and entertained herself and needed no one. Several months earlier she had fulfilled a childhood dream and had won, with astonishing ease, the Israeli junior chess championships. Immediately following the tournament she set aside the black-and-white chess pieces in a cardboard box and informed me she would no longer be playing. I tried to convince her to continue, but she raised an eyebrow from the heights of her four-foot stature and said, "Dad, it's your dream, not mine." She has never played chess again.

Later that same evening, back at home, a colleague phoned, choked with emotion. "Have you heard?" he asked.

"Heard what?"

"Sadat spoke in the Egyptian parliament today. He announced that he intends to come to Israel and sign a peace agreement with Begin."

Just as every American of a certain age recalls where he was and what he was doing on the day that Kennedy was assassinated, so too can every Israeli who lived in the 1970s recall the dark, restrained figure of Anwar Sadat descending the stairs of the presidential plane at Lod airport. The searing depression of the Yom Kippur War had begun to dissipate, making way for cautious optimism. Begin, contrary to what people feared, did not drag us into an additional confrontation of destruction; rather, he led Israel toward the first recognition of the existence of the State of Israel by an Arab state.

Years later, when historians were able to open the archives, they discovered that Sadat had tried to extend a hand to Israel even before the Yom Kippur War, but Golda Meir had refused to believe that his overtures were trustworthy. Once again, the Israeli paradox: only the combative and unrelenting right wing is capable of making a peace that the entire Israeli public can believe in, just as only the liberal and moderate left wing is capable of waging a war that the entire population supports without fearing that it is unnecessary.

As could be expected, the old elites of the country did not give up without a battle, but it was fought on a different field this time: the media. I was approached by Aryeh Naor, the government secretary, at a diplomatic ball in the home of the Italian ambassador to Israel. "Tell me, Tommy," he said, "if you were offered the job of director general of the Israel Broadcasting Authority, would you take it?"

At the time, the IBA was in charge of all radio and television broadcasts in the country. This was the most senior position for a journalist in Israel, a position that enjoyed, in today's terms, incomprehensible influence over public opinion.

We were holding drinks in our hands, and the whole thing looked like bad theater to me; it was exactly how important decision-making was depicted in Hollywood—as matter-of-fact, and at cocktail parties. "Sure," I told Aryeh Naor. "Why not?"

On 9 February 1979, I went to Jerusalem to meet with the prime minister. At 11:30 a.m., Begin received me in his office, rising to shake my hand. His office was large, with a flag of Israel and a variety of gifts he had received in the preceding two years. The wood-paneled walls were elegant, not fancy. Begin was gray and ponderous. He was slightly detached throughout our conversation, withdrawn. "Mr. Prime Minister understands," I said, "that it is not my intention to create television that toes a party line. It will, however, be Zionist and Israeli." He nodded unconvincingly. We continued speaking for another half hour or so and I reminded him that I had once covered one of his official visits, to Romania. His face brightened and he regaled me with a long story about his meetings with the Romanian dictator Ceausescu. At the end of the meeting he rose to his feet again, shook my hand for a second time, and wished me luck in my new job. I had become a director general.

CHAPTER 38

Why does this particular chapter of my life fill me with despair?

After all, I was not depressed as I was living it. My new job had everything to suit my combative temperament: huge and noisy personal disputes; professional coups; confrontations on a national level; and battles of conscience, some of which I won and others on which I took a beating. But I was never bored, not for a moment. In a certain sense this was the moment when the basic anxiety that had been nagging me since the Holocaust—that if I am not important I will cease to exist—finally dissipated and vanished.

And important I was. After years of fighting the elders of *Maariv* for bus money as a correspondent in some outlying area, I found myself heading an organization whose workers numbered 1,600, whose budget was 1.8 billion lira (about $300 million in today's terms), and, most meaningful of all, an organization that was uniquely responsible for shaping Israeli consciousness. Even dissenters from the way I managed the IBA must grit their teeth and admit that I changed it thoroughly. There was not a soul in Israel who did not have an opinion of me: half of them despised me with a passion while the other half supported me with no less enthusiasm.

However—and in contrast to the popular saying—time is not only a healer, it is also a bitter pill. I ask myself today whether everything I did was truly important. Perhaps that is the late insight of an old man, that nothing is truly important. That all the big wars of today are, at best, tomorrow's anecdotes.

And yet, even with the heavy price that time placed on me, I believe that I did have a role in the painful process of wresting control of Israeli society from the hands of the old guard that had established the country. There is nothing more dangerous than aging revolutionaries, and in the winter of 1979, two years after the Likud government was voted into power, they were still treating their failure as a grievous error that would soon be corrected. The infamous statement by Yitzhak Ben Aharon that "if this is what the people have chosen then I do not accept their decision" still echoed in the air like an ominous bell.

The night before I assumed my position at the IBA it was already clear what sort of music would set the tone of my entry into this new job. A stormy conference was organized by various artists and held at a popular Tel Aviv club. There were ardent speeches and petitions and the singer Yossi Banai took the stage and dedicated the Norman Thomas song "The Naughty Little Flea" to me, to the enormous pleasure of the raucous crowd.

On 31 March 1979, the Israel Broadcasting Authority hosted the first Eurovision Song Contest to be held in Israel, and Yitzhak Livni asked that I defer my entry into the position by six hours so that he could be the host of the competition after having toiled at organizing it for months. Naturally, I agreed, and Shula and I attended the evening and watched as Israeli singer Gali Atari took first place with her song "Hallelujah."

The next morning I entered my job from the wrong place. I am not talking about a metaphor here, but a technical fact: I knew so little about the IBA that I went to the studio in the Romema neighborhood of Jerusalem instead of to my office, which was housed in a different building some 500 feet away and was known as the Twine Building because it had formerly been a twine factory. "Good morning," I said to the sleepy guard at the entrance. He looked me over with suspicion. Jerusalem, as is well known, is not lacking in crazy people.

"How can I help you, sir?" he asked.

"I'm the new director general," I told him.

"Yeah, right," said the guard.

CHAPTER 39

On my very first day in the job I noticed a large safe embossed with the IDF emblem in my office. I asked what it was doing there, but nobody knew. Several days later a retired brigadier general phoned and requested a meeting with me. When I asked about the purpose of the meeting, his response was cryptic: "I'll explain when we meet."

"Inside that safe," he said gravely at our meeting, "are all the secret mobilization codes for the different IDF reserve units. Since you're in charge of radio and television broadcasts in the country, it will be your job to broadcast the codes in the event that the threat of war requires a sudden mobilization."

The brigadier general gave me a set of three identical keys to ensure that someone at the IBA would always be available. I kept one in my wallet, gave the second to my deputy and the third went to one of the senior managers.

Months passed and we completely forgot about the matter. One morning my deputy and I flew to Geneva for the annual conference of the European Broadcasting Union. On the plane we were talking about our colleague, the senior manager who had been seriously injured in a car accident and had been lying for two days in hospital, unconscious. All at once we fell silent and looked at one another in shock: the keys! Two of the keys were with us en route to Switzerland and the third was at Hadassah Hospital in Jerusalem. If war broke out that morning, the IDF would not be able to mobilize any reserve soldiers. That was the longest flight of my life. When we reached Geneva we rushed to phone the IBA security officer and had him go to the hospital to retrieve the key from our colleague's pocket.

In those days, the Israel Broadcasting Authority itself was a safe with three keys. I held one, the government held one, and the journalists held the third. Each one claimed that he held the master key and the others were mere copies.

For example, one morning I was summoned to a cabinet meeting in order to discuss confirmation of the IBA budget. What I got instead was a particularly vitriolic attack on the part of the prime minister. Begin presented me with a long list of members of the opposition who had been invited to speak on television as commentators, and he wanted to know why members of the government were not accorded the same screen time. In my heart I agreed with him, but I refused to accept the idea that the government would run the country's lone television station. Begin, however, was unaccustomed to having people argue with him. "My esteemed Mr. Lapid," he said in the sarcastic tone he normally saved for his public speeches, "does it seem reasonable to you that the government should fear what the IBA is doing?"

Silence fell on the room. In those days, no one dared answer back to the prime minister, particularly when he was in one of his killer moods.

"Mr. Prime Minister," I said, "so long as the government fears the IBA more than the IBA fears the government, this country will continue to be a democracy. I don't even wish to think about the other option."

Begin grimaced, but he said nothing. Later that day I got a call from the government secretary, Aryeh Naor. "How dare you talk back to the prime minister like that?" he shouted at me. "We put you in your position and we'll take you down, too!"

I slammed the phone down on him and from that day on I refused to speak to him.

———

I drew fire on other matters as well, simply because people did not know all the facts. One of the most well-publicized of them all concerned a documentary film about the Turkish genocide of the Armenian people during World War One. Historians estimate that at that time, some 800,000 Armenians were murdered or starved to death, while others— including the Nobel prize-winning Turkish novelist Orhan Pamuk—put the figure at more than 1 million slaughtered.

Several days before the screening of the film, I received a call from the director general of the Israeli Foreign Ministry, Dave Kimche. He informed me that for several years Israel had been smuggling Jews out of Syria through Turkey with the help of the Turkish government and that their lives—especially those of the women—would be endangered. "The Turks have let us know," he told me, "that if this film is screened they will seal the border. So you decide what to do."

I decided to cancel the screening of the film without being able to explain the reason to the public. The sanctimonious had a field day: "Of all people, Tommy Lapid," wrote one journalist, "a Holocaust survivor, is helping the Turks deny the Armenian genocide." Dozens of critiques were published, not a single one in my favor. And I did not even try to defend myself in this case, since I could not tell the truth and I did not wish to lie.

Still, if I had to choose again I would do exactly the same thing. With all the pain and grief, saving lives was more important than saving face, and there are women living among us today whose fates would have been drastically different had I screened that film.

The turning point in my relationship with IBA journalists came during the massacres in the Sabra and Shatila refugee camps. My own personal turning point had come several months earlier.

The first months of the 1982 Lebanon War passed in nerve-racking tension, since Yair had gone to war with Armored Corps Division 500 and we had not heard from him. After a week we received a phone call from him, his voice weak, telling us he was in the Rambam Hospital in Haifa. It turned out he had inhaled smoke from a grenade during a helicopter landing, had had an asthma attack and was evacuated by the same helicopter he had helped to land.

The next day, he arrived home, hugged us, and went to sleep. Two hours later, a soldier from the IDF Missing Soldiers Unit knocked at our door holding Yair's kit bag and expressing his sorrow at Yair's death. It turned out that Yair had taken a ride with two officers in a jeep, but had jumped out to have lunch and they had continued on their way. Just a few hundred feet down the road, the officers had hit a land mine and were killed. When Yair's kit bag was found among the destroyed jeep's ruins it was assumed that he had been killed as well. Had he not been sleeping in the next room it is safe to assume I would have had a heart attack on the spot.

I do not wish to stir up drama where there is none, and Yair would certainly not wish me to either. There were far worse stories from the Lebanon War, and far greater heroes, but something had happened to me. I do not like the culture of whining that has taken hold here over the years, one that perceives looking after "our children" in uniform as the primary responsibility of the State of Israel. Rather, it is the soldiers who must look after the state. And yet, the recklessness with which the government sent our children into enemy territory alarmed me.

It is the role of a state to think a thousand times before sending soldiers into battle, and like many other Israelis, I understood that we were waging an unjust war in the wrong place. Until that time my worldview had been that of a liberal, my instincts that of a conservative. Now, the scales tilted toward my worldview. Quietly and to myself I decided that the IBA would cover that war not as a government-sponsored television station but according to the principles of independent journalism.

On 18 September 1982, I went to the Knesset for a toast to the Jewish new year. I grabbed a bite to eat then sat down with Ron Ben Yishai, the IBA military correspondent who, unusually, looked exhausted and glum. "Read this," he said as he handed me six printed pages.

I read slowly, my shock deepening with every page. It was a description of the past two days during which Ron had been present in the Sabra and Shatila camps while Christian falangists slaughtered hundreds of Palestinian women and children and the elderly, and IDF forces stood by and did nothing.

"Are you certain about this?" I asked him.

"Tommy," he said, "I was there."

Ron is a first-rate journalist and I knew I could count on him.

"Does Ariel Sharon know?"

"I phoned him, he didn't say a word."

I knew that someone would have to tell Begin.

"But what about the broadcast?" he asked.

"We'll screen it," I said.

I left the Knesset and went straight to the studios in Romema, where I convened the newsroom employees.

"Ladies and gentleman," I said, "something terrible has happened."

Most were hearing about the massacre for the first time while a few had picked up some scattered details about it from the BBC. No one had been able to receive an official response from the government or from the IDF.

"So what are we going to do?" someone asked.

This was the first time they had regarded me as their editor-in-chief.

"Our job," I told them, "is to broadcast the truth, the whole truth, without fearing anyone. And that is exactly what we're going to do."

There were several moments of silence as people absorbed the fact that before their very eyes I was crossing my own private Rubicon from which there would be no return. Then all at once the bustle that characterizes a newsroom dealing with a big story burst out and everyone began working the phones and shouting.

I stood there and knew that at that moment I had ceased to be the darling of the government. One week later, on 25 September, the Four Hundred Thousand Person Protest took place at the Kings of Israel Square in Tel Aviv. (Years later, the Tel Aviv municipal engineer sat with me and proved in black and white that there was no way of squeezing 400,000 people into the square even if they were standing on one another's shoulders.) The television cameras followed the protest with open sympathy, but this time the IBA director general—me—did not reprimand a soul.

Begin stopped speaking to me and Ariel Sharon was furious with the

coverage. I told his good friend Uri Dan, who had been sent to reprimand me, that I had no intention of pulling back. Someone would have
to pay the price for the massacre. Several months later, Sharon—despite
feeling hurt and offended—invited me to his farm for lunch, to discuss
the matter. His wife, Lily—a Hungarian like me—made a special Hungarian meal of many dishes and lots of cholesterol. We ate and ate until
we nearly burst and the anger in both of us slowly abated. That is the
great advantage of fat people: there is no quarrel that cannot be solved
by a good meal.

There were funnier moments as well. Several months after I took over
the directorship of the IBA, I was paid a visit by my friend Michal Zmora-
Cohen, wife of the retired Supreme Court Justice Haim Cohen. "Did
you know you have an orchestra?" she asked me.

"An orchestra?"

No one had bothered to inform me that I was the director of the IBA
Jerusalem Symphony Orchestra.

"The orchestra is in trouble," she told me sadly.

"What happened?"

"They can't afford a trombone player."

"Let me see what I can do," I told her.

The next day I paid a visit to the mayor of Jerusalem, Teddy Kollek.
"Listen, Teddy," I said, "this orchestra belongs to the city as well. I need
you to give me a position for a trombone player."

"Where am I supposed to find a position for a trombone player?" he
asked.

"I have no idea."

Teddy thought a few minutes and suddenly his face lit up. "Yesterday morning," he told me, "a position for a gardener opened up here at
City Hall." Instead of requesting a new *ganan* (gardener), he would fill a
position for a new *nagan* (musician). "And nobody will notice," he said.

And that is exactly what happened. To the end of my tenure as IBA
director general—and apparently to this very day—the Jerusalem Symphony Orchestra employs a trombone-playing gardener.

CHAPTER 40

It was one of the most ridiculous and embarrassing moments of my life.

One summer morning I had a few errands on Allenby Street in Tel Aviv. As usual, I went there on a public transport minibus and chatted with my fellow travelers, who were surprised to see me sitting among them. After accomplishing what I needed to, I went looking for a minibus back home, but none could be found. The weather was hot and I told myself I was rich enough to afford a taxi. As luck would have it, one was standing right next to me, at a traffic light. I opened the back door, sat down, and said, "20 LaSalle Street, please." The driver did not utter a word as the light changed and he started driving. When we reached my building I asked how much I owed him.

"Nothing," was his surprising reply.

"What do you mean?" I asked.

"Mr. Lapid," the driver said with hesitation, "this is not a taxi."

I looked around and only then realized that I was sitting in a private car with no meter or little yellow sign on the roof.

"So why did you agree to drive me?" I asked.

"I don't know," said the driver. "I was waiting at the stoplight and suddenly Lapid from the television got into my car and told me to take him home. I was afraid if I refused you'd shout at me, so I took you home."

Completely dejected, I walked up the stairs of our building and told

Shula what had happened. Only when she began laughing hysterically did I understand how absolutely absurd the situation had been.

Still, as with most funny events, this one also contained a sad truth: after some twenty years of public service there are many people whose image of me is that of Lapid the wrathful, someone whom it is better not to cross. I am certain I earned that image fair and square, but I do not particularly like it.

And yet, between one crazy struggle and the next we managed, here and there, to make some real television.

One of my biggest campaigns, for example, was the attempt at bringing American films to Israeli television. This will sound completely absurd, but until 1982 it was not possible to broadcast films from the United States on Israeli television. The owners of Israeli cinemas, fearful of the power of television, had appealed to Hollywood film distributors and persuaded them to place an embargo on doing business with the IBA. We made requests, pleaded, offered special prices—to no avail.

One morning, a warm and pleasant American-Jewish television producer from Baltimore by the name of David Jacobs paid a visit to my office. Jacobs was the creator of the series *Dallas*, by then a huge international hit. Jacobs said, "Listen, I'm a Jew and a Zionist and I've decided that my contribution to the State of Israel will be that I'm giving the series to you free of charge."

With great excitement I thanked him and summoned the director of television.

"We've been given *Dallas*, and we're going to screen it on Saturday nights."

"Why then?"

"Because that's when the cinema owners make half their weekly profits. They've been screwing us, now I want to screw them in return."

The series was broadcast and became an immediate hit, with ratings of eighty to ninety percent. Two months later, a delegation of cinema owners came to my office. "You've got to move the series to another day," they said. "The cinemas are empty and we're about to go bankrupt."

I had trouble hiding my joy at this tragedy.

"No problem," I said. "I'll move the series on condition that you remove the embargo on American films."

And that is exactly what happened.

CHAPTER 41

I began writing letters to myself on 14 February 1959, the day before my wedding. The first letter is lying before me right now, written in my illegible handwriting on yellowing stationery. My telephone number, printed at the top of the page, was 28348, which shows just how few telephones there were in all of Tel Aviv at the time. "I love her," wrote the young man I once was, about the woman he was about to marry. "She is the woman I want to be the mother of my children—and I want three."

This became a ritual: once every few years, Shula and I would remove the previous letter from the envelope and read it together. Then I would write a new one and seal it inside the envelope until the next time.

I wrote the saddest letter of them all on 12 February 1984. It was sad because it was written by a happy man who did not know what lay ahead. This is what I wrote:

In three days' time it will be our twenty-fifth anniversary. And on that same day, Michal is getting married. Such a double celebration, so beautiful and fine, happens only once in a lifetime even in the happiest of families. It's a gift from God, and if there is one thing that saddens and confuses me these days it is the fear that life is just too fine for us, too beautiful, and that it cannot always be like this and will not always be like this, so that this knowledge— that these are the most wonderful days of our lives—is a kind of menace, a

*detraction from the wonderful feeling, and perhaps that is exactly the way it
should be. Life does not permit honey without the sting.*

The wedding took place at the Khamam theater in Jaffa in the presence of four hundred guests. President Chaim Herzog was there, most
of the government ministers, members of the Knesset, and the cream of
the crop of Israeli society (I was the creamiest among them; by the time
of the wedding my weight had mushroomed to 250 pounds). Under the
wedding canopy, Michal looked like a painting by Renoir: a frame of
black hair surrounding a beautiful white face in the middle of which were
two dark and shining eyes she had inherited from her grandmother,
Helen. She was just finishing her bachelor's degree in psychology, and her
husband, Shuki, whom she had met while studying, was completing his
master's degree and was about to become a clinical psychologist.

Contrary to tradition with regard to sons-in-law, Shula and I agreed
that we could not ask for a more suitable partner for our daughter. Shuki
was—and still is—brilliant and cultivated in a manner quite unusual
among young Israelis. He was a gifted classical pianist, he could quote
Goethe from memory (in German!) and lead an intellectual debate on
Beckett's plays or simply use his professional knowledge to analyze all
the character flaws of his new father-in-law. The two were also tremendously in love and could not take their hands off one another the entire
night.

It was a splendid evening. I drank too much, ate too much, smiled
until my cheeks ached.

Yair did not leave my side the entire evening. The days of our confrontations and silences had passed, never to return. After that frightening
episode at the beginning of the war, he was transferred to *Bamahane*, the
army newspaper, and after a year and a half working as a correspondent
in Lebanon, he was appointed the magazine's news editor. It was clear
he was on his way to becoming a journalist like his father and both
grandfathers, the third generation of ink-bluebloods. At seventeen, Meirav was more beautiful and witty and clever than all the rest of us, and
had already informed me, with deadly seriousness, that she had decided
to become an actress. I decided, with wisdom born of age, not to argue
with her.

Sometime during the evening I glanced across the room at my wife, and she was glowing. Two years earlier, her first novel, *Valley of Strength*, was published, and became a huge overnight success. The story of red-haired Fania, a fiery and fearless early settler of Palestine who almost single-handedly subdued the rocky hill known then as Jaouni and today as Rosh Pina, became one of the bestselling Israeli books of all time, was translated into a slew of languages over time and garnered ecstatic reviews from critics. Even her fellow writers were impressed and, several months later, elected her secretary general of the Israel Writers' Association. My delicate hothouse flower was suddenly dealing with budgets and signing contracts and establishing wide-ranging international connections—all to my great surprise.

Our eyes met above the jubilant crowd and she smiled at me, that mysterious, private smile shared by longstanding couples. This night, her smile told me, was not over yet. I smiled back. We could not have asked for anything better on our silver wedding anniversary.

That false sense of security had permeated my professional world as well, and I was certain I would be offered a second term as head of the IBA.

There were quite a few reasons for me to think so. In August 1983, at a cabinet meeting, Begin suddenly announced, "I cannot go on," and he went home, never really leaving the four walls of his home again until his death. The prime minister who replaced him, Yitzhak Shamir, seemed bored by us journalists; his many years in Mossad gave him the attitude that they could "write and say whatever they want, it doesn't matter anyway." Government ministers continued to complain that they were not getting enough airtime on television, but they also understood that I—to borrow a phrase from Ariel Sharon—was "unbribable and unflappable."

But life does not permit honey without the sting.

Several months before the end of my tenure, I was invited for coffee with Uri Porat. I had already heard he had his eyes on my job, but I saw no reason to refuse. Porat was, at the time, head of the workers' committee at the *Yediot Ahronot* newspaper, a very pleasant man of the people who was a fine joke- and storyteller. We sat chatting and he asked an endless string of questions about the IBA and my opinions of this or that government minister. When he stood up and went to the bathroom I noticed a tiny tape recorder—still recording—that had fallen from his trouser pocket to his chair. That "very pleasant man of the people" had been secretly recording our conversation in order to provide evidence against me to those who would be selecting the next IBA head.

I was furious with Uri, but I understood him as well. Five years earlier I had been in the same position, though I had played the game more fairly. The sitting head of an organization is always too busy for campaigning, while the potential candidate has all the time in the world. In the few free hours I had I would pick up the phone to this or that politician, but rather unwillingly.

Several weeks before the end of my tenure it was already clear I had lost the campaign and Porat would be the next director general. The next time I saw him I wanted to call him the "Israeli Iago," but I refrained, not because I was suddenly overcome with timidity but because I was not completely certain he knew who Iago was.

On 31 March 1984, I suddenly found myself on the outside.

It is hard to explain the feeling to someone who has not experienced it. That morning I was the omnipotent boss of one thousand six hundred employees, responsible for a television station, five radio stations and one symphony orchestra, while that evening, I gave a farewell kiss to Ruhama, my loyal secretary, gathered my belongings in a small cardboard box and stepped out into a chilly Jerusalem street alone, without the slightest notion of what I was going to do with myself the next morning.

My driver, Gabi, was waiting beside my official car, a Volvo. We both knew it was our last ride together. Fifty minutes later he deposited me at my home in Tel Aviv. I rode the elevator up to the third floor, put my box in the study, sat in my swivel chair and tried to understand what I was supposed to do now. There were no telephone calls to answer, documents to be written, contracts to review. Nothing but a heavy silence.

A few minutes later, Shula entered with a cup of instant coffee that she placed in front of me.

"Call Yitzhak Livni," she said.

"Why?"

"Because he's the only person who's been in the position you're in now," she said.

I dialed Yitzhak's number from memory. Even after I inherited his job he remained one of my closest friends.

"I have no idea where to get started," I admitted to him.

Yitzhak said, "Tommy, we spend our entire lives working to impress people we don't really care for and who don't really care for us. Now, at long last, you can do something for yourself."

"Sure," I said. "But what?"

"I don't know," he said, "but if you ever wanted to be important so there would be something to write on your tombstone, well, you've already achieved that. Now start living for living's sake."

For several weeks I sat at home trying to figure out the meaning of living for living's sake. I read a little, was bored a lot, played hours of chess with one of my four regular partners, all of whom were heavy smokers, so that a blue cloud of smoke hung permanently in my study. I myself had given up smoking on my fortieth birthday, but I was never bothered by people smoking in my presence. Even if one's eyes watered a bit, I always believed that one of the signs of a cultivated person was displaying patience with others' weaknesses.

My body was the first to rebel against inactivity, since it was not cigarettes that were the big killer but idleness. It is a well-known fact that the great advantage of relaxed people who enjoy a moderate pace of life, get physical exercise and eat granola is that they die healthy. As long as I was working like a madman, everything was fine. When I began to rest, the status quo was shaken up.

One afternoon, I felt pressure in my chest and then in my left arm. I panicked. "Shula!" I shouted. "Call an ambulance!"

The ambulance took me to hospital with sirens and flashing lights. As I was rolled into the emergency room the doctors hooked me up to an electrocardiogram machine. "Your husband," they told Shula, "has had a minor cardiac episode."

"A heart attack," I grunted in misery.

"No," they insisted. "An episode. Minor."

"What's the difference?" Shula asked.

"He doesn't need any operations, even bypass surgery."

"So he's all right?"

"We'll keep him here a few days under observation."

The next morning I asked one of the nurses if I could go to the bathroom by myself. She said there was no problem so long as I was able to drag the infusion pole along with me. Several minutes later, I excused myself to my family, got up from my bed, and started to walk. After only a few steps I was overcome with dizziness from all the sedatives and I plunged to the floor. Shula and the children ran over to me; I looked up at them and, in a narcotic-induced fog, decided that these were my final moments.

"Children," I groaned, "I have a few things to tell you," and with that, I broke into a long farewell speech in which I recounted the details of my life, starting with my childhood in Novi Sad, to the Holocaust, my *aliyah* to Israel, my almost grand career. Shula and the children gazed at me in amazement, but shortly they understood what was happening. Michal made the first stifled chuckling noise; Yair was next. By the time the startled nurses reached us, they witnessed a particularly strange scene: the patient was lying on the floor dramatically eulogizing himself while his wife and children surrounded him, doubled up with laughter.

I returned home weak and bewildered, and several weeks later I returned to the offices of *Maariv*. Shmuel Schnitzer, who had in the meantime been appointed editor-in-chief, indulged me in a revealing conversation. "You've got to understand," he told me, "that you've earned yourself quite a few enemies during the years you weren't here."

"Why is that?"

"Because everyone thinks you forgot about us. You've haven't set foot in the building in five years."

"I was busy," I said.

"What did you think, Tommy? That you would show up and everyone would step aside for you?"

"That's not what I said."

"True, but it seems to me that's what you were thinking." After a humiliating exchange, Schnitzer appointed me editor of the new Tel Aviv local supplement that had just been started that month. I was given a tiny office on the roof of the building, one graphic artist whom I knew from my time as editor of *At*, and one part-time typist, and with that I set to work on this sorry four-page pamphlet.

Four days after I started my new job, Yair, in a pressed army uniform, came to visit. I was mortified. Several months earlier he had had a powerful father to whom presidents and government ministers kowtowed, and now he was glimpsing me in all my humiliation. I was certain there was no lower for me to go.

Late at night on 15 November 1984, my son-in-law Shuki phoned. "The police called," he said. "Michal's been in an accident. She's at Ichilov Hospital."

He raced to our house, arriving minutes later, and the three of us went to the hospital, dumbfounded. When we arrived, a doctor in a white lab coat greeted us and asked if we would like to see her. I did not understand. Of course we wanted to see her! "Wait here," I told Shula and I followed Shuki and the doctor. He brought us into a side room and there, on a stretcher, lay my dead daughter.

I gazed at her and still I did not understand. I stepped out into the hall, went to Shula, and said, "Michal is no longer." And with that my quiet wife screamed and screamed and screamed as if she would never, could never, ever stop.

CHAPTER 42

I heard a voice, the sound of a grown man crying. The voice was saying something. "My daughter, my daughter, oh God, my daughter." Outside and surrounding that voice there were other sounds, some soothing, some frightened. Belatedly, I understood that the voice was my own. I found myself lying in the middle of our living room surrounded by people paying a condolence call. I wanted to rise to my feet but I could not, so I continued lying there, an exhausted white whale trying to commit suicide on a beach that looked like a carpet we had once brought from Turkey. "Oh, my daughter," my voice continued to say, and I realized I had no control over it.

I was no longer in the living room; I was in my bed in Novi Sad, an officer in a black uniform had come for my father. "I will be fine," Grandmother Hermina said, and then she died in silence, closing her robe over her body. I was in a basement in the ghetto, hunger gnawing at me. I was walking in a long line of people toward the frozen Danube surrounded by policemen with machine guns. "Wallenberg," my pale mother said. "Wallenberg saved me." Four unnerved young people sat on a bench at the hospital. "She offered us a ride home," one of them said. I was standing on a snowy street, alone, with nowhere to go.

Every once in a while the skies cleared and I could make out what was happening around me. A long line of well-wishers passed before me, people muttered meaningless words that did not help. Shula, who had given up smoking twelve years earlier, lit up cigarette after cigarette. Yair went to the airport with a doctor to bring home his grandfather, David, who had been summoned from Paris, and to tell him what had happened.

A well-known rabbi took Meirav aside and told her, "God gathers the very best to himself so that He'll have angels at his side."

This angered her. "Excuse me," she said, "but that is the biggest load of rubbish I've ever heard."

I wished to tell him that it was not he with whom she was angry but I could not. The voice returned. "Oh, my daughter. My daughter," it said.

She was returning from a visit to a home for mental patients, where she volunteered with several of the residents. There were four other volunteers with her, psychology students like herself. She was driving her Peugeot down Hamasger Street in Tel Aviv when a driver coming the other way hit the median strip, flew upside down into the air, and landed on her car. Of the four young people with her, two were lightly injured, two emerged without a scratch, and she was killed instantly.

Whole months of my life disappeared. I cannot say what I was doing during that time, I was on autopilot. I would rise in the morning without understanding why, go to work without being able to explain to myself what I was doing there, people would pass by and say good morning as if such a thing were possible. At one point I swore I would punch the next person who dared tell me that "life goes on." Life does not go on. When a child of yours dies, your life ends all at once and you become a different person starting a different life.

And your family is different, too. Every family reacts in a different manner to the hole that has suddenly opened up in it. There are some who disappear inside it and others—like ours—that cling tightly together around it. I cannot judge anyone, including those swallowed by grief who cannot emerge from it. In fact, we were close to that. Shula, who was always fragile, lost quite a bit of her will to live. Meirav slept all day and went around with her friends all night and I could only hope they were looking out for her and keeping her safe from the temptations of drugs and alcohol. Yair had finished his army service and was working at *Maariv*. In November 1985, just after the first anniversary of Michal's death, he informed us he was getting married.

"When did you meet her?" I asked.

"Yesterday," he said.

"Yesterday?!"

"Yes."

"And when are you getting married?"

"In three weeks."

I should have sat him down for an incisive man-to-man chat, to explain that this was not really love and that he was only trying to fix what could not be repaired, that this was unfair to his anonymous bride because she was only there to fill in for what was missing in his internal world. I should have but I was unable.

Instead, I attended the wedding, held in the garden of Yair's new father-in-law, and once again I functioned on autopilot. I smiled, I shook hands, I thanked all the well-wishers. My new daughter-in-law, Tamar, embraced me and said she would be my new daughter. I hugged her back and said nothing.

The marriage, as could be expected, did not last. After two years, both Yair and Tamar understood that it had been a youthful error and they parted on good terms. Tamar remained a member of the family to all of us and lives next to Yair and his second wife, Lihie; throughout the years we have celebrated holidays and family events together. I always liked her, and was especially grateful to her for giving me one of the greatest gifts of my life: my first grandson, Yoav.

Over time, the insuppressible part of my personality began to poke through again. I went to Schnitzer and told him I had no interest in this unimportant local Tel Aviv paper, and he decided—perhaps partly out of pity—to give me a column on the political pages of *Maariv*.

At the same time, I published a Hungarian cookbook, *Paprika*. This was the rare case of a man who cannot even poach an egg publishing a bestselling cookbook. Instead of going into the kitchen, I let it be known among old Hungarian women that I was looking for the recipes to Hungarian dishes. In no time I was flooded with recipes for *nokedli*, sweet cheese *palachintas* and steamed cabbage *palachintas*, *rakott krumpli* and *rakott kapusta*, cold cherry soup, hot goulash, and of course Dobos torte, the famed five-level cake layered with chocolate buttercream and topped with thin caramel slices. Hungarians say that if you cannot drum Berlioz's "Rákóczi March"—Hungary's unofficial state anthem—on the top of a Dobos torte then it is clear the icing has failed. In the introduction I noted that "most people eat to live, but the true Hungarian lives to eat."

Also at this time I began hosting a new radio program on Radio Two, called *My Week*.

During my life I did more important things than hosting a weekly radio program, but few things ever gave me as much pleasure or made me work as hard. Sometimes I hear young radio broadcasters, especially on Army Radio, and am amazed at the ease with which they turn on the microphone and begin to talk. Unlike them, I wrote every word in advance, even the broadcasting comments: pause; raise voice this line; smile so listeners can hear the smile in my voice.

Every week I wrote eight or nine pieces, each on a different topic, with musical interludes in between. I tried to capture what Nietzsche called the *zeitgeist*, the spirit of the age, and to include absolutely everything in my program: social satire, political commentary, artistic reviews, historical analysis, gastronomical hedonism, anecdotes, humor and moving descriptions.

Apparently, it worked; in the age of television, this program became an exceptional event. In 1988 it won the Sokolov Prize, Israel's Pulitzer, and it produced over the years four collections of articles, each a bestseller. Radio is often the background noise to our lives, but in the case of *My Week*, tens of thousands of people stopped their lives every Friday at six in the evening, turned on their radios and simply sat and listened.

Here is just one example among many: on 27 December 1985, terrorists attacked El Al counters in Vienna and Rome. The following day—which happened to be my fifty-fourth birthday—I wrote one of the most memorable pieces broadcast on the program. It was called "The Woman in Blue":

This Christmas, Arab terrorists attacked travellers standing at El Al counters in Vienna and Rome. On screens broadcasting around the world, horrified viewers saw the bodies of some twenty casualties, among them a woman dressed in blue at the Rome airport.

In my eyes, this woman in blue, in complete innocence, represents the madness of terror. This young and beautiful woman dressed herself in a blue suit to travel somewhere that she will never reach, because she was murdered. The Italian television cameras lingered over her lovely face as she lies, elegantly positioned, on the floor of the Rome airport, an airport named for Leonardo da Vinci, who could have added to her face the surprised smile of a victim, another innocent victim on the altar of Arab murderousness. The woman in blue probably took no interest in politics and had no idea who was shooting at her, or why. Perhaps she was meeting a lover in Madeira or flying with her children to see their father in Paris, or maybe she was on her way to Eilat for a week of sunbathing. What did the woman in blue have to do with this bloodbath, with bloodthirsty predators, with hate-mongering fanatical assassins spreading their terror throughout the world? They shoot children and kill a woman in blue.

I place on her fresh grave a single white flower.

CHAPTER 43

It was not long before a new play toy fell into my hands: cable television.

Maariv was one of the commercial concerns that received the concession to set up a cable television network as compensation for the losses it could be expected to incur in terms of reduced newspaper sales. I was the only person at *Maariv* who knew anything about television, so quite naturally I was chosen to head the project.

For the purpose of setting up the new company, we decided to meet at the penthouse apartment of Arnon Milchan, the Israeli-born Hollywood film producer who was one of the first investors in the project. Arnon and I—along with the usual entourage that apparently accompanies Hollywood tycoons—rode the elevator up to the fourteenth floor, but at the tenth floor the elevator got stuck. I was overcome with dizziness and felt I could not breathe. For forty years, ever since those long months spent in a basement in the ghetto, I suffered slightly from claustrophobia, but this attack was particularly serious. I fell to the floor of the elevator, my whole body shaking, trying in vain to bring my breathing back to normal. Arnon, worried, loomed over me and more or less held me in his arms (he weighs about a third of what I did) until we were rescued. After that incident I have no idea how he agreed to sign a contract placing a large sum of money in the hands of a man who had acted so strangely, but the company was in fact established and became a great success.

Success, as success does, brought rewards. I traveled each year to the Cannes TV festival (held at a different time from its more famous sibling, the film festival) where I would spend several days negotiating with television producers from around the world. It may sound dull, but this being France, most meetings were held in the most sumptuous restaurants on the Riviera. Anyone who has not bought the rights to the series *Cheers* while eating at the flower-bedecked Mas Provençal Restaurant in Eze, staining the contract with ruddy drops of Château Lafite Rothschild and yellowish drips of the *specialité de la maison*—seafood risotto cooked in a twenty-pound block of parmesan cheese—is simply not fit to conduct international business.

My new position gave me something extra too: it was thanks to the company that I met Robert Maxwell.

I can begin to explain who Robert Maxwell was by sharing a strange phenomenon that I only dared mention when I discovered I was not the only one who had experienced it: after playing chess for several hours on the computer, I would get up, go outside and take a walk, but the passersby on the street looked to me like chess pieces. The woman with the shopping bags was a rook; the clumsy man with the leather briefcase was a queen; the irritable candy salesman was a bishop. My job, apparently, was that of a knight: I could jump over them, this way and that, each time facing a different piece, a different person, and I asked myself who will knock out whom? Would I knock him out, or he me?

When I first met Robert Maxwell there was not a shadow of a doubt what his role was in the game: he was king.

Indeed, Robert Maxwell was a giant, in more ways than one: he was well over 6 feet tall and weighed more than 300 pounds. He had an enormous head crowned with shiny dyed-black hair and spoke nine languages with astonishing fluency in a deep, thundering bass voice that came from somewhere inside the quadruple chins that sat above a polka-dot bow tie. He lived his entire life at accelerated speed like the actors in the old bioscope films, and when he fell—he fell with a giant thud.

Robert Maxwell was born Ján Ludvík Hoch in Czechoslovakia. He escaped from the Nazis, joined the British Army Pioneer Corps, rose to the rank of captain during World War Two and was decorated with the Military Cross for bravery. After the war he acquired a failed publishing house and turned it into a stunning success, becoming a millionaire in the process. He left the business world to become a Labour member of Parliament for Buckingham, and returned to business six years later when he lost an election. He purchased the Mirror Group Newspapers and the Berlitz language schools, Macmillan publishing and even a controlling share of MTV Europe. The millionaire became a billionaire and one of the world's two media barons, along with Rupert Murdoch, his archenemy.

Maxwell came to Israel at the end of the 1980s and quickly fashioned himself as the great lord from abroad who bought up everything: he started with *Maariv*, then the Keter publishing house, a huge number of shares in both Teva and Scitex, and he even decided to acquire the Jerusalem Beitar and Hapoel football clubs and unite them as a single team (luckily, he failed). Israelis found him highly amusing and were affectionate toward the eccentric giant who was so interested in their welfare, and on many cars around Israel the bumper sticker *MAXWELL, BUY ME!* could be seen.

The truth, however, is that Maxwell bought *me*.

One Thursday evening toward the end of 1989, I was sitting in a particularly boring meeting of our company, Matav Cable Communications Systems, when a secretary entered the room to inform me that I was needed on the telephone. I left the meeting and picked up the receiver.

"Maxwell speaking," said a voice as low as the Dead Sea.

I was surprised. Of course I knew who he was, but we had never before spoken.

"Yes, sir, what can I do for you?" I said.

"I've heard that you're Hungarian, you have managerial experience and you're quite intelligent."

"All true," I said.

He chuckled. Maxwell did not like modest people any better than I did.

"I have a group of London lawyers sitting right now in Budapest trying to buy *Magyar Hírlap*. You know what that is, of course?"

"Yes." *Magyar Hírlap* was Hungary's government newspaper, a dull, communist rag of absolutely no value apart from its wide distribution. From the time of the fall of communism, the government had been trying to get rid of it, just as the rest of Eastern Europe had been trying to get rid of assets belonging to the dying Soviet empire, in what would later be remembered as the greatest fire sale in history.

"They've been working on it for two months already," Maxwell said, "and making no progress at all. I want you to go there and solve the matter."

"No problem," I told him. "Let's meet tomorrow. You can give me the details and I'll fly there on Sunday."

A note of impatience filtered into his voice. "We won't meet, and you'll go there tomorrow morning," he said.

"And do what?"

"Close the deal for me."

"For how much?"

"Whatever seems right to you."

I wanted to say something else but he had already rung off. More than anything, I was amused. It had been several years since anyone had put me to the test or hung up on me. I knew he was expecting me to phone him back with more questions—like who was funding my trip—but I decided not to give him the pleasure. In fact, from the first moment, we both knew we were cut from the same cloth: two fat, noisy, decisive, impatient mittel-Europeans who never asked anyone how to behave.

On my own initiative, I informed *Maariv* that Maxwell had instructed me to buy a ticket to Budapest, and the next morning I was on my way.

I landed in Budapest before noon, took a taxi from the airport and asked the driver to take me to the office of *Magyar Hírlap*. On the way, I looked pensively out the window. I love Hungarian culture, its food, its wonderful gypsy music, its poetry, but I do not love the Hungarians themselves. Their fervor in assisting the murder of the Jews—among them, most of my family—is something I cannot forget, and I still believe that in every Hungarian there hides a little anti-Semite just waiting for the right opportunity to emerge. It was explained to me a number of times that this is something that has passed from the world; I always listened politely and did not believe a word of it.

The driver brought me to a dilapidated office building built in the Hungarian baroque style that was only standing up thanks to wooden scaffolding that surrounded it on all sides. The elevator did not work so I walked up three flights of stairs, passing a bored-looking group of journalists in front of ancient typewriters without ribbons and lead printing machines from the nineteenth century manned by workers in gray uniforms.

I entered a peeling conference room, where four embalmed British lawyers in elegant suits were sitting with four Hungarians—three men and a woman—in shabby suits. The moment I walked in, the four Englishmen rose to their feet, expressions of relief on their faces. "This is the senior representative sent by Mr. Maxwell," one of them told the Hungarians. "He is the only one who can decide what to do now."

The Hungarians rose to their feet as well. The first to shake my hand looked like a communist commissar (which, I found out later, was exactly what he was). "Nice to meet you," he said in broken English. "We have been waiting for you."

"*Szervusz*," I said in Hungarian. "I'm glad to be here."

His jaw dropped. Hungarian is a language impossible to fake, so it was clear to them that this distinguished British representative just arrived from Israel (an oddity in itself) was no less Hungarian than they were. The only one to smile was the woman. There was something quick-witted and clever about her, and I knew at once it would be easy to communicate with her. Her name was Katy Bashani, and we remained in touch for years until she committed suicide under circumstances I was never able to fathom.

"You're Jewish," I said to her. It was not a question. Still, she was surprised.

"How did you know?" she asked.

"It's my expertise."

The man sitting next to her burst out laughing. Naturally, he was also a Jew. In fact, it turned out that the commissar was the only non-Jew on the Hungarian side of the table.

"So where's the problem?" I asked the Englishmen.

One of them sheepishly cleared his throat. "We can't figure out who owns the paper," he said.

It was a typical problem during the waning days of communist regimes. Until the fall of the Iron Curtain, the government was the owner of all property, including quite naturally any large newspapers. But one morning people woke up and discovered that the old regimes were passé and they did not know the rules of the new game.

"Let's say," I told them, "that I manage to convince the prime minister that the paper belongs to the journalists it employs. Would you then be willing to sell?"

I did not even know exactly who the prime minister was, or how I could reach him, but they nodded enthusiastically.

"How many journalists are there?" I asked.

"More than two hundred," the commissar was quick to inform me.

There was something in the tone of his voice that I did not like. "Bring me the list of names," I said.

The next morning I reviewed the list and discovered that at least a quarter of the people on it had not worked there for quite some time, including a few dead people who were still receiving full salaries and five government clerks whom no one had ever laid eyes on.

It took a few days, but with the help of Katy Bashani I managed to meet the new prime minister, József Antall, in his elegantly appointed office. Antall, a man my own age, with piercing blue eyes and silver hair that reached his collar, was one of the heroes of the anti-communist uprising of 1956. But he was also a loyal product of seventy years of humorless rule. "I will approve the deal," he told me, "but on condition that you treat my government favorably."

This put me in an awkward position. "Sir," I said, "a free press cannot promise to support a government, but of course we are very much in favor of your reforms."

"Fine," Antall said. "What's important is that we understand one another."

When I left his office I felt that he was only half right: I had understood him but he had not really understood me.

The negotiations took another two months of bickering and shouting, and in the meantime I grew accustomed to my new lifestyle: every Monday morning I boarded a plane in Tel Aviv, stayed in my usual room at the Forum Hotel, and on Thursday evening I would fly back home, or to London to update Maxwell. It was not easy, but when I saw my first paycheck I decided I could handle it.

Toward the end of the negotiations, Maxwell's son, Ian, came with me to Budapest and ultimately we agreed on a price tag of £2 million. While the lawyers were drawing up the contract, Ian phoned his father, overjoyed: "Father," he said, "we closed at £2 million."

"Very nice," Maxwell said. "Now go back and tell them we're only willing to pay £1 million."

Ian nearly cried. "But Father," he said, "you told Tommy and me that we could close."

"That's right," Maxwell said. "But they'll accept £1 million."

"How do you know?" Ian asked.

"What choice do they have?" Maxwell said.

It took another two weeks, but of course it became clear that he was right. We bought the *Magyar Hírlap* for £1 million. As a bonus, Maxwell decided to have the old *Daily Mirror* printing press shipped to Hungary, and he set me the task of finding a suitable place to house it.

One of the journalists, a Jewish sports writer named Nimrod Peter (who became editor-in-chief of the paper two months later), told me that the Hungarian army had a huge barracks in the center of town that they were interested in selling. One morning we paid a visit there. A Hungarian officer in uniform was waiting for us outside, between two sentries. When we approached, all three saluted us. It took my breath away: Hungarian soldiers like these, in these same uniforms, had surrounded the death convoy that led us to the Danube and now here I was, once again in Budapest, and this time they were saluting me. We entered the barracks, took a few steps, and I said, "Excuse me, I forgot something in the car," and I walked out a little way and then returned. Once again, the soldiers saluted. Back in the building, I silently counted to twenty then repeated the process one more time and watched as they stood to attention and saluted. I could have kept it up the entire day.

In the end, I reached the office of their commanding officer, a lieutenant colonel who was drunk as a lord (at ten in the morning). One of our Hungarian representatives, who apparently had received advance information, pulled out a bottle of whisky and placed it on the desk, and the lieutenant colonel pounced on it like a man dying of thirst in the desert and signed everything we put in front of him. Before we finished, he asked that I step into the adjoining room with him for a moment. We walked down the hallway and he unlocked a door using a key on a large ring attached to his belt. There in the enormous hall were two thousand silent plaster casts of Marx and Lenin standing wall to wall; they looked a little bit like the terra-cotta warriors I had once seen in the Shaanxi Province of China. "Mr. Lapid," the lieutenant colonel said, "what am I supposed to do with two thousand plaster casts of Marx and Lenin?"

"Shatter them," I said, and left the room.

One week later, the signing ceremony was held at the elegant general headquarters of the Hungarian army. A red carpet was rolled out and soldiers stood at either side, their weapons at attention, as I strolled down it with the Hungarian chief of staff. Afterward, we stood in front of the photographers, he under the Hungarian flag, I under the Union Jack, while an orchestra played "God Save the Queen." I don't know if God saved the Queen or not but He certainly saved me by keeping me from bursting out laughing.

For the second signing ceremony—the purchase of the paper—Maxwell himself arrived on his private jet, and a convoy of black Mercedes ferried us to his hotel. Like me, Maxwell, who was born in Solotvino, a small town in the Carpathian mountains, and whose relatives were mostly wiped out by the Nazis (with the active assistance of local residents), was motivated by a feeling of "I'll show them." During World War Two, his path to freedom took him through Hungary, so he was particularly pleased with the manner in which he had returned to Budapest. That evening he gave an interview to Hungary's Channel One television station.

"I understand that you can speak Hungarian," the interviewer said.

"Yes," said Maxwell. His Hungarian was very basic, but entirely comprehensible.

"And where did you learn to speak Hungarian?"

"I sat in one of your prisons," said Maxwell.

Later that evening, we were informed that Prime Minister Antall wished to meet with Maxwell. "Fine," said Maxwell. "Let him come to me."

Antall swallowed his pride and came to Maxwell's suite. A moment before he entered, Maxwell turned to me and said, "Quick, tell me something about him."

"Like what?"

"I don't know. Something personal."

"His father gave documents of protection to Jews during the war, he was named a Righteous Gentile and a tree was planted in his honor in the *Yad Vashem* forest."

At that moment the door opened and Antall entered with his entourage. Maxwell stood to his full height, opened his arms wide, and said in his booming voice, "Mr. Prime Minister, the entire Jewish people and I will never forget what your dear father did for us during the war. He was a truly outstanding human being!"

Antall very nearly burst into tears, he was so overcome with emotion.

The contracts were signed two days later. Maxwell and I were sitting in his suite enjoying a glass of cognac and a huge plate of sausages.

"I'm going to leave you here a little while longer," he said.

"As what?"

"As director general."

"Until when?"

"Until you tell me the paper doesn't need you."

The next morning Maxwell left and I went to the offices of the newspaper. I entered the room of the editor-in-chief, a Mr. Sabadusho, who was in essence a communist clerk who was appointed to the job without any connection to his professional expertise. Mr. Sabadusho was sitting behind an impressive desk, a large picture of Lenin hanging behind him.

"Mr. Sabadusho," I said without any preamble, "you're fired."

He had apparently been expecting this, and he rose from his chair without a word, took his briefcase, and began to leave the room.

"Mr. Sabadusho," I said, stopping him in his tracks.

"Yes?"

"Take the picture with you."

He turned around, and while I watched, he stood on the chair, took the picture down from the wall and left the building with Lenin stuck under his arm.

CHAPTER 44

"Mr. Maxwell," the Croatian minister of tourism said, "we cannot sell you the newspaper but perhaps you'd like to buy the island?"

"Which island?"

"Tito's."

Several weeks earlier, Maxwell had phoned me in Budapest and, as usual, he began the conversation in the middle, without preamble. "I want you to go to Serbia," he said. "Buy a newspaper for me there."

"Which one?"

"Whichever you want."

When I arrived in Belgrade, the Serbian capital, government representatives were waiting for me at the airport. They took me in an official car to the palace of the president, Slobodan Milošević. Snow was whirling about in the air as we climbed the marble steps of the palace, and somber Belgrade lay spread out before us like a dark mass lit up only here and there by flickers of light like fireflies. The last time I had visited Belgrade, the city was aflame from bombing and I, a boy of ten, zigzagged between the falling electricity poles.

Milošević, a heavyset man with an amazingly high forehead and a mane of white hair meticulously combed to the back, greeted me warmly in an embarrassingly ornate reception room and seated me next to him on a wine-red velvet armchair.

Ten years later, Milošević would be tried in The Hague, at the International Criminal Tribunal for the former Yugoslavia, for the massacre in Kosovo, where thousands of Albanians fell victim to acts of rape and murder and 164,000 people became refugees. In October 2004, at the age of sixty-five, Milošević was found dead in his cell before the end of the trial.

But all that was still far off in the future. In the meantime, I was enjoying a lively conversation with an intelligent man intent on doing business. The Serbians are perhaps the only people in Eastern Europe with no tradition of anti-Semitism, so I did not have to deal with the well-known Slavic suspicion that "the Jews are buying us up."

"I cannot sell you either of our large newspapers," Milošević told me, "since one belongs to the party and the other to the government. But we have a third one, called *Politika*, that might be more of interest to you."

"I know it well," I said.

Milošević was surprised. "How so?"

"My father used to read it every morning."

I bought *Politika* and returned to Israel for my daughter's wedding. Meirav had decided to marry (for the first time) her high-school sweetheart. Our curly-haired burst of energy had long since given up her dream of becoming an actress and had instead pursued the career path set out by her departed sister and studied psychology at Tel Aviv University. I was happy about her decision but did not ask too many questions. I suppose one needs to study psychology in order to understand why she went to study psychology.

Six days earlier, on 2 August 1990, Iraq had invaded Kuwait. In response, the UN had imposed sanctions on Iraq and the winds of war were in the air. Maxwell, true to his dramatic instincts, arrived at once in Israel to express support, and I invited him to the wedding, which was being held at a garden-like hall fifteen minutes from Tel Aviv. At the start of the wedding his limousine arrived—empty. Then ten minutes later there was a huge boom—trees bent, bushes flew into the air,

shiny satin dresses blew skyward exposing legs—and an enormous helicopter landed, from which Maxwell emerged, looking terribly pleased
with himself.

Had he simply come by limousine it would have taken him half the
time it took to drive to the heliport, rent a chopper, receive clearance
for takeoff and landing—but that was not Maxwell. He was incapable of
passing up an opportunity to make a grand entrance.

At the end of November, UN Security Council Resolution 678 was
adopted, authorizing member states to use all necessary means to ensure that Iraq would withdraw its forces unconditionally from Kuwait,
and Maxwell showed up in Israel once again. We were sitting in his
suite at the King David Hotel in Jerusalem, and he said, "Tommy, we're
flying tomorrow to Croatia to buy a paper."

"Robert," I said, "they won't sell you a paper."

"Why not?"

"Because Tudjman will not sell a paper to a Jew."

One year earlier, the president of Croatia, Franjo Tudjman, had published his very strange book, *Horrors of War or Wastelands of Historical Reality*, in which he claimed, among other things, that only 900,000 Jews
had perished in the Holocaust and that it was the Jews themselves who
had run the concentration camps in Croatia, and that "Hitler's new European order was justified in its need to move the Jews." It is important
to note that these words were not written in the 1940s but in 1989, by
the head of a democratic nation who had been elected in free elections.

"Never mind," Maxwell said, "we're going anyway."

The next day we took off in his private plane from Jerusalem to the Croatian capital, Zagreb. When we were over the city, the control tower
informed us that the weather would not permit us to land and we were
being diverted to Ljubljana, the capital of Slovenia. When we landed in
Ljubljana, the airport was empty; an unmarked truck cleared the snow

from one of the runways, then disappeared. We stood on the runway absolutely alone, Maxwell's butler, Freddy, holding a large black umbrella over Maxwell's head with one hand and a suit in his other, and we waited without knowing for what.

Half an hour later, a sleepy customs clerk arrived. "*Dobro došli*," he said. "Welcome." He perused our passports, stamped them, and disappeared. We left the airport on foot and stood in the darkened street—Maxwell, Freddy the butler, two pilots, a blonde flight attendant and myself—but there was not a taxi in sight.

Eventually I went and found a night watchman who, in exchange for several dollars, agreed to call a taxi for us. When it arrived it transported us to the small and wretched Hotel *Slon*, or Elephant Hotel. After the exchange of another few dollars, a grumpy waiter agreed to open the hotel coffee shop for us. I eyed Maxwell with apprehension; his impatience was legendary, and I was sure he was going to make a scene at any moment. Instead, he kicked off his shoes and poured cheap Slivovitz for everyone. "I'm home," he told us. "It was exactly in a place like this that I grew up."

He sat with us until three o'clock in the morning telling stories, making us laugh, trading crude jokes with me in poor Hungarian over the head of the sleeping stewardess. The next morning, when I came to awaken him, she opened the door dressed only in a tiny robe and an awkward smile. It seemed that the boss's huge appetite was not limited to food and newspapers.

We flew back to Croatia, where we were received by Tudjman, an inarticulate man who looked like an owl with eyeglasses and seemed furious that Maxwell was a head taller than he. From the first moment it was clear he had no intention of selling "his" newspaper to some Jewish billionaire. But then the minister of tourism, who was sitting next to him, suggested we buy Tito's island instead.

"You don't really want to buy an island, do you?" I whispered to Maxwell in Hungarian.

"Why not?" he whispered back.

———

Two hours later, we were in the air again, this time on the way to a Croatian naval base airstrip. From there, a helicopter was waiting to take us along the glittering twists and turns of the Sava River to a small lake near the town of Bled, where we touched down on a natural island only to discover that there, in the middle of Eastern Europe, we had found Croatia's answer to the Land of Oz. White swans floated in the blue water; ducks waddled about in a large and well-tended park reminiscent of Kew Gardens, with a large palace on one side and a small one on the other; deer leaped between the trees and chestnut-colored Irish setters crouched in front of a lit fireplace waiting for their dead master. The sight saddened me: I admired Tito for his role in the war and was grateful to him for letting us leave for Israel forty-two years earlier, so it was awful to see how power had corrupted him in his old age.

"Gentlemen," Maxwell announced to our escorts, "I'm seriously considering buying this island."

The Croatians were overjoyed, while we knew better: if he were really interested in buying the island he would have pointed out all the defects to our hosts and told them he had no interest in the place whatsoever. That was something I learned from him: there is actually no difference between large deals and small ones. The quarrels, the pettiness, the bartering—they are all the same whether the price is $20 or $20 million.

On 6 December 1990, Yair married Lihie.

The wedding took place on the balony of the Relais Jaffa restaurant in Jaffa; the party that followed the ceremony was so noisy that the man living next door, a journalist by the name of Adam Baruch, phoned the police. Little did he know that a year later he would be Yair's editor, and mine as well.

On 15 January Lihie and Yair returned from their honeymoon on a completely empty flight. The UN ultimatum had ended that day and it was clear that war would break out at any moment.

The first Scud missiles fell two days later. I was sitting at home in Tel Aviv and I heard a few distant booms, which Army Radio claimed were thunderclaps. I put on my gas mask; with all due respect, I have far more experience than they with bombs. After verifying that Shula was wearing hers (she was fairly angry at the impediment to smoking), I phoned the children. Both of them sounded strange through the mask, but it was clear they were more amused than frightened. There are some advantages to being a family that has already experienced the worst.

Several days later, we were sitting at the Dan Tel Aviv Hotel with Mayor Chich Lahat and his wife, Ziva, the conductor Zubin Mehta and the American-Jewish comedian Jackie Mason. We were eating and chatting when the sirens sounded again. It was one of the only times that Jackie Mason had absolutely nothing funny to say, but I turned to the server and said, "Could I have some more coffee, please?" She glared at me, said, "Get lost!" and ran off to the shelter. We were still laughing when we put on our gas masks and turned on the television, where we witnessed a most astonishing sight: that same evening there was supposed to be a concert in support of Israel at a large hall in Jerusalem, with some of the finest musicians alive playing. When the siren sounded, the wind section picked up—much like our server—and disappeared. The audience, however, remained seated, simply donning their gas masks. When the cameras panned the audience, it looked like a segment from a science fiction film: hundreds of people sitting in rows, elegantly dressed, with black rubber masks on their faces. Just then, the violinist Isaac Stern took the empty stage, alone, without a mask, holding his violin. He faced the audience—a small white-haired Jewish man of over seventy—and played a Bach violin solo. I never heard a more beautiful, or more lonely, rendition. It was as though the entire fate of the Jewish people was playing along with him that evening.

Thirty-nine Scud missiles fell on Israel, but miraculously, only one man was killed. We all sat in our sealed rooms listening to the IDF spokesman remind us over and over to drink water. I thought that was a slightly odd solution to a missile attack, but I drank water and coffee and wrote an article for *Maariv* in which I claimed that the Shamir government's policy of restraint, its habitual "hold tight, do nothing" approach, was actually serving the country well this time.

The war came and went, and I went back to living the roller coaster that was Robert Maxwell. I continued to spend half my time in Hungary, where I turned *Magyar Hírlap* into the first Hungarian newspaper to be printed in color, and from Budapest I would take short trips all around Eastern Europe, either as Maxwell's emissary or with Maxwell himself. Once we were trying to buy a Serbian radio station, another time it was a newspaper in East Germany, still another, a television station in Bulgaria. One morning he phoned urgently. "Tommy," he said, "buy the Yellow Pages brand for all of Eastern Europe."

"Why?" I asked. "Are you planning on distributing the Yellow Pages?"

"No, but I've heard they're planning to get into Eastern Europe. We'll buy it cheap now and sell it to them in a few months for a bundle."

One evening he sent me to Belgrade in his private jet. I flew alone, arrived at the airport, came down the stairs of the plane and there waiting for me was President Milošević, ruddy-cheeked from the cold, his senior aides at his side. "Mr. Maxwell sent me to tell you that he will not do business with the Croatians if it will harm you," I said.

"Very nice of him," said Milošević. He shook my hand, and I walked up the stairs I had just walked down and flew back to Budapest.

World leaders made pilgrimages to see Maxwell (the custom he had of publishing favorable biographies of them at the publishing houses he owned certainly did not hurt), and he loved every minute of it. Several weeks after my meeting with Milošević, we attended the World Economic Forum in Davos. We were meant to meet with the Hungarian deputy prime minister, but Maxwell was stuck in a meeting with the premier of Quebec, from whom he was buying massive quantities of trees for paper. "Stall the Hungarian," he told me. I was making small talk with the Hungarian deputy prime minister when a crestfallen young woman entered the room.

"My father has been waiting for Maxwell for twenty minutes," she said:

"Who is your father?"

"General Jaruzelski."

It seemed that Maxwell had forgotten that he had made an appointment with the president of Poland. The pace was dizzying, unfathomable, and, as would later become clear, destructive.

Maxwell pulled off three enormous deals that year, and all three proved to be failures. He bought Macmillan publishers for an astronomical $2.6 billion; the *Official Airline Guide* (which the computer made obsolete within months) for $750 million; and he founded *The European*, a pan-European newspaper that tried in vain to compete with the *Herald Tribune*. When his investments flopped and he was in need of money to finance his debts, he took it from his employees' pensions funds and used that to pay the banks.

I tend to believe, even today, that Maxwell was no common criminal, but rather a compulsive gambler. He owned 230 companies, and all their thousands of bank accounts were managed by his sole, feverish brain. He believed with all his heart that he would pull himself out of trouble as he had done many times in the past, and he would return the money without anyone knowing what he had done. But by the time the rumors of his troubles were running rampant on Fleet Street and the British authorities had opened a lively investigation against him, his debts had already reached $2.5 billion.

On 5 November 1991, I returned from the offices of *Magyar Hírlap* to my hotel, where I met in the lobby a small, nervous man who had once served as the Hungarian ambassador to London and whom Maxwell had taken on without anyone understanding what his function was. "Maxwell has disappeared," he told me.

"What does that mean?"

"He was on his yacht and he disappeared. They're saying he jumped overboard."

Since then I have been asked a thousand times whether I think Maxwell committed suicide or whether someone—Mossad, his business rivals, the Russians, the Palestinians, the Italian mafia, former Stasi men, the list is as long as the number of questioners—pushed him into the dark waters. I do not know, but I tend to believe that he simply decided that he deserved a grander end to his life than a moldy cell in Brixton Prison.

I returned to Israel to take part in his ceremonious funeral on the Mount of Olives, where he was eulogized by Prime Minister Yitzhak Shamir, who said, "He has done more for Israel than can today be said," which naturally led to another hundred conspiracy theories. After that, I returned one last time to Hungary in order to sell the paper, according to Maxwell's son Kevin's wishes. I remained in touch with the Maxwell family until my dying day, and each time his wife, Elizabeth, visited Israel, we hosted her in our home. The Maxwells are pleasant and cultured people, but there is nothing in them of their late father's great fervor.

I went back to *Maariv*. My short-lived career as an international businessman was over. My next career would begin in a small office in Jerusalem that was once mine but which I had not visited in many years.

CHAPTER 45

One day, when I was already a government minister, MK Ahmad Tibi of the United Arab List asked to speak with me. Contrary to his customary demeanor, he seemed rather uncomfortable. "I have a request to make of you," he said. "My father is an old man, and he's very fond of you from your days on television. He wants to know if you're willing to visit him in his home in Taibe."

There had been many well-publicized confrontations between Tibi and me over the years, some of them quite hostile. This former adviser to Yassir Arafat is a devoted Palestinian nationalist, and I accused him several times of being disloyal to the very state that made him a member of its parliament, as well as to democracy itself.

However, if there is one thing of which the public is unaware it is that the Knesset is a kind of exclusive members' club, where you meet the same people day after day and develop friendly relations with them that have nothing to do with political differences of opinion. On a personal level, Tibi is a remarkably funny and intelligent man, and I prefer him to any of a large number of pompous asses whose politics were closer to my own.

I consented at once, and several days later we traveled to his father's house in Taibe. The old man received us in the courtyard of his home. Tibi ran and brought two chairs and a small table and we sat facing one another, but something was missing.

"Tibi," I said to the anxious Ahmad, "there's something I've always wanted to say to you."

"What is it?" he asked.

"Ahmad, go make coffee."

Sensitive left-wingers will undoubtedly grimace at this racist joke of mine, but Tibi and his father both burst out laughing and the ice was broken, or at least it melted in the glasses of *araq* that were brought to the table, and we sat enjoying a lively, pleasant conversation for nearly two hours.

Two years later, shortly after my forced departure from politics, I asked Yair to come watch a Maccabi football club match with me. The match was being broadcast on a huge screen at the pub down the street. He brought a friend, a young ultra-Orthodox journalist named Koby Arieli. We sat at a table on the pavement watching the game and passers-by kept commenting on the fact that there was "Lapid sitting with a religious guy." I asked Koby if he wasn't worried about being seen with me.

"Tommy," Koby said, very much at ease, "the world isn't divided between Jews and Arabs or left-wingers and right-wingers or religious and secular. There is only one true division: people with a sense of humor and people without."

I laughed. Koby was right, of course. What he did not know, however, was that the humorless make up the vast majority. I never, in all my many years of life, met a person who admitted that he did not have a sense of humor. But the sad truth is that most people just do not get the joke.

I did, because I learned the lesson on that boiling, roiling, sweaty, noisy and very funny human lab known as *Popolitika*.

Once again I was asking myself if this was to be my fate: an old man sitting at home at his desk, his hair growing whiter and his belly growing thicker as he plays chess on the computer for long hours against Joe from Wisconsin or Ahmet from Istanbul, telling stale jokes to his shrinking audience of listeners and downing pills from a plastic container every morning—two for blood pressure, one to prevent heart murmurs, an aspirin to thin the blood—then deciding to engage in a little sport which means walking to the living room, turning on the television, and after watching Maccabi Haifa play, deciding enough is enough, calling friends and asking if everything is okay with them. "Everything's fine," they answer. I remember that there is a Hungarian salami—Herz—in the fridge, and I cut three slices, but the third doesn't fit on the bread so there is a need for more bread, and now there is room for a fourth slice of salami. It comes to me that the philosopher Seneca once wrote that "old age is an incurable disease." The problem is, I cannot recall when exactly Seneca lived. I will have to look it up, but I have no time because I am too busy doing absolutely nothing.

Meanwhile, Yosef Bar'el, the newly appointed director general of the IBA, was sitting in his office trying to solve a thorny problem of human resources: two of his stars—talk show host Dan Margalit and producer Areleh Goldfinger—were out of work and he was looking for something for them to do. He summoned Goldfinger for a chat. "I want you to create a political program," he told him. "Make sure it's rambunctious and aggressive, something everyone will be talking about, and add in some pop music so young people will tune in, too."

Goldfinger is a soft-spoken but large man with a bad temper and an enormous ego; someone once described him to me as a person who had turned his greatest disadvantage—his inability to listen to anyone for more than two minutes at a time—into a television advantage. Fortunately, during those two minutes he consulted with his aging father, who told him to call the show *Popolitika*, a cross between the words "politics" and *vox populi*, the voice of the people.

It was only years later that Yosef Bar'el revealed to me how it was that they invited me to be on the panel, even though he knew objections would be raised among my detractors at the IBA.

"The truth is," he recounted, quite amused, "the initial idea was to bring three bad-mouthed puppets like those in *Spitting Image*, but it turned out the puppets were too expensive. We sat trying to come up with a similar solution and figured we should bring in you and Amnon Dankner."

No one could have suspected that instead of a folksy puppet, it was I who would be enjoying astonishing popularity in the space of just a few months.

CHAPTER 46

"The State of Israel is *Popolitika*," wrote *Haaretz* critic Yossi Klein, "and *Popolitika* is Tommy Lapid."

It was not Klein's intention to flatter me, of course—like most left-wing Israeli intellectuals he loathed the show and loathed me personally—and yet, I took immense pleasure in what he wrote.

What was *Popolitika*? It was the Athenian Agora, the Roman Forum, the British Hyde Park. It was a battleground for the media, a café-cum-bazaar, and an Israeli living room on a Friday night, in which everyone shouts at everyone else—veins throbbing, eyes popping—and then hugs at the exit, wishing each other well until next week and saying, "It was fun!"

It produced a government minister (me), a member of the Knesset (Rabbi Israel Eichler) and an editor-in-chief of a large daily newspaper (Amnon Dankner); it built, in a sense, the career of Binyamin Netanyahu; and it contributed quite a bit to the demise of other careers. The long list of people who refused to appear on the show includes politicians Yitzhak Rabin, Ariel Sharon and Benny Begin and the writers Amos Oz and S. Yizhar, and yet it served as a stage for some of the most well-known and important disputes in the history of the nation.

Naturally, I am familiar with all the claims made against it: the vulgarity and the shouting; the "I didn't interrupt you so don't interrupt me" heard on every program; the interviewee in our Haifa studio whose existence we completely forgot about, and his ridiculous pantomime of a drowning man, arms flailing, shouting hoarsely, "Dan, hey Dan, what about me?"; the descent of Israeli discourse to abysmal levels.

I am familiar with these claims, yes, but I refuse to accept them.

For better or for worse, *Popolitika* did not create the Israeli culture of debate, it merely exposed it quite accurately. Whoever did not like it apparently did not like what he could see from his own window, either. For example, on the opening show of our second season, one of the guests was David Biton, brother of Charlie Biton of the Black Panthers. Biton made the claim that Russian immigration to Israel was "an immigration of whores," to which I responded that if the matter had been entrusted to me I would have stopped immigration to Israel the day before he himself came to the country, and I stood up and stormed out of the studio. Ephraim Kishon was a guest on that same program and he persuaded me to return, but the country was already buzzing with my dramatic departure and critics took it as yet another example of our collective lack of culture. However, no one noticed that on that same day, Prime Minister Yitzhak Rabin stormed out of the Knesset plenum in the middle of a speech given by opposition leader Binyamin Netanyahu claiming that he "didn't feel like" listening to Bibi.

Israel is a sweaty, irritable and sometimes vulgar country, but it is also a country in which every citizen takes its fate and future personally. Israel has citizens of every shape and kind—right wing and left, religious and secular, poor and rich, Arabs and Jews, geniuses and idiots—but what it does not have is objective people. The British or the Dutch can perhaps laugh at our tendency to take everything to heart, but at least that proves we have one.

Popolitika is thought of as an instant success, but the truth is that our first program was an unmitigated disaster.

Amnon Dankner and I sat there trying to figure out what our role was while host Dan Margalit interviewed guest after guest, turning every once in a while to us for a reaction, a sentence or two, usually an attempt at humor that was met with a raised eyebrow. At the age of sixty-two I was becoming a comedian, and a bad one at that.

The second program was not much better. By the third, I had had enough: there I was, sitting in a television studio surrounded by people, and suddenly I realized I was falling asleep out of sheer boredom. Dan was carrying on a pleasant conversation with Shimon Peres (who himself looked very bored), when I turned to Peres without receiving permission to speak and slammed him with a few angry sentences. The audience, a bizarre gang of right-wing Jerusalemites, woke up and began applauding with great enthusiasm. Dan tried to shut me up but Goldfinger shouted into his earphone from the control room: "Let him go on! Let him go on! They're applauding!" Dankner, always on the alert, decided to join the attack and when a stunned Peres tried in vain to defend himself, the studio erupted. *Popolitika* was born.

From that day onward, there was no stopping me. I decided to myself that I would say to anyone and everyone whatever popped into my head and if they tossed me off the program at least I would know that it was not because I had been boring them or myself. Almost from the first moment it became clear to me that I would earn myself new enemies, but one of the few advantages to being an old man who has already seen it all is that there is no longer anything to fear. I always had great admirers and great detractors, but no one ever remained indifferent to my presence.

More than once I asked myself, just as others were asking, why I provoked such fervent reactions. The conventional answer was that "Tommy shouted," but if you watch all six seasons carefully you will find that I shouted very little on *Popolitika*, preferring instead to insert a well-timed, well-honed line here and there in the middle of whoever was talking.

True, I said things that were really out there and controversial, but in most cases there was no need for me to raise my voice since my voice is loud and peppered with a Hungarian accent that draws attention without shouting. I supported the Oslo accords almost from the start; I attacked the Likud party for putting a stop to the peace process; and the only time I needed a police escort home due to receiving death threats was when I referred to the "ugly monsters" who supported Baruch Goldstein—the American-born physician who perpetrated the Cave of the Patriarchs massacre, killing twenty-nine Muslims at prayer and wounding one hundred and fifty. And yet, when I walked down the street, every right-wing Sephardic taxi driver who saw me shouted, "Hey, Lapid, you're the best! Keep on bashing those left-wing Ashkenazim!"

That is because television is a medium that prefers clear and easily understandable figures. Rightists are always fascists, Leftists are Arablovers, the ultra-Orthodox are parasites. In a way, Bar'el was right: we were satirical puppets of a sort. The public loved the disputes between us but they also knew to appreciate the fact that our arguments contained real content.

In spite of the constant uproar—or perhaps because of it—*Popolitika* put all the true problems that no one wished to deal with on the agenda. On air, Bassam Abu-Sharif, a PLO leader, offered to come to Jerusalem for peace talks; Netanyahu held a live conversation with a senior Syrian representative and suggested they begin a dialogue; the ultra-Orthodox/secular debate returned to the headlines; we were the first to voice the tension between new immigrants from Russia and veteran immigrants from North Africa, the first to talk about the need for a reform in the health-care system, the crisis in education, rising unemployment. Anything considered dull up to that moment became, on *Popolitika*, of interest, and so much so that in the sole season during which we were slotted against the "king of entertainment," Dudu Topaz. At his peak, Topaz complained to reporters that we were killing his ratings. His glittery, commercial television show was less popular among viewers than a political program featuring four aging men talking about the state of education in Israel.

There is no denying that I was the program's star.

Government ministers and members of the Knesset flattered me in the dressing room in the hopes that I would have mercy on them; Shula and Meirav pleaded with me to "talk nice"; guests practiced with their spouses at home on "how to respond to Tommy." Journalists asked me incessantly how it was that I preached European culture on the one hand but was so blunt on the other. My answer, as always, was that I am a mix of both, pleasant company and a rabble-rouser, and I do not see any contradiction between the two. Arguments à la *Popolitika* take place in every smoky café in Vienna or Paris, and when they do, style is no less important than content. Perhaps I spoke in sound bites, but I knew what I was talking about. Behind my one-liners there was an orderly worldview of an educated man that had been honed on forty years of journalistic writing.

Furthermore, more than once I loyally represented the feelings of the average Israeli, who cannot stand the fact that the programs he watches are set to the channels of the politically correct.

When Victor Ostrovosky—the traitor who was a case officer for Mossad and later emigrated to Canada and wrote a book exposing the organizational structure of the Israeli secret services—appeared on *Popolitika*, I told him, "I hope, sir, that Mossad will find you and execute you." Everyone present in the studio hastened to scold me but the vast majority of Israelis felt just as I did.

When I told a prominent astrologist that he was a crook, I was sued and forced to pay some £10,000, but I would do it all again, with pleasure. The horoscopes that appear weekly in newspapers are utter nonsense, and I do not believe that the fact that Saturn is in line with Neptune has anything whatsoever to do with whether I should take a vacation in the Galilee with my wife.

Even when I admonished a pair of Christian missionaries during a debate on the missionary law with "You did us enough damage with the Holocaust," I stood behind my words. Had I had enough time I could have given them, and the audience, an enlightening lecture on the disgraceful role of the Catholic church during World War Two, and on the silence of Pope Pius XII (beautifully rendered by Natan Alterman in his poem "Of All the Peoples"), but that one sentence said enough.

Margalit and Goldfinger, each for his own reasons, were not thrilled with the fact that I was stealing the show. Margalit, the host, found it difficult to be upstaged by one of his panelists, while Goldfinger, like every talented television producer, believed he should be the only person making the decisions, and he flew into a rage on several occasions when I refused to take orders. The fact that I was on a diet at the time and lost nearly sixty pounds did not make me any more tranquil in the face of their histrionics. In one of the most memorable moments of the program, Goldfinger shouted incessantly into Margalit's earphone, "Shut Lapid up! Shut him up! I told you to shut Lapid's mouth!" In the end, Margalit was so enraged that he took the earphone out of his ear in the middle of the broadcast and shouted back at it: "Stop screaming in my ear! Shut him up yourself, I can't control him!"

For the young and uninitiated, it is probably hard to grasp the power of the emotions this program awakened in its viewers. Once, after a particularly heated show, I was walking down a Tel Aviv street when we encountered a man of about forty-five walking toward us with a briefcase. When he was about thirty yards away from us he lost consciousness, dropped his briefcase and fell to the ground, lying unconscious in the middle of the street. I ran to help him, along with another passerby and a soldier who jumped out of a passing car. When I reached him, the man stood up, brushed himself off, smiled, and shook my hand. "I'm sorry, Mr. Lapid, about pulling that stunt," he said, "but I really wanted you to come to my rescue."

CHAPTER 47

I had nothing to say about the Rabin assassination.

In November 1995, two weeks after the assassination, I was sitting in the studio taking part in one of the most pensive and reserved discussions that ever took place on *Popolitika*, and I realized I had nothing to say. The competing voices around me, in which each speaker was trying to prove he was more appalled than the last, seemed idiotic and unnecessary. Of course I was appalled, was there a sane Israeli who was not?

On the other hand, I was not a partner in the attempt to present the entire right as guilty. True, were it not for the riotous incitement against Rabin's peace efforts—from speeches delivered on balconies overlooking Jerusalem's Zion Square to rabbis who gave credence to the assassin, Yigal Amir—perhaps he would not have been murdered. At the same time, however, it seemed like the grief and fury over Rabin's assassination were shadowed by the feeling that the left was taking advantage of the tragedy in order to attack the right. Rightists mourning Rabin's death were branded hypocrites but anyone who had a Bibi Netanyahu sticker on his car or took part in a tumultuous demonstration against the Oslo accords became a de facto accomplice to the murder. Democracy—that very same democracy that Rabin fought to defend his entire life—is a dynamic, simmering institution in which unsuitable and improper things are sometimes given voice. The assassination was terrible enough as it was without anyone exploiting it to earn points in a debate.

Sitting opposite me was the politician Limor Livnat. She was pale and dejected and devoid of her usual spark. Several of those present hurled quotes from the incitement by the right in the weeks preceding the murder, and she did her best to deflect them. On occasion, someone would glance toward me and toward Shelly Yachimovich—a well-known left-wing journalist who, ten years later, would give up journalism to serve in the Knesset—but I continued to hold my tongue. Toward the end, I pointed out that it was not the Likud who had assassinated Rabin but a skullcap-wearing madman who thought he was carrying out God's will. Shelly, to my surprise, agreed. The program ended on an unusually quiet note and the participants began to disperse.

Before we even had a chance to remove our makeup, a furious Gold-finger confronted Shelly and me.

"You didn't deliver the goods," he barked at us.

"What are you talking about?"

"How dare you two defend the Likud!"

From the chair next to mine, the look on Limor Livnat's face was one of pure astonishment.

"Goldfinger," I said, "you're out of your mind."

Goldfinger had already moved away, but he was still muttering to himself in holy wrath.

By that time in my life I had long since stopped being a rightist. I believed that we needed to separate from the Palestinians and enable them to establish a country on most of the land encompassing Judea, Samaria and Gaza, and in the 1992 elections I voted for the first—and last—time and with a shaking hand for the Labour party, and Yitzhak Rabin. While I had a deep affection for the settlers, whom I saw as genuine Israelis filled with good intentions, I felt that their mission to settle was misguided and erroneous and liable to bring about the end of the Jewish majority in Israel and the demise of the Zionist ideal.

On the other hand, I had not really become a leftist, since I did not believe the Arabs. They never accepted and will never accept our presence here. Does anyone doubt that if they could they would have long since murdered every last one of us? That is an unpleasant thought, and perhaps unenlightened as well, which is why the left prefers to repress it, so that it can continue to pretend that the Arab-Jewish conflict is taking place in Scotland or The Hague.

So what, then, is the solution? Unfortunately, the answer is that there is none. Nationalistic conflicts are not a lock for which one must merely find the right key. We must withdraw from the territories because that is the right tactic, and we must continue to be the strongest military presence in the region and remind the Arabs at all times that they do not want to mess with us, because that, too, is the right tactic. I am not a rightist, because their solution—trying to rule millions of Palestinians—is senseless. And I am not a leftist, because their solution—giving up the dream of a Jewish state for a bi-national state—is heartless. So where does that leave me? Sometimes here, sometimes there. To paraphrase Victor Hugo, only beasts of burden are consistent.

Apropos consistency, in January 1996, Meirav came to my study to inform me that she was getting a divorce. Instead of getting angry, I made us both coffee and told her she was my daughter and I loved her and would stand behind her on whatever path she chose. Even being a patriarch takes some finesse.

On occasion I asked myself how it is that both of my children, who grew up with parents in the happiest marriage one can imagine, failed in their first marriages (and succeeded wonderfully in their second). The only answer that came to mind was that they figured the institution of marriage is so strong and sheltering that they did not really bother to make sure they had chosen the right partners. In other words, the parents are at fault. How do I know that? Because the parents are always at fault.

Several months later, Yair walked out on his very successful talk show in the wake of an ongoing battle with the technicians' committee.

Yair wandered about in a daze for several weeks until Arnon Milchan suggested he go to Hollywood and set up the television department of his film company. I was far more upset with the idea than I let on back then; I feared he would fail or, worse yet, that he would succeed. My whole life I scorned the *yordim*—Israelis who leave Israel—and suddenly here was my own son preparing to leave the country. Several months later, I was drinking coffee with friends at the Beit Hanna café near my home. Twenty minutes after I got up and left, a suicide bomber entered the café and blew himself up. Three women were killed and forty-eight people were wounded. Yair phoned from L.A. the moment the news made the headlines.

"Are you all right?" he asked.

"Yes."

"I know that was where you go for coffee."

"I'd just left."

He was silent for a long moment. "I'm coming home," he said.

Dan Margalit was also not particularly consistent: after our second season he left Channel One for the commercial station, Channel Two, in order to start a competitor to *Popolitika*. Yaacov Achimeir was appointed to replace him, and his polite, sleepy style nearly killed the show. Dan came back a year later, bruised from his failed attempt, and we returned to our old habits: on Mondays we met at the station, spent an hour and a half in a volcanic tempest, then from there we went to the home of Ehud Olmert, who had been elected mayor of Jerusalem, to eat cheese and continue the debate.

My close relationship with Olmert was forged from difficult circumstances. In the year I lost after Michal's death, he was one of the few people who did not disappear after the first week or month of mourning. In spite of his busy schedule as a government minister, he managed to make it to Tel Aviv from Jerusalem once a week to visit and give support. I would cry and he would hold my hand and say, "It's going to be all right, Tommy. You'll see, it's going to be okay." And he would cry along with me.

If I were still alive I would ask his lawyers to allow me to testify as a character witness on his behalf at his trial, so that I could have the opportunity to say that in a critical hour he is the best friend a person can ask for.

CHAPTER 48

Of all the thousands of pieces I wrote during my lifetime, the most famous is a little one called "To Live in New Zealand," which I did not put much stock in when I wrote it. Over the years it was printed again and again, was sold in stores on parchment, was included in a number of collections and, in 1995, was recorded as a song by the Israeli pop-rock band Ethnix. It was the only time in my life that I received royalties as a songwriter. For many years I did not look at it (like most writers, I tended not to reread my own texts), but toward the end of 1998 I reached back to the shelf behind my desk, pulled out one of my books of collected humor writing, and read the piece, then broadcast it on my radio program. The more perceptive listeners would have understood that at sixty-seven I was indeed living on LaSalle Street in Tel Aviv, but from every other standpoint I resided in New Zealand:

Sometimes I try to imagine what it must be like to live in New Zealand. To be born on an island hard to locate on a map, in the middle of an ocean. To grow up in a drowsy town of red-roofed buildings, to hike in green fields where you come upon a farmer shearing a white sheep.

To live in the house your grandfather built, to be the grandson of a man who died of natural causes, to learn 220 years of history from a slim volume, to draw wine from a barrel in the cellar—a cellar that is not a bomb shelter.

To be a New Zealander means having the confidence to make plans five years down the road, to be an ardent fan of your local football club, to join the reserves because there is no obligation to serve in the standing army, then to leave it in hopes of finding a life with some tension and suspense.

To read a New Zealand newspaper without understanding what is happening in the Holy Land, why people get killed on every tiny patch of arid land when the world is huge and life is precious.

To believe that human beings are brothers and with a little goodwill it is possible to solve every human problem. To be a New Zealander and to know that a cannon is fired only once a year, on the Queen's birthday. To know that sleeping bags are made for treks, that widows are old women, and that when a parent speaks of a child who fell he is referring to a playground.

To be a New Zealander, small and petty and closed away from the world by the four walls of your home, uninvolved in any cosmic experiences, not indebted to any person and owed nothing by others, expected by no one to make sacrifices or expecting no one else to make sacrifices for you. To be a little New Zealander that cats do not bump up against and noises do not plague.

God, I have no complaints that you chose us from among all the nations. I accept the verdict with submission, love, and pride, and I would not trade Jerusalem with Wellington or the tough life of Israel for an easy life anywhere else in the world. This is my home, my children's homeland, our fate and we accept it. But—now don't get angry, God Almighty—if nonetheless I sometimes think this thought: "Is it fair that in New Zealand people die of boredom?"

And was it fair that once again I myself was dying of boredom? Suddenly, toward the end of 1998 and at the height of its popularity, *Popolitika* was taken off the air. "Everything is personal," says Don Corleone at the end of *The Godfather*, and so it was with the end of *Popolitika*—or at least the motives were personal.

In the spring of that year, Uri Porat was reinstated for a second term as head of the IBA, in place of Yosef Bar'el. "We're in trouble," Dankner told me over the phone when the announcement was made.

Shortly after his reappointment, Porat summoned Goldfinger to his office and informed him that he was taking the show off the air because it was "uncivilized." That must be the first recorded case of a television station manager canceling his most successful program on his own initiative. Since then, Channel One has never had a success that came anywhere near that of *Popolitika*.

Once again, I was stumped. I was beyond retirement age and I told myself that my five years on *Popolitika* were the final chord of an illustrious career, and now all that was left for me to do was, in the words of Rilke, "wander along the boulevards, up and down, restlessly." Nights, I was visited by my old dream: I am running to the train station, running and running, but when I reach it, it pulls away and I stand in the station watching it grow distant, my schoolmates aboard, exuberant and oblivious to the fact that I have been left behind. "The dream is back," I told Shula one morning. She hugged me and said, "Even your dreams are straightforward, without any psychological complications. Yes, the train has left but another one will come along."

Several days later, Dan Margalit summoned Amnon Dankner and me for a talk and suggested we reestablish our triumvirate on Channel Two. We agreed, and we even set up a joint production company, but we all knew it would not be the same. Shiny, fashionable commercial television did not suit the dense political discussion that was our speciality, and Margalit's show was destined to fail, with or without us.

Until this very day I wonder how close I was to disappearing from the public arena. Life is a clock that periodically stops, at random. A single missed meeting, a conversation that did not take place, an idea that did not occur in someone's brain—any of these could have rendered me a very short Wikipedia entry of interest only to my family. It is not artificial modesty that makes me believe so, but the awareness of the dangerous fragility of fate.

My personal clock, however, seemed to tick at its own pace. One morning, Professor Uriel Reichman invited me to a meeting. I knew Professor Reichman only superficially, from his involvement with the Constitution for Israel movement. I was not particularly fond of him, as he came across as full of himself, but it was hard not to admire his drive in establishing his life's dream, the Herzliya Interdisciplinary Centre.

We met at the Beit Hanna café, where the terror attack had taken place two years earlier. Reichman was waiting for me with Aryeh Rotenberg, one of the owners of the Kesher Bar'el ad firm, and we sat facing the impressive monument designed by Eliezer Weishoff depicting three severed roses.

"This coming May," they told me, "there will be elections. We've decided to give our support to Avraham Poraz's Shinui party and we want to ask if you'd agree to be first place on the ballot."

"No," I said curtly.

"Why not?"

"Because I see no point in endangering my standing in the media in order to run with a party that in any case won't get enough votes to cross the threshold."

They glanced at one another and I had the feeling they knew this would be my answer and were prepared for it. "What would you think," Rotenberg said, "if we were to hold a poll that will let us know who'd be the most suitable person to head Shinui?"

I thought about it for a moment. There was a certain risk that news of the poll would leak, but show me a person active in the public arena who would turn down the chance to have his popularity ranked by scientific means.

When I asked my family, opinions were divided. Shula said, as she always did, that she would stand behind any decision I made; Meirav was opposed; Yair was in favor. Unfortunately, I phoned Ephraim Kishon in order to boast. He dismissed the idea before I had even managed to get out three sentences of explanation. "Are you mad?" he asked me. "You are far more important as a journalist than what you would be as a member of the Knesset from some small party sitting on the back benches and doing nothing."

I also consulted with Ehud Olmert, the only professional politician among my close friends. He, too, was opposed in his usual decisive manner. "The party won't cross the vote threshold and it'll make you look bad," he informed me. Naturally, I was careful to remind him of this brilliant estimation of his about once a week for the next ten years.

Two days before I was scheduled to meet with the people from Shinui again, I could not resist telling Dankner and Margalit about it. It was eleven in the evening when I phoned Dankner and told him I was headed to his house. Surprised, he said he'd be happy to see me, and he greeted me with a cup of coffee in his hand when I knocked at his door.

"So, Tommy," he said, "which party asked you to head it?"

"Shinui," I said.

"Take a slip of paper and mark this down: you'll get six seats in the Knesset."

And yet, a day later, if the blue-uniformed guard at the Interdisciplinary Centre had stopped me to ask what my decision was, I would have answered quite candidly that I still did not know.

The meeting was attended by Reichman, Rotenberg, the industrialist Stef Wertheim and several senior party members, including Poraz and the future government ministers Yehudit Naor and Ilan Shalgi. We sat at a long conference table under neon lights that made everyone look green, and the party publicist presented the comprehensive poll he had conducted. It was even worse than the previous one, close to Olmert's dire prediction. "If that's the case," I said at once, "then you can count me out."

For a full hour they tried to convince me I was wrong, that this was only the beginning, that the party would progress—but I refused adamantly. The voices and the faces began to swirl around me, and as happens in all overly long discussions, the arguments repeated themselves like some sleep-inducing Indian mantra. And then, from the midst of this fog, a clear picture came into my mind, several months down the road: it is election day and I am sitting at home watching on my television these very people now pleading with me to lead them, and they are the brand-new members of the Knesset from the Shinui party while I am eating myself up—I could have been one of them! The train has departed and I am still standing in the station.

I raised my head and said loudly, "I agree." Everyone fell silent, astonished, and just then I recalled, not for the first time, the Karl May books I read as a child, and, like a true Winnetou, I banged on the table and said, "I have spoken!"

CHAPTER 49

Arthur Rubinstein, the greatest classical pianist of the twentieth century, once told me, with a smile flickering on his lips, the following anecdote:

"I arrived in New York to give a series of concerts and was staying in one of the best hotels in the city. I rose at seven in the morning and sat down to practice on the piano that had been installed in my suite. The room next to mine was occupied by a journalist who had worked late into the night and my playing woke him up.

"Infuriated, the journalist went down to the lobby and shouted at the reception clerk. 'What kind of hotel are you running here? I'm trying to sleep while some jerk in the next room is playing the piano first thing in the morning and wakes me up. You make him stop, immediately!'"

"The reception clerk took a look at the guestbook. 'That is Arthur Rubinstein in the room next to yours,' the clerk said. 'You say he's playing? I'm sorry, sir, but the price of your room just rose five dollars.'"

Rubinstein burst into laughter, and so did I. It was only thirty-five years later that I discovered what it feels like when the room you are occupying is suddenly worth more, thanks to you.

The next morning I went to the press building, Sokolov House. My car still carried a *PRESS* tag that enabled me to park for free in the adjacent lot. When I get home, I reminded myself, I will have to scrape the sticker off the windshield before anyone can accuse me of exploiting my position. I had been an active journalist for forty-six years when suddenly, from one day to the next, I realized that was all over. I got out of the car and went to the building—the same building where Shula and I were married and where I had spent endless hours engaged in gossip or chess or passionate professional disputes. Dozens of journalists and photographers were waiting on the steps, and I wondered if there was some VIP in Israel who was about to ruin my dramatic announcement. It was only when they stormed in my direction and began clicking away with their cameras and firing questions at me that I understood that the VIP was me.

"So, Tommy," said one young correspondent from Army Radio whom I did not know, "now you're out for a Volvo, too?" In those days, the official car of government ministers was the Volvo.

"You're welcome to accompany me to the parking lot," I said. "You'll see I've already got a Volvo."

They laughed, and I made my way up the stairs into Sokolov House, which was full to overflowing. Poraz and Reichman were already sitting at the conference table, along with the other senior party members. Poraz presented me as the new head of the party, and when I rose to speak, a murmur spread through the room. Journalists may be cynical, but I had been one of them for many years, and they knew this was no easy step I was taking. The room was suddenly worth five dollars more.

The press conference was a great success, providing all the next day's newspapers with headlines. Afterward, Poraz suggested that we adjourn to party headquarters to discuss the campaign. I agreed to meet there, but when I got to my car I realized, with great embarrassment, that I did not know where the headquarters of this party I was now heading were.

Following several telephone calls, I arrived at an unsightly building at 10 Ha'arbaah Street in Tel Aviv. The elevator took us only to the fourth floor and from there we had to climb to the fifth, where I found myself on the deck of the HMS *Victory*, Admiral Nelson's flagship, and now mine. It was a gloomy office of less than 500 square feet, with wall-to-wall industrial carpeting that gave off a smell of glue, and furniture that looked as though it had been purchased at a fire sale.

Waiting for me in the small conference room were the party activists, who gazed at me with suspicion or curiosity, expecting me to tell them what to do. I could not help but recall the day that Ephraim Kishon had gathered the film crew shooting *Sallah Shabati* and said, "Gentlemen, I would like to ask you to teach me how to make a movie."

Who was going to teach me how to make a political party?

CHAPTER 50

"Mr. Lapid," said the young ultra-Orthodox man, "why do you hate me?"

"I don't hate you," I told him. "I don't hate any Jew in the world."

He fell silent and looked at me and I fell silent and looked at him. The cameras were rolling, and from the corner of my eye I could see Moti Kirschenbaum, who had been at my side throughout the campaign, grow tense at the impending confrontation. He summoned the sound-man to come near, but we disappointed them all. The young man gave an almost imperceptible nod of understanding, which I returned in kind, and he continued on his way.

I do not hate the ultra-Orthodox—they are Jews, and all Jews are destined for the same fate. I do not even hate the ultra-Orthodox man I met in the hospital right after my first cancer operation, as I was slowly dragging myself along with my infusion stand, who said to his wife in a loud, clear voice so I was sure to hear, "You see that man? That's the Hitler of the Jews." In my youth I might have punched him in the nose, but at the moment it happened, I felt sorry for him for living in a dark prison of fear and enmity while I am freer in death than he will ever be in life.

I am hardly the turn-the-other-cheek type, but it was not hatred that led my long and well-documented struggles against the ultra-Orthodox. I disagreed with them on the social, cultural and intellectual levels, I had an ink-stained political war with them, and I refused to take it to heart that every time someone dares confront them, they defame him as being an anti-Semite. Much of their strength comes from the fact that we secular Jews let them define what a Jew is and what a Jew is not. But it is bullshit if they think I am any less of a Jew than any rabbi in Jerusalem whose children cannot find China on a map or turn on a computer, and who do not serve in the army or who repress their wives or refuse to work, living off the taxes I pay instead.

"You see?" my detractors will say. "He managed to control himself for a minute, then the hatred oozes out." They do not understand that a democratic society is not founded merely on rights, but on obligations as well. I have no problem whatsoever with an ultra-Orthodox Jew who serves in the army, goes off to work in the morning, then studies Torah all night if he wants. That man is my brother, and I love him better than any non-Jew in the world. He was there with me in the ghetto, and on the rickety boat that brought me to Israel, he sat with me on a boulder facing a ruined synagogue on the island of Rhodes when I sobbed at the memory of 500 Jews led from the building by the Nazis and drowned at sea in an Italian ship.

The fact that a man wears a *shtreimel* on his head and grows a beard does not absolve him from the responsibilities carried by all the other citizens of the state. It was not with ultra-Orthodoxy that I had a complaint but with the fact that the ultra-Orthodox turned it into a permit for ignoring all the chores we are obliged to carry out on a daily basis on our bowed backs. More than once I spoke of my own ultra-Orthodox son. I never met him, but I paid his bills from the day he was born since his biological father was exempt from doing so simply because he felt like studying the Torah on a full-time basis. I do not believe that and I do not accept it. Parenting is a responsibility, and if you brought children into the world then it is up to you to take care of them. Even so, I am willing to pay those bills for this child of mine I have never met, but only if he fulfils the three criteria I set down for my other children: to serve in the army, to work and pay taxes, and not to throw stones at policemen or IDF soldiers.

The ultra-Orthodox even added insult to injury when they tried— and often succeeded—to pass religious laws forcing their way of life on others. I am not presumptuous enough to tell other people what to eat, when to work or rest, when a person may drive his car and how he must dress, but I am also unwilling for someone else to tell me how to run my life.

"But what do you want from us?" the ultra-Orthodox politicians said, rolling their eyes. "These laws were passed in a democratic fashion." This is how I answered them: "Would you be willing to accept a law passed democratically that forbids you to wear a skullcap or requires you to eat pork?" Of course not. The ultra-Orthodox are willing to play the democracy card only when it works to their benefit. As soon as the tables are turned, democracy becomes worthless.

At the end of 1999, the first polls conducted after I became head of the party were published. Not a single one of them predicted we would pass the necessary threshold for even a single seat in the Knesset. Months later, Poraz admitted to me that when he opened the paper that morning he was overcome with despair and asked himself if he had not made a mistake by bringing me in; he could have failed to enter the Knesset all on his own. When we adjourned our first campaign meeting in the Shinui headquarters, the mood was somber and I felt that they were holding me accountable for failing to deliver the goods.

We began discussing the party, its character, and mostly how to differentiate ourselves from the other parties. All kinds of ideas were exchanged, then in a loud voice I said, "People, we're going to run on the ultra-Orthodox issue, and that issue only. We're not a supermarket party that can allow itself to present a huge range of ideas to the public. We are a small and angry party, and that is how we will appeal to the Israeli voter."

The next day we got to work. We hired a veteran television producer and director to film our election broadcasts. I informed them that I would write the scripts, and when their laughing died down I went to the computer and banged out a few pieces on how the ultra-Orthodox have taken control of our lives, how they get out of serving in the army, how each succeeding Israeli government has given into their dictates.

My daily schedule came together with surprising speed. At seven in the morning I would be picked up in a van covered in bumper stickers and ferried from conference to conference, from assembly to assembly. A large loudspeaker was affixed to the roof of the van and it played our election jingle, a play on the name Lapid as a torch leading the secular population.

Almost always, more people were awaiting us than had been invited. I knew that the majority were not Shinui supporters but people curious to meet "Lapid from television," but I didn't mind. I would stand before them on a platform or a bench or an upturned orange crate and tell them that a government coalition without the ultra-Orthodox might seem like a pipe dream to them, but it was absolutely feasible. After speaking, I would climb down, shake hands, speak with the people present, ask them about themselves and their lives in Tiberias (or Afula or Beersheva; I didn't always remember where I was). To my surprise, I discovered I liked these meetings. Hungarians are a warm and outgoing people, always hugging and kissing, and I never had a problem with strangers jostling me. For some reason, though, nobody asked me to kiss their baby. I know that politicians are always photographed kissing babies, but throughout the campaign I wasn't asked to kiss a single baby. Could it be that all the babies kissed by Bibi Netanyahu and Ehud Barak that winter were rentals?

The police warned us that on the ultra-Orthodox streets, threats to my life were increasing, a few arrests were made and, on Poraz's advice, I was provided with a bodyguard, a 330-pound guy named Moti Paz who could have protected me not only from a potential attacker but from an entire firing squad. A few years later, I met him at some social affair and barely recognized him: he had shed 150 pounds through diet and sport and was sculpted with an impressive collection of muscles. I thought he looked terrible and told him so.

Midday, we would return to Tel Aviv or travel to Jerusalem, and I would be interviewed. I believe there is no Israeli television program on which I did not make at least three appearances, including a cooking show (with my recipe for Hungarian cherry soup), a travel show (with the *Lapid Guide*), talk shows (with funny stories from my days as a London correspondent), a Jewish heritage program (with a heartwarming story about Novi Sad), a children's show (Grandpa Tommy talks about his grandchildren), and of course political shows.

After that we would head north again to meet, say, 300 worried citizens in Haifa, and in the evening I was back at party headquarters in Tel Aviv, where I would write press copy with the publicists, review announcements made by our spokesman, and take a last glance at our daily broadcast before heading for the studio to record it and then to the editing room to make sure it had come out the way I had planned. Finally, I would return home and sit with my team to plan the following day. I would climb into bed at three in the morning only to rise at five thirty to a new day.

Those were frantic, feverish, tension-filled days and—as predicted—I had never enjoyed myself more.

In the meantime, the world seemed absolutely determined to come to our assistance. I thought then and still think now that we ran a campaign that should be studied at institutions teaching politics and government, but I must admit that reality worked to our advantage.

In February, the ultra-Orthodox staged a huge rally in Jerusalem—some claim it was the biggest in the history of the nation—against the High Court of Justice. Some of the things said there that day frightened a large portion of the populace. Most alarming of all was a statement made by David Yossef, son of Rabbi Ovadia Yossef, spiritual leader of the Shas political party, in which he used a particularly odious Biblical curse to call Supreme Court President Aharon Barak an "enemy of the Jews."

It was not only the ultra-Orthodox who attacked us, however, but the left as well. A long list of influential left-wing journalists published articles dripping with poison that did everything to damage our reputation and make me out to be a fascist in camouflage who had stolen his way into the fortress of liberalism. I decided to publish a response in *Yediot Ahronot*, but the paper refused to print it and we were forced to turn it into a flyer. This was the only time in my life I had to pay to have an article of mine appear in print, instead of being paid for it.

And still, nobody believed it was possible. So great was our lack of faith, that four days before the elections, Mody Zandberg—fifth place on our list of candidates—informed me that he was flying to London. "Are you mad?" I asked him. "Who leaves the country at a time like this?"

"Come on, Tommy," he said. "Fifth place is unrealistic. I've been invited to an event at Buckingham Palace and I'll get to meet the Queen. Something like that happens once in a lifetime."

He did indeed travel to London. I continued to remind him of it for the entire time we served in the Knesset and the government, and he always laughed. Blushed and laughed.

On the evening of the elections, I was invited to a special television studio set up by Channel Two. Three days earlier, someone from *Maariv* had leaked to me the information that according to polls we were going to earn six seats—but that sounded too good to be true. When I got to the studio, half an hour before the polling station sample votes were due to be announced, I got a thumbs-up and a wink from the show's host. That was, I believe, the first time I had an inkling that the rumors might be right. Thirty minutes later the results were broadcast: Ehud Barak would be the new prime minister and Shinui would enter the Knesset with six seats.

An hour later, I was on the roof of our building, drunk and ecstatic. So many people had gathered there that one of the party activists, an engineer by profession, came to inform me that the roof could cave in. "So what do you want me to do about it?" I asked, and he walked away mumbling to himself. At some stage, Poraz disappeared, then returned. "I popped over to the Barak victory celebrations at Rabin Square," he told me. "There are thousands of people there shouting, 'No to Shas! No to Shas!' We're going to be in the government."

I hugged Poraz and kissed Shula and someone shoved a microphone in front of my face. Everyone fell silent and looked at me. "Ladies and gentlemen," I said, "this is the happiest day of my life."

CHAPTER 51

What exactly is the Knesset?

It is a serious parliament and a home to irresponsible clowns; it is the most respected institution representing Israeli democracy and the most ridiculed; it is a place where highly vocal confrontations erupt between people who, two hours later, sit together in a committee meeting to word joint communiqués; it is out of date yet ceaselessly renewing itself; it is an academic institution that deals—in a deeply serious manner—with the most important problems facing the nation and a marketplace in which the most unbearably foolish pronouncements are made; it is an elite and exclusive club and a place where a member of your party may grab you by the collar to complain that the municipality will not let him close off a balcony and this is a scandal for now and for generations to come. The Knesset is filled with contradictions and contrasts, is both high- and lowbrow, clever and stupid, friendly and threatening. In short, the Knesset suits Israelis and we Israelis suit the Knesset.

On 7 June 1991, I stood for the first time on the Knesset podium and was sworn in as a fully fledged member of the parliament of the Jewish state. Of course I thought about my father, but also about the fact that on the inner side of the podium, hidden from the television cameras, the Formica was peeling.

After the swearing-in ceremony, my friends and colleagues greeted me while the ultra-Orthodox MKs ignored me. The next day, before giving my first speech, I saw them dashing into the plenum. Poraz explained, in a whisper: "They want to be here so they can make a demonstrative exit the moment you take the floor." This reminded me that the day before, during the singing of the national anthem, the cameras had been focused on them and it caused quite a stir when not one of them joined in the singing of "*HaTikvah.*" When I took the floor they rose to their feet and stampeded toward the exit. "*Nu,*" I said scornfully, "I understand the ultra-Orthodox MKs are running away because they're afraid I'll sing '*HaTikvah.*'" The MKs remaining in the room burst into laughter.

I did not find the fact that they ostracized me particularly troublesome. With all the disputes I have with the ultra-Orthodox public, I still think it is a thousand times better than their representatives. Here and there you meet someone intelligent from their ranks, like former Shas leader Aryeh Deri, but mostly they're a noisy bunch of self-proclaimed big shots without a touch of God in their hearts. What's more, I figured that life is stronger than all those huge demonstrations and that they would get used to me. "The problem with you, Tommy," one of them said to me with a mixture of anger and wonder, "is that you speak out against Jews all the time but you're one of the most Jewish people there is." I told him it was absolutely true but that it was not a problem. In that very same session of the Knesset I put forward a bill, together with one of the ultra-Orthodox party members, prohibiting the attempt to convert minors to other religions.

This huge change in my life quickly turned out to be not such an upheaval after all. I was dealing with the same political problems I had dealt with previously, I was meeting the same journalists and politicians I had met in the past, I was speaking on radio and appearing on television as usual. I was invited to the same events and saw the same faces at the same cocktail parties. Even the corridors of the Knesset, which I knew from my days as the parliamentary correspondent in the 1960s, had not changed much, and the schnitzel served in the cafeteria was the same dried-out schnitzel that I sent back to the kitchen years earlier.

I had ample time, however, to deal with the schnitzel issue, since the new prime minister, Ehud Barak, broke his promise to the voters and opted for a coalition with the ultra-Orthodox rather than with me. Although I should have expected it, I walked around stunned and disappointed for days. Was this what I had left journalism for, to watch from the back benches how Shas was taking over the country? Plenty of people told us we should have joined the coalition (Barak had been very persistent) and I explained to all of them that I had made a promise to our voters that we would not join a government with the ultra-Orthodox and I was absolutely going to keep that promise. In most cases that attitude was met with bemusement and raised eyebrows. Poor Tommy, the expressions on people's faces said, he really doesn't understand a thing about politics.

On the Saturday night following the elections, I spoke with Ehud Barak over the phone. "Within a year," I told him, "you're going to be mired in the muck of all kinds of outrages these people are going to bring down on you, and you'll be sorry for the day you brought them into your government."

In fact, it took far less than a year.

United Torah Judaism left the government in September, after the Israel Electric Company transported turbines on the Sabbath. It seemed absurd to me, but I respected them: at least they left on moral grounds. The Shas party operated differently: it was not the *peace* process that interested them but the *pass* process: how much money could be passed into their coffers. For example, in December, when President Clinton announced that Syrian president Hafez Assad was interested in renewing talks with Israel, Shas head Eli Yishai hastened to point out that the support of Shas depended on government support for the party's educational institutions. There was something refreshing in the candid cynicism of Shas party leaders stating that the fate of the Golan Heights and its thousands of residents depended on one thing and one thing only: the size of the bribes it could extort.

The more time passed, the more I took pleasure in abusing them. A pattern set in: Ehud Barak would make a political move that led nowhere, Eli Yishai asked for money to go along with it, and I made the most of it in the media—at their expense. When the first 15 million shekels were transferred to Shas we hired a private investigator to check up on each and every institution that was on the receiving end. The investigator came back with a huge stack of photos. That same evening we presented the photographic evidence on television of the Talmud Torah school at 19 King Jeroboam Street in Ashdod, which the state had funded with munificent lavishness. Too bad that King Jeroboam Street ended at No. 17, and that No. 19 was an open field in which sheep sometimes grazed.

Like every citizen of Israel, I, too, often had trouble understanding Barak. The new prime minister incessantly zigzagged from one matter to the next, perturbed, perspiring, perpetually restless, and most of all, incomprehensible to anyone but himself. During the spring recess, Shula and I traveled as we did every year to our favorite hotel in Switzerland, a pastoral gem of red-roofed buildings in snowy mountains, with an aged pianist in a white tuxedo playing Strauss' "Blue Danube" waltz at dinner. Three days into our visit, my spokesman phoned, very excited, to say that "Barak has announced he is returning to his public agenda and he wants you to come home immediately to set up a secular government." I lowered the receiver and told Shula, "The holiday's over," and that evening we flew home. We had not even unpacked when a phone call came from Barak's office telling us that the matter had been canceled. Why? No reason. When I met him two days later I complained to him about his inconsistency and his slapdash style of management, and I told him about our ruined holiday. He gazed at me with a blank expression and neither apologized nor bothered to explain.

To be fair, it should be noted that I had some more positive experiences with him as well. In January 2000, he brought me along to a Holocaust memorial conference sponsored by the Swedish government. We stayed at the Grand Hotel, the most beautiful in Stockholm, which became a military fortress during our visit, but I took advantage of the fact that I was not a member of his entourage and I toured the city alone in freezing temperatures wrapped inside my overcoat in a European city sparkling with soft snow. Which was how I arrived at the conference site ahead of everyone, and I had a chance to pay a visit to a photo exhibition of Swedish diplomats who aided in rescuing Jews during the Holocaust. Naturally, I sought out Wallenberg, and when I found him I was dumbstruck due to the testimony of one of the survivors: "They came and rounded up all the young women, the ones who could still march.

They gave us only a few moments to say our farewells. Mother hugged me and Mother kissed me and Mother went off and left me completely alone. But then, that evening, Mother suddenly returned and said, 'Wallenberg saved us.'"

That was my story, my own words as I had recounted them many times in print and over the radio; they even appeared in one of my books. But this text was attributed to someone by the name of Yoni Moser. To this day I have no idea who he is or whether he experienced exactly what I did or whether this was some kind of very odd joke.

One week after my return from Stockholm, I met Yassir Arafat for the first time in my life.

If someone had told me just one year earlier that I would be the guest of this mass murderer in his compound in Ramallah and that after chatting for an hour he would lead me, hand in hand (two fingers grasping my pinky finger) to a table laden with wonderful Middle Eastern delicacies, I would have said he was delirious. Truth be told, there were moments during the meeting when I myself was certain I was dreaming.

On the appointed day, I found myself sitting at the Ramallah barrier, where a policeman on a bicycle was waiting to escort us to the compound, ignoring all red lights along the way. I looked out of my window with curiosity and glimpsed a lively town where most of the buildings looked new but which still managed to preserve its basic character as a Levantine city.

Arafat was waiting for us at his headquarters, a building that had served the British, Jordanian and Israeli armies, and now Arafat. He greeted us in an elegantly appointed lounge, some half a dozen members of his entourage in attendance, most of them the security detail. We exchanged gifts: I brought a replica of a Philistine icon that my secretary had bought at the shop of the Israel Museum, and he presented me with a large, shell-encrusted jewelry box. "You must fill it with jewels for your wife," he told me, and we both laughed. I'm sure he repeated that joke to every guest.

He seated me in an armchair to his left and I presented the members of my party to him and explained that we had come to learn about the

Palestinian position firsthand and also to warn him that a serious terror attack by Hamas or the Islamic Jihad could derail the peace process (some things never change). Arafat said that both sides should be interested in the success of the talks through mutual respect. "As Barak was a general, so, too, am I," he stressed.

He was dressed in his army uniform, was unshaven, and sported a *keffiyeh* on his head—as always. His small, round hands were far whiter than the skin on his face. In spite of his trembling lips, he made an impression of being a man in control of the situation and he expressed himself exactingly, all the while remembering names and details.

"I opened for my partner Rabin the doors to China, to Indonesia, to India, to Senegal and the Arab world," he said.

"But Rabin opened for you the door to the White House," I said.

"Yes," he said, "but I opened many more doors than he did."

"Yes," I said, standing my ground, "but he opened the largest door of all for you."

Arafat's English was mumbled and substandard, but he got by with it. He complained bitterly to me about various injustices, like the transfer of tax monies, but here and there a bit of humor poked through his words. When I asked why he didn't allow freedom of expression in the Palestinian media, Arafat told me I was mistaken. "The citizens enjoy full freedom of expression," he said, "that is how they can lie all the time."

After an hour-long conversation, Arafat took my hand and led me down a long corridor lined with a huge number of security personnel to the large dining room, where a beautifully laid table was overflowing with excellent food: pea soup, rice, grilled chicken and grouper, fried mullet, a number of salads—and shrimp. "Here it is known that you do not keep kosher," I was told. Arafat picked up a *kibbeh* dumpling with his hands and passed it to me. "Try this," he said.

Joining us at the table were his military adjutants, his bureau chief, the Palestinian Authority head of information, the head of Force 17, which guarded Arafat, and the head of the Palestinian secret services, Jibril Rajoub, who told us a juicy story: a brother of former Shas head Aryeh Deri had won $65,000 at the casino in Jericho!

Arafat's meal was served on separate dishes, apparently due to security issues. His appetite was remarkable: he ate more than I did.

CHAPTER 52

On 16 February 2000, German president Johannes Rau addressed the Knesset, in German.

Life's circles opened and closed all around me, one merging into another. Here I was, sitting in the Israeli parliament beneath the Israeli flag watching a tense Rau, his military adjutant at his side dressed in the uniform of the German army. People stole glances at me; of all the MKs I was the only one who had been in the ghetto and they wondered how I would react to the speech. Knesset Speaker Avraham Burg spoke before Rau, noting that while German was the language of Hitler, Himmler and Eichmann, it was also the language of Heine and Goethe and Schiller. He forgot to mention that the man in the portrait on the wall behind him, Theodore Herzl, wrote *The Jewish State* in German.

I scrutinized myself during the speech. I was neither emotional nor shocked, merely pensive. Here I was, fifty-five years after the Holocaust, listening to the German language spoken by the president of Germany. It was not rough like that of the SS officers I sat with at the train station in Novi Sad, but soft and lyrical, almost apologetic. Naturally, I thought of Father. What would he have made of all this? His bones are in the ground at Mauthausen while I was in Jerusalem, free to shout, free to protest, free to enjoy this odd feeling of victory. I hoped that Father forgave me.

I felt old, and "old" is the word. Not "vintage" or "golden-aged" or any other euphemism that people who fear growing old use to mask a bitter truth. After 1945, I had no use for masks. My wrinkles were the paths I took to get where I was that day. I did not wish to compare myself to young people, only to the young person I once was. As an old man I was smarter, I wrote better, I knew who I was and where I stood, dependent on no one and expecting nothing. All that provides tremendous power.

My assistants—my spokesman, my parliamentary aide, my driver—were all younger than my children. At times I wondered how that gap affected them. Did they talk about me at home? Did they relate to me like some piece of antique furniture? Secretly mock my idiosyncrasies? One day I met Ariel Sharon in the canteen, and we talked at length. As old people will do, everything reminded him of some anecdote from the past. Was I like that as well? Should I have stopped?

On 24 May 2000, the Israel Defence Forces withdrew from Lebanon. The hasty retreat, moved up by a month, was the sole success that Ehud Barak could take credit for during his tenure as prime minister. He did not have much time to enjoy it, however, since his coalition disintegrated in June in the wake of his visit to Camp David. It was actually our Shinui party, which had been tossed into the opposition by Barak, that refused to vote against him. Had we, the government would have fallen and his trip would have been canceled, but I did not want to bring down an Israeli government for trying to make peace.

During the talks, Barak offered the Palestinians more than any previous prime minister had offered, but he returned with a stamp of failure embossed on his face. His explanations about having "revealed the true face of Arafat" convinced no one, and the Second Intifada broke out in September. The old man who had fed me *kibbeh* with his own fingers had dragged his people once more into a dance of blood and hatred. In October, Arab Israelis joined the fray and the police reacted harshly by killing thirteen protesters. Barak lost even the support of the Arab parties.

Several days later, I called a meeting of the Shinui central command and told everyone we had to prepare for new elections. "When will they take place?" someone asked. "In a year," I responded.

In fact, unlike other parties, we had never stopped campaigning. We continued consulting with our public relations firm weekly in order to plan strategy, buy ads in newspapers and put out our own paper—of which I was the editor—to the tune of 100,000 copies per issue. It was clear to us that in the next elections the ultra-Orthodox issue would not suffice, and I began going from branch to branch talking about "the return to Israeliness."

I explained that the Israeli left had lost its way since it combined Zionism with socialism; Zionism was fading out and socialism had gone bankrupt. The Israeli right had lost its way, too, as it had thrown its fate in with the vision of the Greater Land of Israel that could not be actualized. The religious Zionists lost their way because some of them had turned into ultra-nationalists while others had become ultra-Orthodox. The educated secular youth adopted a cosmopolitan, anarchistic worldview of enlightened selfishness that had no connection to the state. As a result of all these, a vacuum was created at the center of Israeli consciousness. It was up to us to fill it.

We needed to get back to some basic values, I explained, while standing on a bench and holding a microphone. Israel needs to be a state where a moderate and enlightened person who was also a patriot and a good Jew could find his place. We needed to be good Israelis without resorting to nationalism or ultra-Orthodoxy or socialism or cults, and without trading in our Israeliness to become citizens of the entire world.

The message caught on, and polls showed that Shinui was gathering momentum. The cynics that claimed I knew nothing about politics were wrong: in a world gone mad, people knew to appreciate a party whose head maintained his principles and knew how to iterate them as well.

Barak announced his resignation in December, and in the special elections that were held (for prime minister, not the Knesset), Ariel Sharon was the victor. I was pleased: Sharon was my friend, and I believed his vast experience and his peace of mind even at times of crisis would prevent him from making the same mistakes made by his two younger predecessors.

Right after the elections he invited me to a private chat, and for the next hour and a quarter he pleaded with me to join his government on the grounds that this was a state of national emergency. I refused. "I will support you from the opposition on any security measure you want to adopt," I told him, "but I will not join a government with the ultra-Orthodox. It is inconceivable that at a time when thousands of Israelis have been called up for additional active service, I should sit in a government with people who are not willing to send their children to the IDF." Sharon was disappointed but sympathetic. Even without us, he went on to form the largest government in the history of the nation, keeping the Knesset carpenters busy widening the old conference table that could seat only forty ministers and deputy ministers around it.

On one matter, there was utter agreement between us: if we were not going to be sitting together in the government, we should revive our famous dinners at his farm.

"What about that diet of ours?" I groaned one time as his young daughter-in-law, Inbal, piled my plate high with food for the fourth time. Sharon sounded that little snuffle of his that served as a chuckle. "My most successful diet," he told me, "I did just before the Yom Kippur War. All I ate was lettuce. Then the phone call came telling me that the Egyptians had invaded the Sinai. I said, 'Give me half an hour,' and I went to the fridge, ate everything in it, and went off to war."

That December I turned seventy.

On the eve of my birthday we went to dinner with the Kishons, two couples enjoying an ancient friendship (Ephraim and I, forty-eight years; the wives, more than forty). Two days later, the family threw me a party with seventy-five guests, and Ephraim gave one of the funniest speeches I ever heard. "Tommy and I," he said, "have a relationship of love and jealousy. He loves me and I am jealous that he has someone to love."

Shula also made a speech. Petite, fragile, painfully shy Shula, who ran away from public appearances her whole life, stood in front of the crowd like someone who had prepared for that moment her entire life. I quote here from her speech not because it says nice things about me (though it certainly does that), but because it says something far more beautiful about the person saying them.

> *Bad people say about Tommy that he is fat, but that is an optical illusion. He simply needs more space than most beings in order to contain so many emotions, so much love: for his wife, his children, friends, the Jewish people, the water level of the Sea of Galilee, Herz sausages; for the poems of François Villon and songs by Rita; for Mozart, Beethoven and Ben Gurion; for Hungarian dishes and the Jewish State.*
>
> *In our family, you have always been and always will be the Lapid guide. You are the captain, you are the anchor, you are the helm and you are the compass. You are the wind in the sails and the star chart. Whether the sea is calm or stormy, whether it is as expected or surprising, you are the oarsman. The sea is large, dangerous, tempting, nourishing, entertaining, comforting— and so are you. In my life of nearly forty-three years with you, there has never been a dull day. Unfortunately.*

I cried, of course I cried as always, and I laughed and hugged everyone and thought that in the end, life is love: the people you love and the people who love you.

During the sing-along that followed, I stood to the side and watched my family. On one side of the room stood Meirav leaning against her husband, Danny, a true man of culture, genteel and intelligent, who brings her much happiness, and their two daughters, three-year-old Noga, whose playground was the world, and six-month-old Netta, a chubby-cheeked redhead fast asleep in her carrycot. Of all my grandchildren, she resembles me the most, but unlike her grandfather she is actually pretty.

On the other side of the room were Yair and Lihie. My son the rebel had become over the years no less famous than his father. His latest detective novel, *The Sixth Riddle*, was at the top of the bestseller list that week, which is exactly where Lihie's first book, *Secrets I Kept Inside*, had been until very recently. I tried for a moment to think if I had ever met another couple with concurrent bestselling books, and I could think of only one: Shula and me.

And still, I looked at Yair and my heart cinched. This young man, treated by all the world as a golden boy to whom everything comes easily, copes in secret with a tragedy that will remain with him his entire life. His two sons, Yoav and Lior, are talented and successful, but his five-year-old daughter, Yael, is autistic. She does not speak, she is detached from the world, and she relates only to a small number of instructions. She is delicate, very beautiful and lively, a sort of little fairy that will need to be looked after and protected her entire life. Taking care of Yael so intensively, with the help of an army of caregivers, saps most of Lihie and Yair's strength, and most of their money as well. And yet, Yair never complains. "Are you happy?" I asked him not long ago. He seemed surprised to be asked that question. "Sure," he said. "Very."

The ability to be happy, I understood not for the first time, is not at all connected to the circumstances of our lives. I knew people who had gone through things far less horrible than the Holocaust, or losing their daughter in a car accident, and they were far less happy than me. In the world there are thousands of books that deal with the "secret to happiness," but most of them bring happiness only to their publishers. Happiness, in my opinion, is a character trait. Just as there are people who know how to paint, and there are people with a musical ear, there are people adept at happiness.

I was happy that day, and I missed Michal; a scrim of sadness lay over me because she was not there. Had she been alive she would have enjoyed the party, and everyone would surely have fluttered around her like butterflies to a flower, but there is no connection between the two. The opposite of happiness is not sadness, it is loneliness, and I was not alone.

While I was happy in my private life, the state (and I hope I do not sound like Louis XIV when I say that the state was a private matter for me) filled me with grief and desperation, and not because anything had changed but precisely because it had not.

That Passover we took a holiday in the north of the country with the Olmerts and another couple. We spent our days pleasantly enjoying the ancient vistas and the mountain air as clear as wine that served as an echo to our conversations, but in the background the Second Intifada loomed like a threatening black shadow. "So what is the solution?" we asked ourselves again and again, and each time we understood that we—perhaps the most experienced people in Israel—had none.

When I returned, an email from an old acquaintance from Miami awaited me. She suggested that we come and stay with her for a few weeks to air out "from that war of yours." Her letter caused me no small amount of distress; it reminded me of the letters that American Jews sent to Europe before World War Two, and the telephone call from Shula's parents suggesting that we "send the children so at least they'll survive" before the Six Day War.

After all, was there a year in which such a statement was not fitting? The Arab riots of 1929? The War of Independence, 1948? 1956? 1987? 2001? 2010? 2015? Why is it decreed that we will keep returning to Jenin, attacking Gaza, lamenting the death of friends killed in this or that terror attack? Why must we continually apologize for the deaths of innocent people when the IDF is dealing with operational activity it was compelled to carry out?

Political correctness prevents us from discussing the fact that our biggest problem is Islam. Were we simply talking about the national aspirations of the Palestinian people, we would have long ago reached a peace accord. God and Allah know that we offered them more than they once even dared to dream could be theirs. But for every secular Palestinian interested in finding a solution, two zealots who want us dead are born. Radical Islam has waged a war of destruction against everything that the Western world represents: freedom, democracy, equality, science, technology, feminism, progress.

Of the fifty-seven Islamic nations in the world today, not one is a democracy. They are all mired in dictatorships—some more enlightened, some less—rife with corruption and poverty and hatred and, primarily, envy. Twice before, Islam has tried to conquer Europe, once when it conquered Spain and once when it reached the gates of Vienna, and each time it failed.

In the past 700 years, Professor Michael Har-Segor once bravely wrote, Islam has not made a single meaningful contribution to human culture, to philosophy, to science, to medicine—no discovery from which a civilization worthy of being called such is created. And even though hundreds of millions of Muslims around the world (and in Israel) live peacefully as regular citizens, the people who claim to represent them are leading their innocent believers in the name of holy war toward a catastrophe the likes of which perhaps the world has never before seen.

Islam itself is not the scourge of humanity, but fanatical, militant Islam is, an Islam that only finds relief for its frustrations in the complete destruction of Western civilization, which reminds it of its failure. In contrast to all the prim denials, we are witnessing today a battle of religions, a battle of cultures, and a battle between two civilizations.

"If that is the situation," Olmert said on a balcony during the holiday with wonderful Galilean red wine in front of us, "then surely you must join the government and help this war."

"You're wrong," I told him, "since I am fighting to ensure that our side will remain part of the enlightened Western world, and that cannot be done with the ultra-Orthodox parties. Pretty soon the elections will take place, we'll win ten seats and the political map will change."

"You won't get ten seats," Ehud said.

"You're starting up with me again?" I said. "We're sure to."

We were both wrong.

CHAPTER 53

On the day that Shula's mother, Helen, died, her father asked her to prepare a few pots of food at home so there would be something to give to the mourners paying condolence calls. While she was standing and cooking, a small bird flew in the window and raced about the kitchen. Shula tried to shoo it out but the bird, instead of escaping, sat on the refrigerator and watched her. "Actually," Shula said to herself, "why do I care?" and she continued with her cooking. A few minutes later, the bird flew on its way.

Half an hour later, Shula phoned her father to ask how he was doing. "The strangest thing happened," she told him. "A bird sat on my refrigerator watching me with an expression like Mother's."

"What did it look like?" my father-in-law asked.

"Small and black," she said, "with a bluish beak."

"And a yellow breast?" he asked.

"Yes," Shula said, astonished. "How did you know?"

"Because it's sitting on my refrigerator right now."

Religious people believe in providence, not coincidence. Secular people know that sometimes the strangest things happen, but that God has no connection to them. And yet, if I were a religious man, I would certainly have asked myself in the winter of 2002 why all the pieces of the puzzle had fallen into place almost on their own, and how it was that all the coincidences and events worked to the advantage of the most secular party in the country.

The decision to hold elections caught the public by complete surprise, even though the fifteenth Knesset had been nothing to be proud of in terms of Israeli democracy: nineteen MKs had resigned (a new record); two prime ministers came and went; parties fell apart and realigned; two economic reforms were trumpeted then quietly shelved.

From the start of my career in politics, I loved campaigning.

A political campaign is an unsettling event, fraught and hectic, that requires the making of dozens of quick decisions every day under ever-changing circumstances. These are the moments that "separate the men from the boys."

It is a roller coaster on which everyone is enslaved to the polls that hit the desk every morning. If a slight decrease in popularity is registered, people begin shouting about making changes to the strategy or rethinking the ads or dumping the copywriter and, if possible, bringing in a new party leader. If the polls are good, people become cautious and anxious, walking around on tiptoe and saying to everyone they meet, "What's important now is not to make mistakes" (which is, of course, the biggest mistake a campaign manager can make). You have to learn how to ignore both the optimism and the doomsday prophecies to remain focused on the target, while at the same time exhibiting flexibility when the need arises.

What's more, you need to be speedy. As Yashi Eilat, one of our two publicists explained, "Political propaganda has to be up to date. Unlike an ad for Coca-Cola, for example, which can be 'the national refresher' half a year ago and a half year from now as well, our campaign must be capable of reacting to events of the day, even the hour."

And so it was that twenty-four hours after the elections were announced, when other parties were trying to figure out what their campaigns would look like and where their budgets would come from, we had already hung billboards throughout the country and flooded the print media with our slogan. By the time our competition recovered, they discovered we had already bought up all the best billboard real estate.

In fact, we were pretty much alone in the field for the first two weeks of the campaign, and it was then that we made our huge leap in the polls, from six to eight and then eleven seats.

The speed of our reaction stemmed from the fact that long before Obama we were one of the first parties in the world to make use of the Internet. A year earlier, when Yashi's partner, Alex Biletzky, wanted to talk me into making our party Internet-efficient, he spoke slowly and clearly, the way you would to some museum specimen who still writes with a quill pen. He was surprised to discover, however, that the white-haired head of the party was one of the first people in Israel to be connected to the Internet and was proficient and efficient at using it long before Alex himself.

What started out looking like some flash in the dark by a small and pretentious party began to impress people as a realistic possibility. In a major interview they conducted with me, *Newsweek* magazine proclaimed that Shinui might garner enough votes "to make Lapid the kingmaker of Israeli politics." I sent that article to everyone who knew me and a few more who did not. "We're not a boutique party anymore," I emphasized over and over. "We're a large party that wants to govern, and that's how we have to behave."

Several days later we held our focus groups. A number of slightly bewildered citizens sat around long conference tables and were asked dozens of questions about their lives and their preferences. I stood behind a pane of glass watching my voters—or at least the people I was hoping would become my voters. "Are you rich or poor?" the interviewer asked as she scribbled on her clipboard. "I'm neither," said one man. "I'm middle class." The man sitting across from him raised his head and concurred, a note of surprise in his voice as if he were thinking this thought for the very first time. "Yeah, that's right," he said, "I'm middle class, too."

That evening we gathered in the living room of my home. After a long discussion, we decided to run the campaign on three principles: the struggle against the ultra-Orthodox; the war on corruption; and the status of the middle class. I told them that the Israeli bourgeois was sick of being the only ones paying taxes, the only ones doing army reserve duty, the only ones respecting the law, the only ones carrying the burden of the nation on their shoulders while others take advantage of their silence to line their coffers. In parting, I reminded the team of something said by Emmanuel Joseph Sieyès at the height of the French Revolution: "What is the Third Estate? Everything. What has it been hitherto in the political order? Nothing. What does it desire? To be something." The response was bleary-eyed stares, probably because of the late hour.

The elections were held two weeks later. This time, I did not go to the television station. Instead, I sat at home, surrounded by friends and family, and I watched—for the second time in my life—as my name rose and rose until we hit the number fifteen. Fifteen seats! Everyone continued laughing and shouting until Shula noticed that a cloud had descended on my face.

"What is it, Tommy?" she asked.

People fell silent and looked apprehensively at me.

"Suddenly I feel the burden of responsibility," I told them. "It's not a game any more, and it's not my pension fund, either. With fifteen seats I can change the country."

Meirav said, "Change it tomorrow. Tonight we're celebrating."

We went to Sokolov House for the victory party, the most joyous I ever attended.

"This is the happiest day of my life!" I shouted to Poraz.

"Tommy," he said, "you told me the same thing after the last elections."

"That's right," I said. "And it was true, until today."

I suddenly noticed a small man, someone unfamiliar to me, was standing at my side. He threw himself on Yair and began kissing and hugging him. Yair was taken aback.

"Remind me who this guy is," I said to Poraz.

"That's Yigael Yasinov. He's number fifteen on our list. He just found out he's got a seat in the Knesset."

CHAPTER 54

Shortly after the elections, Meirav gave me a gift, a statue of the three wise monkeys: see no evil, hear no evil, speak no evil. That statue was the only thing I took with me to my new office after being appointed minister of justice, and I placed it on my desk. I caught sight of it every time I looked up, and every time I saw it I remembered that this was exactly what must not happen to the system of justice over which I was presiding. It could not turn its gaze away, it could not shut its ears, it had to be the mouthpiece of those who have no voice.

No, I had not turned into a bleeding-heart socialist or a social revolutionary. I was the same fat and satisfied bourgeois I had always been, but what I had said to my family on the night of the elections stayed with me; it was no longer a game. As deputy prime minister and a member of the security council, I felt a huge responsibility for the fate of millions of people and I was determined not to let them down.

I felt at the time—and things have not changed—that we are the citizens of two countries. One is modern Israel—successful, strong, a nation that has gone in sixty years from orange-grower to hi-tech superpower. A nation of the good life, with trips abroad and two cars per family and a cell phone for each child.

But there is another Israel, one under siege, subject to terror, disintegrating from within, threatened from without, impatient, intolerant, a nation of unemployment, and poverty (officially, twenty percent of the population). A country that instead of offering every Jew a safe haven had become a place unsafe for a Jew.

It was not a matter of looking at the half-empty or half-full glass, nor was it optimism or pessimism; rather, it was both at once, deeply embedded in all of our souls. We identify with both of these, a schizophrenic situation that makes life difficult since you never know whether you are happy or miserable, safe or frightened, desperate or hopeful.

This phenomenon of split personalities explains a lot with regard to our unsettled private and public lives. It explains the sharp mood swings from elation to deep depression, the exaggerated self-confidence and the extreme paranoia, the national pride mixed with thoughts of leaving the country, the altruism and the petty selfishness. We may have only one identity card, but each of us wobbles between our two identities.

The balance between my own two identities had suddenly shifted. My famous "this and that," which enabled me to be the loudest and quickest mouth in the country while at the same time a grounded intellectual with an orderly worldview, was no longer sustainable. I was obliged to choose the latter, to become more cautious. To hold back.

It did not always work. My natural tendency to make enemies because I could not hold my tongue still took hold of me on occasion. During one very long evening of negotiations leading to a government coalition, I went to Jerusalem's famous Sima's restaurant for a bite to eat with my aides. At one of the tables sat MK Yuval Steinitz—later, a finance minister—dining alone.

"Why don't you join me?" he offered magnanimously.

"Yuval," I said, "just because you're boring yourself doesn't mean that you need to bore us as well."

Everyone burst out laughing, but I could see that Steinitz's laughter was slightly artificial.

Coalition negotiations are a dance of liars. They meet in the middle of the night, lie to one another, phone their party cronies from the hallway and tell them half-truths, then give interviews to the press and lie to them as well.

And so it goes and goes and goes, in this case, for an entire month during which everyone leaked fabrications, made pledges with nothing to support them, slandered each other publicly then held hands in private, embodying the famous principle set down by British politician Alan Clark: "There are no true friends in politics. We are all sharks circling, and waiting, for traces of blood to appear in the water."

In the end, the government that was formed was exactly the government that any ten-year-old child knew would be formed just ten minutes after the elections, a center-right coalition of sixty-six seats that put Shinui, the second largest party, in a position of real power.

I still ask myself what would happen if we'd gotten rid of that liars' dance and simply told the truth to the public on the very first day, without continuing to hope that we could earn one or two more points in the game. I do not know the answer because it has never been tried.

Actually, the aspect of negotiations where the biggest disagreements usually exist was the simplest to solve. Sharon's liaison officer put a blank page in front of me. "Which ministries do you want?" he asked.

I wrote: "Deputy prime minister, Justice, Interior, Science, Infrastructure, Environment." He looked at the list and said, "Okay."

"Okay what?" I asked.

"Okay. They're yours," he said, and left the room. Only later did I hear that Sharon tried to send him to me again for a second round, but he threatened to resign if the agreement he made with me was not honored.

On 27 February 2003, I was sworn in as justice minister and deputy prime minister. I was probably the only one there to recall that seventy years earlier to the day, the Reichstag in Berlin had been burned by the Nazis. We tend to forget this but the Nazis came to power legally. I asked myself what would have happened had there been a resolute and powerful minister of justice in Germany during the 1930s who had prevented them from taking part in the elections.

CHAPTER 55

The late Willy Brandt, chancellor of Germany in the 1970s, was active in the anti-Nazi underground during World War Two and was one of the people most wanted by the Gestapo. Once, we were having coffee together and I asked him how he managed to escape their clutches.

"When the noose began to close around my neck," he said with a grin, "I escaped to Norway. But then the Nazis took control of Norway and the Gestapo began to search for me again. I knew I would be caught within days, and it was then that I had an original idea: I wore the uniform of a Norwegian soldier and infiltrated a German POW camp. It was the only place in all of Europe they would never think to look for me. And that was how I survived."

I recalled that story many years later as I sat in my new executive chair in my new executive office and looked out of the bulletproof window of my bureau. (The justice minister's bureau is the only government ministry located in predominantly Arab East Jerusalem, which is why my windows were bulletproof and why I was "lucky" enough to be given a special armored Volvo that was so heavy—two tons—it needed to be repaired every other day and was barely capable of making the climb from Tel Aviv to Jerusalem.) For the first time in my life I understood the meaning of the expression "a prisoner of success."

My main problem was that we had succeeded in fulfilling ninety percent of our goal on the day the government came into being. Everyone had thought that my showy promise—a government without the ultra-Orthodox—was merely election sloganeering, devoid of content. The ultra-Orthodox had been members of every Israeli government from the very first, and no one believed it was possible to keep them out. The significance was dramatic: social, economic, moral, but it was also—in more than one sense—the beginning of the end of the Shinui party. Parties that fulfill their missions are doomed to extinction. If we had already fulfilled our main role on our first day as part of the government, then where did we have to go?

In the meantime, my relationship with Ariel Sharon deepened. He and I had always shared a covenant of the fat. It was the last time in my life I looked at someone and saw something there—maybe just a hint—of the father that was taken from me. Had it not been so pathetic I would probably have mocked myself. Here I was, a seventy-three-year-old grandfather some thirty years older than the father who left our bedroom and never returned, and yet there was still something, some slumbering but powerful nucleus inside me hoping he would appear on my doorstep.

Sharon, who had the sharpest sensors I ever saw on a person, noticed this tendency of mine and took me in at once. We spent many long hours together eating and gossiping, swapping jokes and anecdotes, and talking deeply and with great concern about the fate and future of the nation. He was as fat and clever and funny and warm as my father, but the problem was—he was not my father.

Sharon, like me, was the last of his kind. I was the last of those who remembered the Holocaust firsthand and he was the last of the era of legendary giants who founded Israel and whose identification with the country was so complete that they could not differentiate between it and themselves. He assumed, almost automatically, that what was good for him was good for the nation as well. There was something kingly about the way he would sit at the large dining table under a thatched roof at the farm, a whole lamb stuffed with rice in front of him, surrounded by children and grandchildren and aides and fans and senior officials in suits and ties rubbing elbows with farmers with gnarled hands and spotted coveralls from the surrounding communities.

In all the years I knew him I never once saw him shout; his famed viciousness came out in venomous comments that were occasionally astonishingly funny. Furthermore, he was polite to such an extreme that it almost seemed like parody. Each time a woman entered his office he would immediately rise to his feet—a complicated task involving shoving back the chair, placing his hands on his desk, pushing his heavy rear up into the air and then straightening slowly to a standing position (and breathing heavily). By the time this whole act could take place, the poor woman was usually red-faced from embarrassment for having caused him to make so much effort on her behalf.

On the other hand, Sharon was also an unbridled politician who never shied away from petty backroom politics. Because he identified so closely with the nation, he related to the people around him as chess pieces he could always sacrifice for the greater good. That included even his son, Omri, to whom he sent the investigators looking into a scandal involving fictitious non-profit organizations. If he was willing to send his own son to the firing line, should I have foreseen that in spite of our friendship he would drop me like a dirty rag the moment it suited him to do so?

I am not angry with him. Most likely, the fact that he was so cynical and unrestrained is the reason that he became prime minister, while I was only his deputy.

Months passed, and I grew accustomed to being a government minister, to the security detail that was always around, to the (unreliable) official car, to the ceremonious way people suddenly addressed me. I warned myself against the tendency of people in power to distance themselves from life. A screen of honors and aides and spokesmen cuts you off from the world and you try incessantly to see beyond them, to recall how normal people act.

In other, more serious, matters, it takes time before you can understand the scope of your job.

I was appointed to the security cabinet, which numbers only five and whose job it is to give consent to non-standard IDF activities. In

October 2003, immediately following the attack on the No. 2 bus in Jerusalem, Sharon convened the security cabinet and told us that the IDF had prepared a "bank of targets" enabling swift response to every act of terror aimed at Israel. Foreign Minister Silvan Shalom said that he was unwilling to give his automatic consent with regard to operations he knew nothing about. "It doesn't make sense," he said, "that IDF officers and clerks will know more about these operations than a government minister." I agreed with him and Sharon nodded, so I assumed he had affirmed the decision.

Several days later, Sharon's military attaché, Brigadier General Yoav Gallant, phoned me. "We're about to attack an Islamic Jihad base inside Syria," he said. It was clear to me that this was some operation that had been approved a long time earlier so I said, "Okay," and put down the receiver.

Two days after the operation I read in *Yediot Ahronot* that a vote had been taken among members of the security cabinet by phone and that I had been in favor. "I wasn't voting," I told Gallant later. "I was just telling you I was affirming the report."

"But you said, 'Okay,'" he said defensively.

I did not argue with him because he was, in effect, right. For a person who was a regular citizen for more than seventy years, I assumed, instinctively, that there was some distant, higher power that was the only one permitted to approve secret missions behind enemy lines. I had to err once in order to find out that the higher power was essentially me.

In December 2003, I gave a somber speech at the Herlizya Conference. I said that time was working against us; that the Iranians would soon have a nuclear bomb; that the Palestinians were winning the war of wombs; that we had lost Europe a long time earlier because we had no response to photographs of Palestinian mothers carrying their injured children; that the power base of American Jews was waning; and that the settlements were a price we could no longer afford to pay.

"Although Israel is a model democracy," I said, "it is in fact run by a small minority of leaders from the territories in Judea and Samaria, who in turn represent a small minority within the settler movement. Their solution to the demographic problem is to bring 1 million Jewish immigrants to Israel but no one knows from where. In their heart of hearts they dream that the Palestinian population will be transferred to the other side of the Jordan River, a solution that is not only barbaric but also completely impossible. And, when all other arguments have been put to rest, they put their faith in God. With regard to anything concerning the existence of the State of Israel now and in the future, I would not recommend relying on God."

The settlers were furious, of course, while members of the right wing of my party scratched their heads and wondered what had become of me. In fact, nothing at all had changed in me—it was the country that had changed. During my long talks with Sharon, we came back again and again to the fact that there was no way of continuing with the status quo. Negotiations were stuck, Israeli society was stuck, the world was stuck watching us as if they were watching a horror flick in which rivers of blood paint the screen red every few scenes.

The disengagement—Israel's withdrawal from the Gaza Strip—got its start in those talks. It was Sharon who came up with the idea and I who made it possible. In the not-too-distant future, the disengagement would cost me my political career.

CHAPTER 56

"When *I* use a word," Humpty Dumpty said in a rather a scornful tone, "it means just what I choose it to mean—neither more nor less."

We tend to believe that words are just words and that they are always less important than deeds, but that is not true. Words are everything; without them there is nothing. The Bible is just words, the Magna Carta is just words, and so are Marx's *Das Kapital*, Churchill's speeches and Ben Gurion's declaration of independence for the State of Israel. Words have changed the world more than all the bombs and guns and fighter planes combined.

Now if I may allow myself to add my name as a footnote to this honorable list, a single sentence of mine prevented the destruction of thousands of homes in the Gaza Strip and headed off a human tragedy that would have stained the nation forever.

Conventional wisdom has it that this was some heart-wrenching cry on my part at the very moment I could take it no longer. But that is not the truth. I had planned it out, like Humpty Dumpty, and I even knew in advance what the reactions would be.

May 2004 was a tense month. Early in the month, Sharon brought his disengagement plan to a vote among Likud party members and, contrary to all predictions, garnered only forty percent of the vote. Sharon was furious—particularly with his aides, who had been certain he would win—and told me he had no intention of capitulating. He took the original plan, made a few small changes, and announced it would be brought to the government for a vote as the New Disengagement Plan. This was a typical Sharon ploy: he knew it was fraudulent, we all knew it was fraudulent, but he did not care. He had a goal, and the opinions of others seemed to him like a minor obstacle that needed moving by a bulldozer.

Several days later, on 18 May, other bulldozers began to move. In the framework of Operation Rainbow, the IDF entered the city of Rafah, at the southern end of the Gaza Strip, with terrifying armored D9 bulldozers, and began destroying homes for the purpose of widening the Philadelphi Route, the buffer zone between Gaza and Egypt controlled by Israel. That evening I arrived home early, turned on the television and watched as an old blind woman named Hadija searched on her hands and knees through the ruins of her home for her medications.

I thought about Grandma Hermina. I was not thinking about the IDF and about how I always claimed one could never compare anything to the Holocaust. I was merely thinking about what I would feel if this woman were my grandmother. The business with the incursion into Syria came back to haunt me in a new, expanded version: why was it that I, deputy prime minister of Israel, knew nothing about this massive invasion into Rafah? After all, I was responsible for what was happening in this country; there was no shirking it—I shared ministerial responsibility for the fact that this old woman was picking through the rubble of her house.

Agitated, I went to meet friends at the Basel café. Ehud Olmert was there, and Dan Margalit. While bodyguards stood on the pavement outside, we sat drinking cappuccinos with foamed milk, and I told them what I had seen on television. They shook their heads and said, "Ugly," and, "Really terrible," and this, for some reason, irritated me even more. "Terrible things happen," I said, "when bad people do bad things and good people don't speak up. The silence of good people is a significant part of the tragedy. Whoever remains silent is responsible for what happens, almost as if he were the perpetrator." They said nothing, and stared at me like you look at a person who has stated the obvious. My irritation was turning to fury.

The next morning at a governmental meeting I took the floor. "The images of an old woman on all fours looking for her medications reminded me of my grandmother," I said, then leaned back, waiting for the storm of reactions that was not long in coming.

"Those are very strong words that should not have been said," Sharon fumed. "They are practically incitement."

Even Defence Minister Shaul Mofaz, a man normally unflappable, was angry. "That is a very strong statement to make about the security forces of the IDF," he said, "and I ask that you retract them at once." I shook my head.

Then Danny Naveh, the minister of health, joined the fray: "My grandparents and their five children were kicked out of their home in Hungary just like your family," he said, "and they were sent to Birkenau. Any analogy to that time period is completely inappropriate."

Unlike them, however, I had had twelve hours to prepare for the uproar. "I wasn't comparing Israel to Germany or the Nazis," I insisted. "What I did say was that there is no excuse for bringing suffering to a defenseless old woman."

As expected, everyone kept shouting and reprimanding me for several long minutes—this was the only part of the meeting covered by the media—but then, everyone calmed down and as I had hoped there ensued a serious discussion about the operation in Rafah and its humanitarian significance. For the first time, it became clear to all of us government ministers—to our horror—that the IDF had planned to destroy some 3,000 homes in Rafah without us knowing about it. Slowly but surely, the ship changed course, and by the end of the meeting it was decided to stop the bulldozing of homes. Not only the Palestinians, but the State of Israel as well, were spared the sight of hundreds of old women on all fours searching through rubble, broadcast on television screens around the world.

So, what had happened to me? Had I become some bleeding-heart leftist? Of course not. To my dying day I was an Israeli patriot who saw everything through the narrow prism of Jewish destiny. And yet precisely because of that I became more and more anxious about the nature and character of this country. People say things like "We've got to kick their asses" but they take no interest in how many children will die or how many old blind women will lose their homes. So we win a campaign here and there but we lose the war.

The State of Israel was not founded for us to adopt the moral standards of fanatical Islam. I am not interested in being an Arab or thinking like an Arab or taking on the cruelty of some Arabs. In the long run, we will only be able to survive the struggle against the millions of Muslims surrounding us if we strive to be an enlightened Western democracy, humanistic and free. In the short run, we must at times give up our need for retaliation. It is painful, but essential.

Several days later, I managed to put that same idea down on paper far more eloquently, in the form of a letter to my oldest grandchild, Yoav, who was going on the March of the Living and would visit Auschwitz. We were very close by then, and we tried to run away—he, from high school, me from the government—to meet for lunch as often as we could.

My Dear Grandson Yoav,

This is a trip you will never forget. When you reach the train tracks of the Birkenau camp, imagine for a moment your great-grandmother arriving there in a cattle car packed with seventy Jews who have been travelling for two or three days without food or water and who, upon finally arriving, at last breathe in deeply the fresh air and do not know that the smoke billowing from the nearby chimneys is all that remains of their relatives who arrived earlier.

The State of Israel is meant to be the response to the Holocaust, but, paradoxically, it is a nation in which the Jews are more threatened than anywhere else in the world. Our job is to ensure that Israel continues to exist and that Jews can live here in peace and security. It will take a number of years until we reach that point, but the effort is worthwhile, as are the sacrifices.

And yet, we must uphold the moral imperative handed down to us from Hillel the Elder in Hebrew and Kant in German, in almost identical words: "Do unto others as you would have them do unto you." This I implore you to remember: evil people could not have carried out the Holocaust were it not for good people who kept silent. The simple Poles you will meet are the descendants of citizens who knew and kept quiet. When you see the tranquil villages surrounding Auschwitz, know that they were like that—tranquil—even when millions of people were being slaughtered inside the camp.

With great love,
Grandpa Tommy

While Yoav was off to see the train tracks on which my grandmother had traveled, I flew off to Washington to give a speech at the annual AIPAC conference. My purpose was to convince the audience—many of whom were traditionally affiliated with the right wing in Israeli—to support the disengagement. "There are countries with no differences of opinion," I told them, "but we are a nation proud of our differing opinions, as is your country. I believe that Sharon's disengagement plan is the right thing, and my party supports it."

To my surprise, a round of applause rose from the audience.

"The opposition supports it as well," I said. "In fact, the only party that doesn't is Sharon's own."

The audience laughed, and after my speech I sat down to dinner with my good friend, Tom Lantos, chairman of the Foreign Relations committee of the US House of Representatives. Many years earlier—when I was still called Tomislav Lampel and he was still called Tomislav Lantos—we were children together in the ghetto in Budapest, nightly escaping the clutches of the Nazis in order to find food. One of our partners in crime was a beautiful girl named Annette, who later became his wife. At the end of the war, each of us got on a boat that took us in a different direction. He became an important congressman from the state of California while I became Israel's minister of justice, but we always felt that our lives were a sort of revolving door; who knows what would have happened if he had sailed on my ship and I on his.

A year earlier, when I was appointed to my position, Lantos had requested and was granted the opportunity to be the official congressional representative to congratulate me on behalf of the American government. He came to Jerusalem and entered my office surrounded by journalists and aides. I rose to shake his hand, and to everyone's astonishment, Lantos got down on his knees and kissed my shoes, crying all the while. "Oy, Tommikeh, Tommikeh," he muttered in Hungarian. "Look where we've gotten."

After the meal we took a walk, quietly chatting in the frigid Washington air. The enormous Capitol building loomed above us, its white pillars radiantly lit, and once again I thought about the power of words. America, like Israel, is not merely a place but first and foremost an idea. It was founded thanks to the thoughts of brilliant people who knew how to formulate the words necessary not only for bringing about the birth of a nation but also to what end, what purpose.

Back in Israel, I found myself in a steamy, sweaty political imbroglio. Sharon had presented his "reworked" disengagement plan for a government vote and found himself facing a rebellion by some of his cabinet ministers. I sat near Bibi Netanyahu at that meeting and when I looked at him my heart cinched. The opponents to the plan expected him to lead them, but he had sincere doubts about what to do. Unlike many people, I believe Bibi is a decent young man whose interest is the good of the country, and he was not the only one at the time who was unsure whether the disengagement would help or harm the country.

In order to make matters easier for him, a ridiculous compromise bill was ultimately passed in which we would clear out of the Gaza Strip but the words "evacuation of settlements" would not appear—as if we were going to leave the area while the settlements remained intact, suspended in air. Sharon chuckled and so did I, but the proposition passed and Bibi voted for it.

Shortly thereafter, I noticed that Sharon's attitude toward me had changed. He continued to be pleasant and charming, but became rather distant.

Toward the end of November 2004, Sharon summoned me for a chat and announced that he was adding NIS 290 million as a special allocation for the United Torah Judaism party.

"You can't do that," I told him. "You know we'll quit the government."

"Tommy," Sharon said, "you'll cause the disengagement to fail."

This time, however, I had no intention of giving in to him.

"No, Arik," I said, "it's you who'll cause it to fail."

He was silent for a moment. "The fate of the nation is on your shoulders," he said.

Once again we fell silent. Yisrael Maimon, the government secretary, who was writing the protocol of the meeting, sat with his pen in the air. I decided to try another tactic. "This is the time to put together a government of the three elders," I said, referring to Sharon, Peres and Lapid.

Sharon smiled. "You know my party isn't ready for that."

I left his office knowing everything was over. I gathered the Shinui cabinet ministers and informed them that we would vote down the budget, a move that meant leaving the government. Victor Brailovsky, who had been appointed minister of science just two days earlier, raised his head and said, "Well, at least I'll go down in Israeli history as the only government minister never to have made a single mistake."

That was the only time I laughed the entire week.

The next day, we voted down the budget and on 1 December 2004, Sharon sent me a one-line letter: "This is to inform you that I have decided to remove you from your duties as minister of justice."

"The torch has gone out," said Rabbi Ovadia Yossef in his weekly speech, mocking me with a double entendre on my name. For a change, I actually agreed with him.

CHAPTER 57

Ephraim Kishon was dead.

"He was sitting with me in the living room in a good mood," Lisa, his young third wife, told me, "then I asked him something and he didn't answer, and when I looked at him I understood he was dead."

Even with humorists, death is a serious matter.

He was my best friend for more than fifty years. Fifty years of exchanging millions of words in Hebrew and Hungarian, fifty years of worrying about what would become of this country, fifty years of watching him pull from his top pocket the slip of paper with his latest brilliant idea, fifty years of him amusing me and enraging me. Without him I would not have had our first apartment or my first job at *Maariv,* and if he hadn't come with me to the Rabbinical Court that day, I might not have had my first and last wife, either.

On my seventieth birthday he said to me, "Tommikeh, it doesn't matter how you feel, it only matters how old you are."

He was eighty years old at the time of his death. I write "he was" and I cry—for him and for me and for our entire generation that arrived in Israel after the Holocaust, to this unknown land. I cry for the thin young man who memorized the Hebrew dictionary, yet it is impossible today to compile a dictionary without including expressions coined by that very same man. It is also impossible to talk about Israeli humor without beginning with him—in dozens of languages, millions of volumes, films, plays.

As with most great comedians, he was a sad man, because he had no illusions. And he was also a happy man, because he knew there was no one else like him. How many people can you say that about after their death? Or before it?

The year 2005 was not shaping up well.

Shortly before the new year, I cleared out my office. I took leave of my staff, who flooded me with pleasant words that touched me deeply, and I went back to being a member of the Knesset.

"How will you manage as a regular MK?" Avraham Poraz asked me.

"Don't worry," I told him. "In a few weeks, Peres will enter the government instead of us and I'll become head of the opposition."

"But Peres promised he wouldn't join the government."

"Sure. But that's Peres," I said.

Naturally, I was right. The Labour party groveled its way into the government by paying the ultra-Orthodox everything I refused to, and I became leader of the opposition. It was a strange opposition, quarrelsome and splintered, but one that did not want by any means to topple the government. Among my colleagues in Shinui there was at first a dispute whether we should vote against the budget that had been the catalyst for our departure from the coalition. I decided we would not, and I even obliged others to do the same. "I am not willing to be responsible for the failure of the disengagement," I told them. "Let's let Sharon get it through, then we'll have ample time to bring him down."

Several months earlier, at the height of the crisis, I sent a letter to Herr Andreas Ludwig, manager of the Hotel Margna in Switzerland, where we took our holidays. "My Dear Herr Ludwig," I wrote, "as you undoubtedly know, there is a serious governmental crisis in Israel at the moment and I cannot leave the country. Unfortunately, I must cancel our reservation." Now I could finally make that vacation up to Shula, and we traveled to the land of blue lakes and snowy mountains. When we arrived, it became apparent—of course!—that Herr Ludwig had no knowledge of the crisis I had written about or how it had ended. It was a good reminder that the things that seem most significant to us mean nothing to normal people living in a normal country where "significant" means that the hot cocoa was served too early and has cooled down.

Upon our return we found a nation divided, the streets restless and raging. The settler population was out protesting in record numbers: some 130,000 demonstrators participated in a "human link," 150,000 in a protest prayer service on the first day of the month of Shvat (which, I discovered for the first time, was in January), and 200,000 came to protest in Rabin Square. Most of these demonstrations were non-violent, but there were some pretty serious protest measures, like when members of the This is Our Land movement blocked roads and agitated for civil unrest, or when a number of prominent rabbis called upon their students to refuse orders when required to act.

Like everyone else, I looked around me in fear and grief. The settlers, whom I had once loved and admired, seemed to have lost their minds, and once again I was reminded that there is no chance for dialogue with God. However, beyond the torrent of emotions and experiences an important truth shone through: the State of Israel could not acquiesce. The prime minister had initiated the decision, the government had approved it, the Knesset legislated and the High Court of Appeals ruled in its favor. When a popular movement imbued with treasonous faith and incited by messianic rabbis challenged the authority of law, the state was obliged, like some genie awakening from a deep sleep, to extend its long arm—the military and the police—for the purpose of restoring law and order.

Similar scenes had unfolded years earlier in the southern United States, when local authorities, supported by inflamed mobs, protested against the integration of black children in white schools. Southerners claimed that the liberals in Washington—the White House, the Congress, the Supreme Court—were trying to force measures upon them that were contrary to their faith, their tradition, their way of life, their democratic right to prevent blacks from getting what they wanted. President Eisenhower sent in the military, which enforced the rule of law. Ever since, black children and white children study together.

When a nation is in dire straits it must flex its muscles. The enormous power amassed by the authorities enables it to act with restraint. In spite of the threats, the demonstrations and the protests, routine life in Israel was not disrupted. There was no coup d'état, no apocalypse, neither the messiah nor the end of days arrived. A properly functioning country was put to the test of a difficult reality, and succeeded. We are entitled to note with pleasure that in our hour of crisis, the nation functioned well. Democracy squared off against a determined, faith-inspired, agitated mob that was well organized and well funded, and the rule of law was victorious.

The disengagement began on Monday, 15 August 2005. Two evenings later Ariel Sharon asked me to meet with him in his office in Jerusalem.

It is well known that when a tornado hits, sending trees and houses and cars in its path in every direction, there is absolute silence in the eye of the storm. That is exactly how I felt during that meeting. While a tornado was passing over Gaza, bringing fierce winds and media from around the world to report on the struggle for survival being waged by the settlers against the army and the police, we sat for more than an hour chatting, mostly about David Ben Gurion and Moshe Dayan. Sharon asked his aide to fetch his autobiography so that he could show me a photograph in which Ben Gurion was turning to Arik as Meir Amit looked over their shoulders. "Look at Amit's eyes," Arik said, "look how jealous he is of me." He chuckled. And all the while, soldiers and policemen were forcing their way into settler homes in Gaza.

Sharon at that moment was both the media's most sought-after man, and the world's loneliest. He was physically isolated due to the fear for his life, politically isolated due to the split of opinions in his own party, personally isolated due to the plight of his son Omri, and isolated as a statesman who has carried out a decision that will be judged historically. He was in a good mood.

I thought that if I were in his place I would step down, quit, return to the farm, raise sheep and help my son. I would do it at that very moment, while I still could, at the height of my career, respected internationally, sought out by statesmen who once refused to have anything to do with me, popular with the public, sated with wars and generally satisfied with myself. Before Bibi Netanyahu could pluck my feathers, before causing a rift in the Likud party, before sinking into the putrid muck of party politics. What did he need it for? Just because "Sharon doesn't ever give in?" Why retreat in defeat when he could go out a winner?

Even today, when Sharon's demise is known, I ask myself why he carried on, why he did what was required of him in his situation. What kept him going? Inertia? Stubbornness? Fear of the moment he would become irrelevant? Fear of decline? A lust for power? A feeling of purpose, of mission?

I said all of this to Sharon. He merely listened and smiled. He knew I had not come to defend or blame him. My words contained no accusation or defiance, merely friendly advice between two people who had seen it all.

CHAPTER 58

When I was a boy, during that year and a half when Father was school-
ing me at home, he once read me a tale from a tattered volume of Hungarian stories, in which a simple man—a carpenter by profession—died
at a ripe old age. He had no relatives, and on the day of his death he was
forgotten, though not entirely. A few months after his death, his friends
sat in the neighborhood pub. One of them mentioned their dear drinking buddy who had passed away, and for a brief, flickering moment he
lived again in their memories. A year passed, perhaps two, and one night
an old song came on the radio, and an elderly woman suddenly recalled
a young carpenter who had pressed his lips to hers, bestowing her with
her very first kiss, and once again the man lived on for a moment or two
in her memories. A few more years went by, and one day a young lawyer was sitting in the office of his dead father, going through papers.
Among those papers he found a yellowing bill that the carpenter had
sent to the father for bookshelves he had built in the man's office. The
young lawyer understood that the bill was worthless, and he tossed it
from the window. The piece of paper landed on the pavement and rain
fell on it and wiped out the fading numbers one by one until the very
last memory of that carpenter had disappeared.

Deposed politicians are those letters fading slowly in the rain.

At first, you are still asked questions, people take an interest, want to know what happened; quickly, however, their interest wanes. Someone else gets the car, you go from having four aides to one, and in the morning you have to pursue the same radio programs that you refused to allow to interview you just a few months earlier. The more time passes, the more they discover that everything that seemed important once is no longer so.

Most politicians, during such dead periods as these, devote time to party matters. They visit branches they haven't visited in ages, attend bar mitzvah celebrations of their activists, invite board members to lunch. But I did none of these. I had gone pretty far in politics without making appearances at ethnic celebrations or weddings and I believed there was no need for it. After all, Poraz dealt with party matters, I told myself, and anyway, everyone knew that without me, Shinui would never have won a single seat.

Suddenly, I had time on my hands. I wrote, went back to playing chess, proposed legislation, and sat in sessions of the plenum for hours listening to other MKs. From time to time I took the podium and roundly pounded the government, but without real conviction. At the time, the coalition was so good at causing itself damage that the opposition had no choice but to applaud from the sidelines. A group of rebels from within the ranks of the Likud, led by Bibi, resigned from the government after the disengagement and tabled vote after vote. "Let them carry on like that," Poraz said. "It'll only bring us more votes."

Out of boredom I traveled to China as head of a large diplomatic mission. At one of the hundreds of stalls in the Shanghai market I bought a green Mao cap with a red star in the middle, which I wore the whole time. Everywhere I went, people giggled. They looked at me, looked at the cap, and giggled. I was the only person—among 1.2 billion Chinese—wearing a Mao cap. His jacket has also gone out of style (I went looking for one, but in all of China I did not find a single one my size), and throughout my long stay there I saw his picture only once, hanging in Tiananmen Square, with policemen patrolling beneath it. If Mao, one of the greatest and most reviled leaders of the twentieth century, had been wiped from consciousness so efficiently, then what was there to say about me?

———

In November 2005, Ariel Sharon stunned everyone when he announced he was setting up the Kadima party. Two days later, new elections were announced, the third in only six years. Polls published two days later had Kadima delivering us a crushing blow, but I refused to give up. I knew how to conduct a good campaign and I thought our voters would remain loyal under any circumstances.

On 16 December, I wrote a report for the Shinui newspaper in which I attacked Kadima and its head. I claimed that the party Sharon had established was not really a party but a one-man show behind which there was no defined ideology. Their campaign was one of total populism: Sharon hugging people, Sharon petting sheep, Sharon promoting an image of the strongman without anyone explaining what it meant. My report began with the words, "And what if, heaven forbid, something happened to Ariel Sharon?"

Two days later, Sharon collapsed for the first time.

The public was informed that he was in good condition, but the rumors were far worse. Of course I phoned him, and he sounded woozy but stable. He even repeated my old saw, "There's no hope for worry."

Two weeks later, Olmert was interviewed on Yair's talk show. "This Thursday," Yair told him, "Sharon will be going into surgery and you will become the de facto prime minister of Israel."

Olmert laughed him off. "Come on," he said. "Sharon is completely healthy. He'll lead us through the elections."

Later that same evening, in our living room, I told him it wasn't funny. Sharon was not a healthy man and the entire party was dependent upon him.

"If that happens," Olmert said, "you'll have to run in the elections against me."

This gloomy scenario became reality on 4 January, when Sharon had a second stroke and went into a coma from which he did not emerge, and Olmert was appointed chairman of Kadima. With all my love for Olmert, I figured he would be an easier opponent to run against.

I knew that before we could start another campaign we would have to choose a new list of candidates for the Knesset, but I did not attribute much importance to it. With Shinui, unlike other parties, there were no primaries, only a council numbering 169 members. I figured that as usual I would place my list of candidates before the council and it would be approved without difficulty. I knew that a group of malcontents— people who had hoped for jobs provided by Shinui ministers—had infiltrated the ranks of the council, but I did not believe they could do much harm. I should have recalled what the Jewish philosopher Moses Mendelssohn said about revenge, that it "seeks its object, and when it cannot find it, it eats its own flesh."

The internal elections were held in January 2006 at a Tel Aviv hotel. The night before the election I read an article online penned by a prominent journalist who claimed that the Shinui elections were of no interest because "Shinui always was and continues to be a party of one—Tommy Lapid." I nodded to myself and began to write the victory speech I would deliver to the council.

But twenty-four hours later, everything collapsed.

Opposing me for first place in the party was Itzik Gilad, one of the scriptwriters for an Israeli soap opera and a mediocre author who claimed, rather surreally, that he had predicted the hole in the ozone layer. I beat Gilad—who nobody had ever heard of beforehand, or afterward, for that matter—by a humiliating margin of only point five three of a percent. But that was only the start of the disaster, since Ron Levintal, the leader of the malcontents, was running against Avraham Poraz, and beat him. Poraz and I sequestered ourselves in a rented hotel room for a little while to talk.

"I'm not running for third place," he said. "They'll do it to me again."

"So what'll you do?"

"I'm going home."

"Then I am, too."

"You can't, Tommy. You've been elected to head the party."

"If you're out then I am, too."

I descended to the conference room in silence. The uproar was in full swing, as our party loyalists were swept away one after the other by the insurgents. Never before had a political party committed *hara-kiri* so swiftly, so efficiently, so destructively. But I did not stay around to absorb any more humiliations. My aides were waiting for me in the car; I bid farewell to Poraz with a big hug and went home, where Meirav and Yair were already waiting—they had heard the news on the radio and came straight over. I sat on the brown sofa in the living room trying to take in what had happened only moments earlier.

"What do you think I should do?" I asked them.

"Dad," Meirav said, "it's over."

"What is?"

"You and politics."

And so it was that in a single sentence uttered by my daughter, my political career was over.

I could, of course, have continued. The day after the elections, Levintal realized that his was a Pyrrhic victory and he began sending emissaries to persuade me not to step down. "In any event, the public has no idea who's number two in our party," they said, "and you'll continue to be our uncontested leader." I refused to listen or even answer them. I hadn't brought Shinui to where I had in order to carry a bunch of third-rate traitorous wannabe politicians on my coattails into the Knesset, people I did not believe were worthy or even intellectually capable of representing our voters. Furthermore, I was not willing to turn my back on Poraz. He was a friend, and I never betray my friends.

Several days later, I held a press conference and announced my retirement. To the cameras I said, "I have decided I do not have the moral right to head a list of people for election to the Knesset in whom I do not believe. Shinui, in its present formation, is not fit for public support."

I began to sit down, but then straightened up again to add another few words: "This chapter of my life is over and done with, a chapter of which I am proud."

CHAPTER 59

Weeks passed, then months.

This was a time during which I was meant to begin enjoying life a little, to wake up late in the morning, finally read Proust's *In Search of Lost Time*, trek the Kelt wadi, sign up for a course in Kabala, do Vipassana, mow the lawn, make cold cherry soup, visit Aunt Bluma, fix the missing slat in the blinds, water the plants on the roof, listen to all of Mahler's symphonies, play chess with my grandson, arrange photo albums, replace the postbox.

And what, of all of these, did I actually do? Nada. I soon realized that these things, which had been waiting for me for years, were not there to be done but to wait. Instead, during those long months, I sat and stared. I spent time with people who spoke to me but who fell silent because they realized I was not listening, just staring. I was staring into the void. I woke up early so as not to admit to the fact that no one would miss me and I would miss nothing by awakening late. I sat and stared because I knew my fate was sealed. From then until the end of my life I was doomed to inaction.

I stared at all sorts of things taking place around me: the elections that brought Olmert into the prime minister's office; the ultra-Orthodox, who celebrated my downfall and naturally referred to it as proof of "the hand of God" (odd, though, that they did not say that about my spectacular rise just a few years earlier); the crash and burn of the Shinui party, in which Levintal and his cronies managed to garner the astonishing total of 4,907 votes, which means that after subtracting the votes of the candidates and their families, the only other person who voted for them was Mrs. Zlibansky from Kfar Saba, who actually thought I was still heading the party.

I stared at my dear friend Amnon Dankner, who came by daily to persuade me to stop sitting and staring and to start living. I stared at Yair and at Meirav, fuzzily aware of the cautious, heartening tone they took when speaking with me. I stared at Shula, whose latest book—*The Maidens' Farm*—had just come out, and we celebrated as it became a bestseller. She stared back at me, trying to understand how she could possibly rescue her staring husband from the mud in which he found himself.

I could have volunteered somewhere, of course. The Civil Guard, if it still exists. The Police. Magen David. An environmental protection group. A geriatric ward. Maybe even the Fire Department.

Desperation, depression. My old friend Dosh used to say that old age was even worse than Auschwitz. Why? Because at Auschwitz you could go left or right, but with old age the only option was left.

Those long months of staring taught me something that beforehand I only knew in theory but which I now understood. Men who retire at sixty-five and women at sixty are ten and fifteen years younger than I was at retirement, which means that they have loads more energy, more vigor, more strength. What do they do with themselves? How long can they delude themselves that they are doing something that justifies their existence?

All right, go ahead and say it: You just figured that out *now*?! Well, not really, but only then did I understand the practical meaning of forced unemployment. I understood why the Pensioners' Party got seven seats in the Knesset elections. Hundreds of thousands of men and women with millions of years of experience are sitting at home staring.

And then, I stopped staring.

How did it happen? Am I now capable of writing a bestselling book, *How to End Depression*? I'm afraid not. Mark Twain's adage that "old age isn't so bad when you consider the alternative" finally sank in. I knew how to write and I knew how to think, and I knew I would have lots of time in the future to be dead. When a Hungarian is in trouble and wants to encourage himself he says, "There will once again be grapes with soft bread." Well, the world began rolling grapes in my direction again. First there was Dan Margalit, who asked me to be a regular participant on the *Council of Sages* program on Channel Ten, then Dankner asked me to write for *Maariv* on a regular basis, and Voice of Israel phoned to see if I would be interested in reviving my radio program.

I said yes to everything.

My old-new radio program was scheduled for Saturday mornings at eleven o'clock, probably so that the ultra-Orthodox would not know it existed. I opened the first show with these words:

> *In order to avoid misunderstandings, I have decided to clarify the following at the outset:*
>
> *I confess to being an elitist. I confess to being fat. I confess to being bourgeois. I confess to being old. I confess to being a celebrity. I confess to being an intellectual. I confess to being a friend of Olmert. And thank goodness for that.*
>
> *What else? I confess to being Ashkenazi, to loving goulash more than couscous, to preferring classical music to Mizrahi Middle Eastern tunes. I confess that I do not celebrate the Moroccan Mimouna holiday, do not visit the tombs of the just, do not fit into the Middle East, do not believe in God. And thank goodness for that.*
>
> *I confess to being a man. I confess to liking beautiful women. I confess to having kissed a young lady without first obtaining notarized authorization. I confess that fervent feminists repulse me, that pampered women irritate me, that complicated women scare me. And thank goodness for that.*
>
> *I confess that I can't stand bleeding-heart liberals. I confess that I do not like strikes. I confess that I am not crazy about the Palestinians. I confess that I do not believe that all men are created equal. I confess that postmodernism does not speak to me. I confess that rock 'n' roll drills holes in my head. I confess that I prefer a new, nicely paved road to a field of wood sorrel. I confess that in street fights I take the side of the cops. I confess that I have prejudices. And thank goodness for that.*

And that's not all. I confess to being an Israeli patriot. I confess to being a secular Jew. I confess to being me. And thank goodness for that.

So, what are you going to do about it?

In July 2006 I was appointed chairman of the *Yad Vashem* council.

To my mind, the task of *Yad Vashem*, the Holocaust Martyrs' and Heroes' Remembrance Authority, is not merely to preserve the memory of the Holocaust but also to prick the world's conscience. It must remind the world that the Holocaust took place and that the next one must be prevented from happening. When Ban Ki-moon, secretary general of the United Nations, visited, I spoke about the massacre taking place just then at Darfur, instead of delivering the usual speech on 6 million dead. "Three hundred thousand men, women and children have been murdered to date, two and a half million are homeless, tens of thousands of the ill lie dying for lack of medicine, tens of thousands of children are dying of malnutrition, tens of thousands of women have been raped, tens of thousands of homes have been razed. The Holocaust took place while the world kept silent, it is our special task to sound the alarm about what is happening in Sudan. It is your duty to do everything in your power to put an end to these atrocities taking place as we speak."

A seasoned diplomat, Ban Ki-moon kept a straight face, and I will never know what he thought about my speech. But I was quoted prominently in the most important newspapers in the world, and if what I said had even the slightest impact on raising consciousness of the tragic events in Darfur in an indifferent world then I feel I did my part. Israeli playwright Hanoch Levin once wrote that "all people are brothers once they're pushing up daisies," and I felt it was my obligation to speak on behalf of yesterday's casualties in order to prevent tomorrow's.

I enjoyed a different sort of pleasure when I discovered that in my capacity as chairman of the council I had a deputy. It turned out that several years earlier, *Yad Vashem* had bestowed upon my friend, the Nobel laureate Elie Wiesel, the title "honorary deputy." I wrote to him: "Elie, my dear friend, I always dreamt that Elie Wiesel would be my deputy, and now my dream has come true."

Life did not resume its normal path, because life has no one normal path. Still, I felt as though I had once again found my place in the world. On the eve of the Sukkoth holiday I went to the Beit Daniel synagogue to listen to Yair lecture on the Biblical story of Saul and Samuel. I enjoyed his talk immensely, but all the way home I could not stop thinking about an expression he had used, "living on borrowed time."

I hid it from my wife and children, and to some extent from myself, but my body was beginning to inform me that something was wrong.

CHAPTER 60

Exactly one year passed between the time that I was told I was ill and my death.

When I look back on the process, I realize, with no small amount of surprise, that essentially it's quite boring. Illness and death are an enormous personal drama for the patient and his family, but all tales of illness are in essence one and the same: an emotional roller coaster, the first prognosis, the second opinion, Prof. Fliss's look of joy at pronouncing the operation a success, Dr. Pfeffer's look of concentration as he helps me into the radiation machine, the broad and friendly face of the Japanese doctor who took care of me at Memorial Sloan-Kettering Cancer Center in New York, the vulnerable faces of Professors Ravid and Inbar, the only two to tell me the truth, the look of desperation on the face of Prof. Barabash, director of Tel Aviv's Ichilov Hospital, when he realized there was no way of persuading me to continue chemotherapy, the tearstained face of Ehud Olmert as he sat by my bed, the fake smile on Dankner's face (he had not been in a hospital since the death of his father), the face of Aliza Olmert, stunned and pale, and the beautiful faces, those most precious faces in the world to me, of Shula and Meirav and Yair at night, and the face of Michal, who suddenly surfaces in the shadows then fades.

After my death, it was written in the papers that I had died after "a long battle with cancer." But that is a groundless statement. In fact, I did not battle with cancer; it did battle with me. A score of years earlier, Kishon had said to me that the most important words a person could ever hear in his lifetime were those of his doctor holding his x-ray and saying, "I see something here that I don't like." For years I repeated that as a joke, then suddenly it happened to me. The first tumor, the size of a pea, appeared on my right ear. It was removed, but the doctor apprised me that it had metastasized to the lymph glands beneath the jaw. That evening, we had tickets to see *King Lear* at the Cameri Theater. I told Shula I felt fine and was not frightened but that I would not attend the performance. I had had enough Shakespearean tragedy for one day.

The second tumor was also removed in a seven-hour operation, after which I was told I was "clean" and healthy. Several months passed, and I returned to *Council of Sages* and, on occasion, to writing, but then I was told that there was metastasis in the lungs. That evening, I took Meirav and Yair to a pub in Tel Aviv, where Yair and I drank whisky and Meirav had a strawberry-colored cocktail. "I don't know how to tell you this without sounding melodramatic," I said, "but I only have a few months to live."

We sat there talking until quite late. We talked about our lives, our fears, what the family would be like without me. "I know you won't believe me," I told them, "but I have nothing to complain about. I was supposed to die at the age of thirteen, and here I am, seventy-three years of age, surrounded by family and friends, surrounded by love, overflowing with the feeling that I did quite a bit more than what fate had in store for me."

"My only qualm with you," Yair said, "is that you haven't prepared me for life without you in it."

"In fact, I have," I said. "You just don't know it yet."

That same evening I spoke with Shula, and I hope it won't upset my children and grandchildren to know that I made love to her as well, this woman I loved with all my heart for nearly fifty years.

I also decided not to hide my disease. To anyone who asked how I was, I answered, "Great. Except that I have cancer." I must admit I was highly amused with the variety of reactions I received to that response. In my opinion, there is something ridiculous about writing that someone "succumbed after a long illness." I had cancer, and I failed to understand why I should be embarrassed to say so.

In February 2008, I went to New York for a relatively new treatment not available in Israel. As you already know, it didn't exactly work, but at least it enables me to make a medical recommendation to anyone who has heard about new cancer treatments abroad: take the $20,000 it would cost you, give it to your children, and tell them to throw a lavish party a year after your death. That would be a much better way of using the money.

When the rumor of my impending death got out, God's faithful staged one last assault on me, led by "Rabbi" Dankner. Rabbi Aryeh Deri came, Rabbi Lau came, and everyone tried to persuade me to pray for absolution just once, or at least let Yair say the Kaddish prayer after my death. Despite what you may think it didn't anger me. I appreciated their efforts, and I believed their intentions were good. These are the junctures at which most people need religion, particularly birth and death, when they are confronted with the miracle of creation or with the drama inherent in the fact that we are all ephemeral souls.

I refused for two reasons. First, because I knew what a celebration the ultra-Orthodox would stage at my expense when they found out, and second—and more importantly—because I had always refused to allow primal fears to control my life and was not about to begin at my death. God is a fairy tale created in order to enable people to put an end to the fear of powers they do not understand. I was not afraid, so I was not in need of God.

The day before I went into the hospital for the last time, I phoned Aliza Olmert and asked her to meet me at the Lebanese restaurant in Abu Ghosh, outside Jerusalem. "If my family won't let me die," I told her, "you'll have to tell them that that is what I wanted." She cried. "At least have an olive," she said for some reason, and I recalled the very first olive I had ever eaten, sixty years earlier at the Beit Lid military camp.

Several days before my death I had one final opportunity to be who I had always been: a person who made his own rules.

The cancer had spread to the lungs and from there to the liver and kidneys, and the doctors hooked me up to chemotherapy. I lay there for a whole day staring up at the ceiling, with Shula and Meirav at my side. In the evening, Yair came to relieve them, and we watched Maccabi play for the Euroleague Cup. In one of the time-outs, the announcer said, "Next week, Maccabi will be playing on its home court against Real Madrid."

"You'll be watching that game," I told Yair, "on your own."

He smiled, held my hand, and my eyes shut. Late that night I awoke and heard him crying quietly in the dark. At the same time, I could feel the chemotherapy dripping into my arm, and suddenly I realized how idiotic it was. What was I trying to gain? A few more months in hospital during which I would grow bald, turn gaunt and lose what was left of my brain, all the while torturing my exhausted family? What good was that?

That night, I discovered the biggest secret of terminally ill people. They always say to themselves, "When the end comes, I'll decide if I want to carry on or put a stop to it," but when the end comes they are too exhausted or too drugged to make any decisions on their own, so the decision is left to the doctors—and doctors always try to keep them alive for as long as possible since that is the oath they swear, and that is the training they receive, and they do not know how to behave otherwise.

I woke up in the morning and asked to see Ehud and Aliza. When they arrived, I had them sign as witnesses on the form proclaiming that I refused to receive life-prolonging treatment. My grandson Yoav, who was with us in the room, asked why family members could not sign as witnesses.

"Because," I explained, "that's how you prevent a situation where a wife wants to get rid of her husband, or children are trying to get their hands on their inheritance early, and they force the patient to sign against his will."

"You know what?" he said after thinking about it for a moment. "That's a really smart law."

"I know," I told him. "I'm the one who made it."

————

After they left, I summoned the doctors and instructed them to disconnect me at once from the chemotherapy. "But Tommy," said Prof. Barabash, who had been alerted and had rushed to my room, "we can help you live another six months."

"Like this?" I said, gesturing to the room. "You call this living?"

The other doctors tried to dissuade me as well, but I had already made up my mind. One young doctor surprised me by bursting into tears at the end of our conversation. "You know," she said, "here in Oncology I should have been seeing people making that decision every day, but you're actually my first, and the first to go ahead with it." I smiled and continued speaking with her until she calmed down.

During the last week of my life I didn't want to see a soul apart from the family. Meirav sat by my side for endless hours, stroking my hand and saying, *"Bushik, Bushik"*—the children's pet name for me—over and over. Shula held my other hand and caressed my forehead, and Yair was at my side in the evenings, telling me what was on television when I could no longer open my eyes. I received morphine to dull the pain, and each time I fell into a slightly deeper, slightly darker sleep, knowing that this would be the way it would end: a slow immersion surrounded by love. I don't particularly recommend death to anyone, but if there's a way to go, this was it.

On 1 June 2008, before sunrise, I started my final immersion.

From time to time I had glimpses of consciousness, but I knew—or felt—that this was the end. There is something deceitful in the way in which the human brain operates during its final hours. I thought about Father, in fact I saw him, lucid and vital like I had not seen him since he was taken from me. Mother, too, beautiful as ever. I thought about how I was thinner than I had been in forty years, and how it was too bad I couldn't enjoy it. I felt the hands of my family and heard their voices vaguely as my breathing became more and more labored. I was suddenly aware of how each breath was noisy and ragged, and I felt bad that I could no longer hear what Meirav was saying. I cannot claim that I "saw my life pass before my eyes" but I was in a tranquil place. I understood my life, I understood my death, and I was at peace with both.

And then I stopped breathing.

And there was darkness.

I know there are those who would like to know what happens after that.

After that, there is nothing.

I told you so.

ACKNOWLEDGMENTS

This book could not have been written if it were not for a series of recorded conversations between Amnon Dankner and my father during his last year of life. These conversations are a model of journalism and friendship that Amnon made available to me generously and unconditionally.

I thank my mother, Shulamit Lapid, who was with me during every step of the process of writing this book, almost daily providing additions, corrections, and just listening, always tremendously supportive of this project her son had taken upon himself.

Thanks to my sister, Meirav Roth, her husband Danny Roth, my wife Lihie and my elder son, Yoav, who patiently kept me supplied with good advice and, no less importantly, withstood my disappearance from their lives into my cellar of memories.

A special thanks to my editor, Ronit Weiss-Berkovich, for her insight, support, patience and friendship, and, especially, the delicate manner in which she steered her opinionated client to his target. Thanks, too, to my English translator, Evan Fallenberg, for his wisdom, sensitivity and devotion to this project.

Thanks to my research assistant, Avital Eilat, without whom I could not have coped with the staggering amount of material in such a biography, and to Ethel Hooven who, as always, stood between me and life so that I could be free to write.

Thanks to Ehud and Aliza Olmert, Eli Zohar, Avraham Poraz, Raz Ben David, Gal Segal, Tzahi Moshe, Tommy Yagoda, Peter Gutman, Danny Tokatli, Shimon Weintraub—without whom I could not have survived the trip to Novi Sad—and to many others who read and encouraged and sent material and whom I bothered with questions at strange hours.

Thanks to my two agents, Boaz Ben Zion and Ilan Bushari, who as always stood at my side throughout the project.

And thanks to Father—for everything.

—Yair Lapid, Tel Aviv, October 2009

INDEX

Tommy refers to Josef (Tommy) Lapid.